7003/6533   £66-00   1/11

Poverty and Human Rights

Poverty and Human Rights

Sen's 'Capability Perspective' Explored

Polly Vizard

OXFORD
UNIVERSITY PRESS

OXFORD
UNIVERSITY PRESS

Great Clarendon Street, Oxford OX2 6DP

Oxford University Press is a department of the University of Oxford.

It furthers the University's objective of excellence in research, scholarship, and education by publishing worldwide in

Oxford New York

Auckland Cape Town Dar es Salaam Hong Kong Karachi
Kuala Lumpur Madrid Melbourne Mexico City Nairobi
New Delhi Shanghai Taipei Toronto

With offices in

Argentina Austria Brazil Chile Czech Republic France Greece
Guatemala Hungary Italy Japan Poland Portugal Singapore
South Korea Switzerland Thailand Turkey Ukraine Vietnam

Oxford is a registered trade mark of Oxford University Press in the UK
and in certain other countries

Published in the United States
by Oxford University Press Inc., New York

British Library Cataloguing in Publication Data

Data available

Library of Congress Cataloging in Publication Data

Data available

Typeset by SPI Publisher services, Pondicherry, India
Printed in Great Britain on acid-free paper by Biddles Ltd.,
King's Lynn, Norfolk

ISBN 0-19-927387-1   978-0-19-927387-4

'Poverty itself is a violation of numerous basic human rights'
(*Mary Robinson, Honorary President of Oxfam International and
Former UN High Commissioner on Human Rights*)

M.Robinson, Romanes
Lecture, Oxford,
11 November 1997.

Acknowledgements

The research monograph is a revised version of a Ph.D. thesis (Vizard 2000) written at the Institute for Development Studies (DESTIN) at London School of Economics (ESRC Award No. T026271155). The material was further developed whilst I was PostDoctoral Research Fellow and Research Associate at the Centre for Analysis of Social Exclusion (CASE) located in the Suntory Toyota International Centre for Economics and Related Disciplines (STICERD) at London School of Economics (ESRC Award No. T026271155).

I am especially grateful for long-term support, and for detailed comments and input, from Meghnad Desai, Michael Anderson, Raymond Plant, Edward McClennan, Tania Burchardt, John Hills, and Julian Le Grand. I have benefited enormously from institutional support from CASE, from the interdisciplinary research environment at STICERD, and from the support, comments, and research projects of friends and colleagues around LSE, including those at DESTIN and the LSE Centre for the Study of Human Rights. Important stepping-stones in the development of the monograph have included the development of a Briefing Paper (Vizard 2001) published by the Overseas Development Institute, with comments received from Clare Ferguson, Andy Norton, Simon Maxwell, Julia Häusermann, Robert Sugden, Sakiko Fukuda-Parr, and Sabina Alkire. Helpful feedback was also received at a seminar on poverty and human rights organized by CASE, especially from Peter Townsend; at the Third and Fourth Conferences on the Capability Approach held in Pavia in 2003 and 2004, including useful discussions with Frances Stewart and Siddiq Osmani; and from Martin Van Hees and Arjun Sengupta. I am also extremely grateful to Dominic Byatt, Claire Croft, Lizzy Suffling, and Donald Strachan at Oxford University Press, both for their commitment to the project, and for their help with the editorial and publication process, and for the input of three anonymous referees. Support from

Richard Derecki and close family has also been critical. Finally, Amartya Sen has provided encouragement over the years as well as the body of rich and stimulating work that the monograph sets out to analyse.

Responsibility for content and interpretation is, of course, solely mine.

Polly Vizard
January 2005

Contents

1

Introduction and Overview: Poverty, human rights, and Sen's 'capability approach'

This monograph analyses the ways in which the work of the Nobel Laureate Professor Amartya Sen has advanced international thinking about global poverty as a human rights issue. Sen's work in ethics and economics has emerged as a key influence on international debates about global poverty and human rights, and has deepened and expanded theoretical thinking about this issue in important and innovative ways. His research programme has made a major contribution to the development of new paradigms and approaches that focus on global poverty and human rights, and has promoted interdisciplinary cross-fertilization and theoretical integration on these subjects between ethics, economics, and international human rights law. The monograph explores Sen's research agenda from a human rights perspective and assesses the significance of his work for a contemporary human rights project that includes the elimination of global poverty as a central and critical objective.

The analysis of 'states of denial'—of modes of avoidance that result in denials of responsibility and in the rationalization and sanitization of atrocities and suffering—has recently come to the forefront in the field of human rights.[1] In the context of global poverty, the cultures of indifference, passivity, and inaction that underlie the failure to address global poverty have themselves been reinforced and perpetuated by theoretical perspectives that fail to give adequate weight to global poverty as a human rights concern. The monograph explores the ways in which Sen's work over more than forty years has challenged these perspectives. It shows that

---

[1] See especially Cohen (2001).

Sen's contributions in the field of human rights have been twofold. First, Sen's work in ethics has challenged the exclusion of forms of basic deprivation and impoverishment such as hunger and starvation, premature mortality and 'excess' morbidity, and illiteracy and inadequate educational attainment, from the characterization of fundamental freedoms and human rights, and has contributed to the development of a normative framework in which authoritatively recognized international standards in the field of poverty and human rights can be meaningfully conceptualized and coherently understood. Second, in economics, Sen has highlighted the limitations of dominant income-focused and utility-focused paradigms from the perspective of fundamental freedoms and human rights, and has pioneered the development of an expanded framework for theoretical and empirical analysis that takes explicit account of the instrumental and intrinsic value of these concerns.

This introductory chapter is divided into five main sections. Section 1.1 examines how global poverty has moved up the international human rights agenda over the past decade. Section 1.2 provides a brief review of the ways in which the international human rights system, supported and reinforced by international law, establishes international obligations on governments and other actors in the field of global poverty and human rights. Section 1.3 addresses the need for the development of a cross-disciplinary framework for analysing global poverty as a human rights issue. Section 1.4 provides an analytical overview of Sen's contributions. Section 1.5 surveys the contents of the monograph as a whole.

1.1 The Emerging International Agenda on Global Poverty and Human Rights

Global poverty has moved rapidly up the international human rights agenda in recent years. Whereas in the past, poverty was systematically downgraded and neglected as a human rights concern, the proposition that global poverty represents a violation and denial of human rights on a persistent, systematic, and massive scale is having an increasing influence on international debates, policies, and programmes aimed at poverty reduction and elimination, and on the advocacy work of major international human rights and development NGOs. Virtually all governments have recognized the protection and promotion of human rights aimed at the survival and development of the human person—including the human right to life, the human right to a standard of living adequate for

health and well-being (including adequate food, water, sanitation, an(
housing and access to health and social services), and the human right t(
education—as ethical, legal, political, and economic imperatives for the
twenty-first century. Global poverty causes these internationally recognized human rights to be violated and denied and has been described by
Mary Robinson (2004: 2), the former United Nations High Commissioner
for Human Rights, as the worst human rights problem the world faces
today.

The nature and scope of global poverty

The approach to the conceptualization of poverty adopted throughout
this monograph is based on the characterization of poverty as 'capability
deprivation'. This approach relates the notion of poverty to the notion of
'impoverished lives' and to deprivations in the basic freedoms that people
can and do enjoy—such as the freedom to be adequately nourished (unaffected by endemic hunger and starvation), the freedom to enjoy adequate living conditions (with access to adequate shelter, housing, and
sanitation), the freedom to lead normal spans of life (unaffected by premature mortality or 'excess' morbidity), and the freedom to read and write
(unconstrained by illiteracy and inadequate educational provision). It
recognizes that deprivations in basic freedoms of this type are associated
not only with shortfalls in income (i.e. with income poverty) but also with
systematic deprivations in access to other goods, services, and resources
necessary for human survival and development—including deprivations
in access to essential medicines and vaccines and adequate health facilities, housing, sanitation, and educational arrangements—as well as with
interpersonal and contextual variables.[2]

- **Income poverty.** World Bank estimates suggest that despite recent
  gains from growth in China and India, 1.1 billion people worldwide—
  around one in six of the world's population—live in 'extreme' income
  poverty on less than $1 a day, and 2.7 billion people—nearly one half
  the world's population, including more than two-thirds of the populations of South Asia and sub-Saharan Africa—in 'severe' income poverty on less than $2 a day. The absolute numbers of people living in
  'extreme' income poverty is estimated to have fallen from 1.5 billion
  people in 1981 to 1.1 billion people in 2001. The numbers of people

[2] See, for example, Drèze and Sen (2002). The conceptual basis of this characterization is discussed
in Chapter 3, whilst its practical application in empirical investigations is discussed in Chapter 4.

living in 'severe' income poverty is estimated to have increased from 2.5 billion to 2.7 billion over this period.[3]

- **Deprivations in other essential goods, resources, and services necessary for survival and development.** Around 840 million people worldwide suffer from chronic malnutrition, with a severe shortfall in the minimal nutritional requirements necessary for normal levels of activity, including more than 10 million in industrialized countries. In 2002, more than 1 billion people were still using unsafe sources of drinking water, and more than 2.6 billion people—over 40 per cent of the world's population—did not have access to basic sanitation. Millions of the poorest people worldwide are affected by a complete lack of housing, whilst 924 million people lived in slums in 2001—in overcrowded and sub-standard housing, often with unsafe, inadequate water, hygiene, and sanitation, and without access to adequate health services. Inadequate housing and living conditions are also associated with other major risk factors, such as increased exposure to adverse environmental conditions and hazards (including the effects of climatic change, disasters, indoor smoke inhalation, and urban air pollution). Despite improvements in primary school enrolment rates, the denial of the human right to basic education remains a reality for millions of children worldwide. In sub-Saharan Africa, primary school completion rates remained at around 40 per cent in 2000–2. The World Bank estimates that on current trends children in more than half of developing countries will still not complete a primary education by 2015—with a financing gap in low-income countries of more than $2.4–3.7 billion a year.[4]

- **The capability to avoid premature mortality and excess morbidity.** The failure to access the basic resources, goods, and services necessary for human survival and development is the cause of avoidable mortality and morbidity on a persistent, systematic, and massive scale. In 2002, communicable diseases, maternal and perinatal conditions, and nutritional deficiencies accounted for 18 million deaths—32 per cent of all deaths worldwide, and 41 per cent of the global burden of disease (with the loss of 610 million 'healthy life years' or 'DALYs'). Many of these deaths are caused by the deprivations discussed above. For example, inadequate nutrition and unsafe water, sanitation, and hygiene

[3] See Chen and Ravallion (2004: 29), Tables 2 and 3. The poverty lines are calculated on the basis of 'purchasing power parity'. See Chen and Ravallion (2004: 8–9) for details.
[4] Statistics from: World Bank (2004: 4, 5, 10); WHO and UNICEF (2004b).

remain a major cause of premature mortality and excess mortality. In 2002 alone, undernutrition in the form of protein-calorie malnutrition and micronutrient deficiency was the direct cause of 500,000 deaths, accounting for 0.9 per cent of deaths globally, and 2.3 per cent of the overall global burden of disease (34 million 'DALYs'). Diarrhoeal diseases were the direct cause of 1.8 million deaths, accounting for 3.2 per cent of deaths globally and 4.2 per cent of the overall global burden of disease (61 million 'DALYs'). In addition, undernutrition and unsafe water, sanitation, and hygiene are major risk factors in all-cause mortality and morbidity. Taking account of the interactions, the World Health Organization (WHO) attributed 3.7 million deaths in 2000 to the risk factor 'underweight'. This accounted for about one in fifteen deaths worldwide, and 9.5 per cent of the overall global burden of disease (138 million 'DALYs'). 1.7 million deaths in 2000 were attributed to unsafe water, sanitation, and hygiene, accounting for 3.7 per cent of the global burden of disease (54.2 million 'DALYs'). Inadequate housing and living conditions are associated with other major risk factors, with 1.6 million deaths (and 39 million 'DALYs') in 2000 attributed to indoor smoke from solid fuels alone.[5]

- **Essential vaccines and inadequate health care arrangements.** The mortality and morbidity risks associated with global poverty are compounded by persistent, systematic, and massive inadequacies in access to essential vaccines and medicines and adequate health care arrangements. WHO estimates that 4.2 million deaths in 2002 were preventable by vaccines that are either part of a national immunization schedule, or for which a licensed vaccine is available. This includes 2.5 million deaths of the 10.5 million deaths of children under five (including 0.5 million from measles).[6] Maternal mortality continues to claim the lives of more than 500,000 women a year, the risks multiplying with poverty, malnourishment, disease, multiple pregnancies, and lack of access to adequate health care facilities. Malaria, which claims 1.1 million lives a year, is a disease of poverty, with almost 60 per cent of deaths occurring among the poorest 20 per cent of the population, and could often be prevented by low-cost mosquito nets; whilst the resurgence of TB, which kills 2 million people a year, is being fuelled by systematic inadequacies in health care systems and management. In Africa, the spread of HIV/AIDS has reversed decades of

[5] Statistics reported in WHO (2004a), Overview, Annex Table 2: Deaths by cause, and Annex Table 3: Burden of disease in DALYs; and WHO (2002: 54, 68) and Annex Table 9.
[6] WHO (2004b).

improvements in life expectancy. The HIV/AIDS pandemic is characterized by massive global inequalities in access to essential antiretroviral drugs. According to WHO, almost 6 million people in developing countries will die in the near future if they do not receive treatment—but only about 400,000 of them were receiving it in 2003.[7]

- **The position of children.** Global poverty disproportionately violates and denies the human rights of millions of children worldwide. New estimates for UNICEF suggest that the human rights of over 1 billion children, more than half the children in developing countries, are violated and denied because of severe deprivation in access to the basic resources, goods, and services they need to survive, grow, and develop (including nutrition, safe water, essential vaccines and health care, housing, and education).[8] These deprivations are the cause of mortality, morbidity, and underdevelopment of children in the developing world on a persistent, systematic, and massive scale. In 2003, 10.6 million children died before they were five, mostly from preventable diseases such as diarrhoea, measles, malaria, and acute respiratory infections; and nearly 4,000 children die every day because they lack access to safe drinking water and adequate sanitation.[9] Inadequate educational provision continues to be associated with systematic failures in the capability to avoid illiteracy and achieve basic levels of education. Recent estimates suggest that 134 million children aged

---

[7] World Bank (2004: 8–9) and WHO (2004a: Overview).

[8] UNICEF (2004b) based on the findings reported in Gordon et al. (2003: 10–11). The survey found that over half of the world's children in developing countries (56%)—just over one billion children—were found to be severely deprived in relation to one or more basic need. Key deprivations included:
- Shelter deprivation—more than half a billion children in the developing world (34%) were living in dwellings with more than five people per room or which have mud flooring;
- Sanitation deprivation—over half a billion children (31%) in the developing world had no toilet facilities whatsoever;
- Information deprivation—almost half a billion children (25%) in the developing world lack access to radio, television, telephone, or newspapers at home;
- Water deprivation—nearly 376 million children (20%) in the developing world are using unsafe (open) water sources or have more than a fifteen-minute walk to water;
- Food deprivation—over 15% of children under five years of age in the developing world were severely food deprived, over half of whom (91 million children) were in South Asia;
- Health deprivation—265 million children in the developing world (15%) had not been immunized against any diseases or had had a recent illness causing diarrhoea and not received medical advice or treatment;
- Education deprivation: throughout the developing world, 134 million children aged between seven and eighteen (13%) were severely educationally deprived and had never been to school.

[9] UNICEF (2004b), Basic Indicators Table; and WHO and UNICEF (2004).

between seven and eighteen in the developing world (13 per cent) are 'severely educationally deprived', defined as lacking any primary or secondary school education. Sub-Saharan Africa was found to have an above average rate of 30 per cent (50 million children), as did the Middle East and North African regions (23 per cent or 19 million children) and South Asia (19 per cent or 57 million children).[10]

1.2 The Evolution of International Concern with Global Poverty as a Human Rights Issue

The human rights model suggests that in order to reduce and eliminate global poverty, the underlying distribution of global rights and responsibilities must be addressed. The international human rights system, supported and reinforced by international law, establishes far-reaching international obligations of national governments, other governments, and the organizations of which they are members (including international organizations such as UN agencies, the World Bank, the International Monetary Fund (IMF), the World Trade Organization (WTO), and regional development organizations) in the field of global poverty and human rights. Global poverty has in the past been and often continues to be downgraded and neglected as a human rights issue. This monograph does not address the underlying issues of power and inequality that underlie this process. Rather, the emphasis is on the ways in which the embryonic but expanding and deepening framework of ethical, political, and legal commitments in the field of human rights can provide a basis for strengthening international accountability and securing the individual and collective actions necessary for a sustained programme of global poverty reduction and elimination.

The international human rights framework

Authoritative international recognition of global poverty as a human rights issue dates back to the adoption of the Universal Declaration of Human Rights by the United Nations General Assembly (UNGA) in 1948. Article 3 of the Universal Declaration recognizes the human right to life and Articles 25 and 26 recognize the human right to a standard of living adequate for health and well-being—including adequate food, clothing,

---

[10] Gordon et al. (2003: 21).

housing, and medical care and necessary social services—and to free and compulsory basic education. During the second half of the twentieth century, this cluster of human rights was codified in major international treaties including:

(1) International Covenant on Civil and Political Rights (ICCPR);
(2) International Covenant on Economic, Social, and Cultural Rights (ICESCR);
(3) International Convention on the Rights of the Child (ICRC);
(4) International Convention on the Elimination of All Forms of Racial Discrimination (ICEFRD);
(5) International Convention on the Elimination of All of Forms of Discrimination Against Women (ICEFDAW).

These treaties create legally binding international obligations on state parties to implement progressively the human rights to life, to adequate food and nutrition, to safe water and sanitation, to adequate health care facilities, and to education, both individually and collectively through international assistance and cooperation. By 2004, these international treaties had been signed and ratified by the vast majority of states, with 153, 150, 192, 169, and 178 state parties respectively. This expansion and deepening of international legal obligation in the field of global poverty and human rights has been consolidated by a process of authoritative international standard-setting and the emergence of a body of case law. Human rights-based approaches to poverty elimination are also having an increasing impact on domestic legal and policy agendas. In South Africa, the human rights to an adequate standard of living, food, water, housing, education, and health are protected in the new constitution and the jurisprudence of the South African Court has established important precedents in these areas. In the UK, increased emphasis on the international human rights framework is reflected in government anti-poverty strategies and international development policy (e.g. DFID 2000) and the introduction of new standards in UK domestic law.

The strengthening of international concern with global poverty as a human rights issue

Poverty issues have rapidly moved up the international human rights agenda over the last ten years. Whereas global poverty was systematically downgraded and neglected as a human rights issue during the cold war period, there has been a strengthening of international concern with global poverty as a human rights issue over the past decade. In 1993, the World Conference on Human Rights in Vienna was something of a watershed (with 131 governments agreeing that all human rights—civil, political, economic, social, and cultural—are indivisible, interdependent, and interrelated (Commitment 5)). This principle is widely interpreted as implying that the promotion and protection of one category of human rights does not exempt or excuse states from the promotion and protection of the other. All human rights have equal importance and should be given the same level of urgent consideration by the international community.[11] Following Vienna—and despite the attempts by some countries to limit the scope of the international human rights agenda—the idea that freedom from severe poverty is a basic human right, giving rise to moral and legal obligations on governments and other actors, has become increasingly influential. Robinson (1997: 6) stated that 'poverty itself is a violation of numerous basic human rights' and increased emphasis on global poverty as a human rights issue has been reflected in a series of resolutions by the UNGA and the UN Human Rights Commission.[12] In 2000, the 'Millenium Declaration' adopted by world leaders as a statement of values, principles, and objectives for the twenty-first century included the promotion and protection of all internationally recognized human rights (economic, social, and cultural as well as civil and political) and set deadlines for collective actions in the field of poverty eradication (UNGA 2000).

The human rights framework for international poverty reduction and elimination strategies

This strengthening of concern with freedom from poverty as a human rights issue has been reflected in increased emphasis on the international human rights framework, supported by international law, as an overarching framework for international programmes aimed at poverty reduction and elimination. The United Nations International Children's Education Fund (UNICEF) explicitly adopts a human rights framework for its policies and programmes (e.g. UNICEF 2004a). WHO and the Food and Agricultural

---

[11] UN Committee on Economics, Social and Cultural Rights, Statement to the World Conference on Human Rights, 1993/22, Annex III, p. 82.

[12] Resolutions of the Commission on Human Rights on extreme poverty: E/CN.4/RES/2004/23, E/CN.4/RES/2003/24, E/CN.4/RES/2002/30, E/CN.4/RES/2000/12, E/CN.4/RES/1999/26, E/CN.4/RES/1998/25, E/CN.4/RES/1997/11, E/CN.4/RES/1996/10, E/CN.4/RES/1995/16, E/CN.4/RES/1994/12, E/CN.4/RES/1993/13, E/CN.4/RES/1992/11, E/CN.4/RES/1991/14, E/CN.4/RES/1990/15, E/CN.4/RES/1989/10, E/CN.4/RES/1988/23. Relevant Resolutions of the General Assembly: A/RES/57/211, A/RES/53/146, A/RES/47/134, A/RES/47/196, A/RES/46/121.

Organization (FAO) are placing increasing emphasis on the international human rights framework (e.g. as reflected in the recent adoption of the 'Right to Food Guidelines' by the FAO Council (FAO 2004)); the United Nations Development Programme (UNDP) recognizes that poverty eradication should be addressed as a basic human right—not merely as an act of charity (UNDP 2000: 8); and the United Nations Economic, Social, and Cultural Organization (UNESCO) has initiated a programme of work on poverty and human rights (e.g. UNESCO 2004; Sane 2005). Establishing the responsibilities of the international trade and financial institutions is an intrinsic element of the human rights 'mainstreaming' process being spearheaded by the Office of the United Nations High Commissioner for Human Rights (OHCHR). Robinson (1998: vii) has referred to the process whereby the World Bank recognizes that it has an express role to play in the promotion and protection of human rights as a 'defining moment' in history. The Bank's Articles of Agreement state that, in all decisions, 'only economic considerations shall be relevant'. Whereas in the past this phrase has often been interpreted in a way that precludes a focus on human rights, there has been increased recognition of the relevance of international human rights standards to the mandate and activities of the World Bank in recent years (e.g. World Bank (1998: 2–4)). The integration of international human rights standards into the Poverty Reduction Strategy Papers (PRSP) accompanying agreements between national states and international development organizations, including the World Bank and the IMF, would be another important step forward (e.g. OHCHR 2002, 2004).

The link with global economic and financial arrangements

The international human rights framework is also increasingly at the centre of campaigns for global economic and financial reform. NGOs including Oxfam, Human Rights Watch, and Amnesty International have placed increased emphasis on global poverty as a human rights issue in recent years, with human rights objectives being linked to campaigns for the deepening and widening of debt reduction cancellation, for reform of international rules relating to trade and investment, for increased and more effective development assistance, and for reform of the global economic and financial architecture. For example, Oxfam's *Basic Rights Campaign* has focused attention on the impact of international economic and financial arrangements and practices relating to intellectual property rights (e.g. the WTO patent rules set out in 'TRIPS' agreements), agricultural subsidies, dumping practices, restrictions on developing country market access, as well as the impact of structural adjustment and other economic and development policies, and the need for reform of the global development architecture. The idea that global poverty eradication requires new forms of international partnership in relation to issues such as trade, aid, and debt was underlined in the Millenium Declaration (Goal 8) and has been subsequently reflected in a range of international initiatives (e.g. the Doha 'development round' of trade negotiations, new international agreements relating to essential medicines and vaccines, the 'Monterrey Consensus' on mutual responsibilities in relation to development finance, proposals to widen and deepen the Highly Indebted Poor Countries Initiative, the Commission on Africa, etc.). Significant progress is anticipated in these areas as a result of the G8 Summit, the UN Special Summit on the Millenium Goals, and the WTO Ministerial Conference during the course of 2005. In the UK, suggestions for moving forward include government proposals for fairer international trade, for debt reduction and cancellation, for meeting the UN overseas development aid target (of 0.7 GNP) and for long-term development financing (including new forms of international economic arrangements aimed at achieving secure access to essential vaccines based on an 'international financial facility') (e.g. HM Treasury 2004). Other proposals include the idea of an 'International Children's Investment Fund' funded by an 'international financial transactions tax' (e.g. Townsend 2004).

1.3 The Need for a Cross-disciplinary Framework for Analysing Global Poverty as a Human Rights Issue

Yet the plausibility of the international agenda on global poverty and human rights depends on the development of adequate theoretical frameworks for thinking about what people mean when they claim that poverty is a *violation* or a *denial* of human rights. In the past, the cultures of indifference, passivity, and inaction that underlie the failure to address global poverty as a human rights issue have themselves been reinforced and perpetuated by theoretical perspectives that fail to give adequate weight to global poverty as a human rights concern. Dominant discourses in ethics have often overlooked and downgraded global poverty as a human rights issue, whilst theoretical perspectives in economics have paid inadequate attention to the range of normative perspectives addressed in ethical debates or to established standards in international human rights law.

The limitations of traditional mono-disciplinary analysis

The failure to give adequate weight to global poverty as a human rights concern has been reinforced and perpetuated by the tendency to analyse human rights issues from traditional mono-disciplinary perspectives. In the past, philosophers have focussed on foundational debates in ethics, lawyers on questions of legal obligation—and both disciplinary perspectives have tended to neglect institutional, economic, and structural processes that impact on human rights outcomes. Meanwhile, economists have often failed to incorporate the ideas of individual freedom and human rights into theoretical analyses and empirical investigations. Dominant approaches have evaluated the adequacy of economic processes and arrangements in terms of income expansion, whilst standard frameworks in welfare economics have evaluated interpersonal advantage and the efficiency and fairness of competitive market outcomes in terms of utility—with no explicit recognition of instrumental and intrinsic value of fundamental freedoms and human rights. These mono-disciplinary approaches have resulted in conceptual fragmentation and theoretical and empirical impoverishment. The analysis of human rights issues has failed to incorporate economic analysis, whilst theoretical and empirical economics have failed to take adequate account of important ethical variables and concerns.

The need for a 'scholarly bridge' between human rights and economics

The more practical need for a 'scholarly bridge' between human rights and economics has been highlighted by Robinson (2002). Whereas there is a wide perception of a conflict between human rights on the one hand and economics on the other—with fundamental freedoms and human dignity being viewed as opposed to development, growth, and the optimal allocation of resources—Robinson suggests that the case for human rights could often be advanced by economic analysis. For example, arguments for shared international responsibility could be supported by the analysis of resource constraints, whilst economists could build on philosophical and legal advances in the field of human rights with empirical methodologies for assessing outcomes. Areas of common ground should in Robinson's view be developed through a programme of interdisciplinary research and consensus-building. The development of a scholarly bridge between human rights and economics could ultimately impact on the shaping of new and emerging 'big' ideas such as 'ethical globalization'—the idea that economic processes (including globalization) should be subject to moral considerations including the ethical and legal principles entailed by the idea of human rights.

1.4 The Importance of Sen's Research Agenda in Ethics and Economics

Against this background, this monograph analyses the ways in which th work of Amartya Sen has contributed to the development of a cross-disciplinary theoretical framework for analysing global poverty as a human rights issue. The aim is to establish the ways in which Sen's intellectual project over more than forty years addresses the theoretical underpinnings of the idea that global poverty represents a violation or a denial of basic human rights on a persistent, massive, and systematic scale. Sen's research agenda is shown to have systematically addressed the 'theoretical obstacles' to viewing global poverty as a human rights issue—through the examination and rejection of frameworks in ethics that exclude freedom from basic forms of deprivation and impoverishment, including hunger and starvation, premature mortality and 'excess' morbidity, and illiteracy and inadequate educational achievement, from the class of fundamental freedoms and human rights; and frameworks in economics that exclude fundamental freedoms and human rights as objects of central concern. In addition, Sen's work has deepened and widened human rights discourse in both ethics and economics by making a major contribution to the development of new paradigms and approaches that focus on global poverty and human rights concerns. The monograph explores these contributions and establishes the ways in which correspondences and analogues between Sen's 'capability perspective' and embryonic—but nevertheless developing and strengthening—standards in international law provide a basis for a major new cross-disciplinary framework for thinking about global poverty as a human rights issue.

1.5 Sen's Contributions to Cross-disciplinary Theoretical Integration and Development in the Field of Global Poverty and Human Rights

The monograph demonstrates the importance of Sen's work for a contemporary human rights project that includes the elimination of severe poverty as a central and critical objective in eight key respects.

Contributions to the development of a normative framework for characterizing poverty as a violation or a denial of fundamental human rights

Sen's work in ethics has challenged the exclusion of forms of income poverty and basic forms of deprivation and impoverishment including hunger and starvation, ill-health, and illiteracy from the characterization of fundamental freedoms and human rights, and has contributed to the

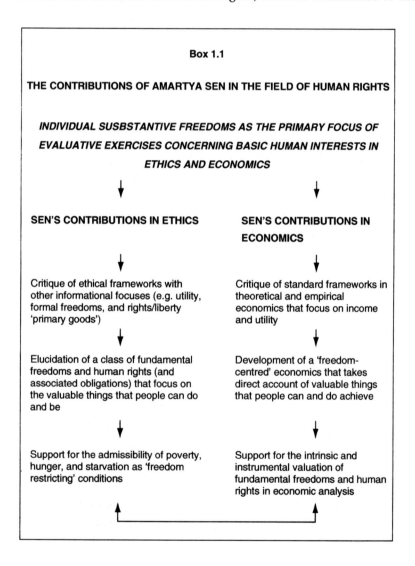

Box 1.1

THE CONTRIBUTIONS OF AMARTYA SEN IN THE FIELD OF HUMAN RIGHTS

INDIVIDUAL SUSBSTANTIVE FREEDOMS AS THE PRIMARY FOCUS OF EVALUATIVE EXERCISES CONCERNING BASIC HUMAN INTERESTS IN ETHICS AND ECONOMICS

SEN'S CONTRIBUTIONS IN ETHICS

SEN'S CONTRIBUTIONS IN ECONOMICS

Critique of ethical frameworks with other informational focuses (e.g. utility, formal freedoms, and rights/liberty 'primary goods')

Critique of standard frameworks in theoretical and empirical economics that focus on income and utility

Elucidation of a class of fundamental freedoms and human rights (and associated obligations) that focus on the valuable things that people can do and be

Development of a 'freedom-centred' economics that takes direct account of valuable things that people can and do achieve

Support for the admissibility of poverty, hunger, and starvation as 'freedom restricting' conditions

Support for the intrinsic and instrumental valuation of fundamental freedoms and human rights in economic analysis development of a normative framework in which authoritatively recognized international standards in the field of poverty and human rights can be meaningfully conceptualized and coherently understood. Twenty-five years ago, Sen (1982d) raised the question of whether *adequate food* and an *adequate standard of living* can be meaningfully and coherently analysed as basic human rights. Many of the central themes in Sen's work in ethics—including substantive freedom, capability and functioning, well-being and agency, meta-rights and entitlements, human rights and 'imperfect obligations'—have contributed to theoretical development on this issue. The monograph explores how Sen's 'capability perspective' supports the elucidation of a sub-class of fundamental freedoms and human rights that focuses on valuable personal states (such as being adequately nourished, clothed, or having the opportunity to benefit from basic health and education). It establishes how this perspective contributes to the development of a normative framework in which freedom from income poverty and other forms of basic deprivation and impoverishment including hunger and starvation, ill-health, and illiteracy can be meaningfully and coherently conceptualized as fundamental human rights that governments and other actors have obligations to respect, protect, and promote.

Expansion of the economics agenda to take account of fundamental freedoms and human rights

Sen's research agenda in economics has highlighted the limitations of dominant income-focused and utility-focused paradigms in theoretical and empirical economics from the perspective of fundamental freedoms and human rights. His work over more than forty years has analysed how these frameworks concentrate on an overly narrow informational base, and consequently on an overly narrow characterization of both the *means* and the *ends* of development and growth. Both the *instrumental* role of fundamental freedoms and human rights (in influencing the effectiveness of development and growth) and the value of fundamental freedoms and human rights (in assessing the benefits of trajectories of development and growth for individuals, groups, and populations) are neglected. In contrast, Sen has pioneered the development of an expanded framework for theoretical and empirical analysis that takes explicit account of the instrumental and intrinsic valuation of fundamental freedoms and human rights. His work has moved the economics and human rights agenda forward through the development of a series of far-reaching proposals for new paradigms and approaches in theoretical and empirical economics—away from paradigms and approaches that focus exclusively on income, growth, and utility, with an increased emphasis on individual entitlements, capabilities, opportunities, agency, freedoms, and rights. The monograph examines how Sen's development of these proposals has expanded the theoretical and technical underpinnings of theoretical and empirical economics, whilst practical applications have advanced knowledge and understanding of the phenomena of income poverty and other forms of basic deprivation and impoverishment, including hunger and starvation, premature mortality and 'excess' morbidity, and illiteracy and inadequate educational achievement, resulting in an important body of new statistical findings on human rights-focused concerns.

Promotion of cross-disciplinary theoretical integration and consensus-building between economics and human rights

As well as deepening and expanding theoretical thinking about human rights within the disciplines of ethics and economics, Sen's research agenda has promoted cross-fertilization and theoretical development and integration on human rights issues *across* these traditional disciplinary divides. His work has resulted in the emergence of new and richer paradigms in ethics (that take greater account of the outcomes of economic processes and arrangements) and in economics (that incorporate a broader range of normative concerns, including fundamental freedoms and human rights). This establishment of a cross-disciplinary analytical bridge between ethics and economics on human rights issues has methodological importance (for the development of integrated theoretical frameworks that transcend traditional mono-disciplinary analysis) as well as substantive importance (for the promotion of cross-disciplinary theoretical integration on the subject of human rights). The monograph assesses Sen's contributions from the cross-disciplinary perspective, exploring the ways in which his work provides a prototype and stimuli for cross-disciplinary research, as well as a basis for cross-disciplinary dialogue and consensus building between economics and human rights at a more practical level.

Contributions to the emerging reform agenda around 'ethical globalization'

Sen's establishment of a cross-disciplinary bridge between human rights and economics has long-term implications for the development of a reform agenda focusing on the new and emerging 'big' ideas highlighted by Robinson, including 'ethical globalization'—the idea that economic processes (including globalization) should be subject to moral considerations including the ethical and legal principles entailed by the idea of human rights. Sen's pioneering contributions towards the reconstruction of traditional economics to take account of an expanded range of ethical values and concerns (including fundamental freedoms and human rights) provide theoretical underpinnings for a reform agenda of this type. The central and overarching idea that evaluative exercises concerning basic human interests should focus on individual substantive freedoms (such as the ability to avoid premature mortality, to be adequately nourished, and to benefit from basic health, social services, and education) rather than alternative informational focuses (such as income, growth, utility, liberty, and 'primary goods') has precipitated important paradigm shifts in ethics and economics and has had a far-reaching influence on international policies and debates. This central idea provides an alternative informational focus to dominant approaches of the twentieth century ('libertarianism', 'utilitarianism', and 'income-focused'/'resourcist' approaches) and underlies influential proposals for assessing the outcomes of economic processes (including processes of growth, development, and globalization) and national and international economic institutions and arrangements in terms of substantive human freedoms and human rights.

Establishment of broad international acceptance of 'freedom-focused' approaches to poverty and development

Sen's elucidation and applications of the 'capability perspective' have also resulted in broad international acceptance of major new approaches to poverty (that focus on 'capability deprivation') and development (that focus on 'capability expansion'). The argument that poverty entails not only income deprivation but also deprivations in central and basic freedoms that people can and do enjoy (e.g. deprivations resulting from a lack of access to adequate nutrition, water and sanitation, health care, housing, and education) has had a major impact on international poverty analysis and has resulted in important shifts of thinking—away from an 'income' and towards a 'human rights-focused' approach. Likewise, the characterization of development as 'capability expansion' has also had a major impact internationally and has functioned as an important catalyst for human rights-focused concerns.

Correspondences between the 'capability approach' and evolving standards in international human rights law and jurisprudence

The monograph establishes the ways in which Sen's development of the 'capability perspective' in ethics and economics might be reinforced and supported through the embryonic and underdeveloped—but nevertheless widening and deepening—body of international standards in the field of global poverty and human rights. Sen's work in ethics has emphasized the important role of the idea of human rights outside the legal domain, and suggests that the justification and elucidation of this idea is not contingent on the degree of precision necessary for codification and judicial enforcement. At the same time, his work in economics has resulted in an important body of empirical research findings highlighting the role of different complementary institutions (economic, political, social, legal, etc.) in avoiding 'capability deprivation' and achieving 'capability expansion'. The monograph moves forward on these issues by highlighting and analysing the ways in which the idea of the 'capability perspective' might be appropriately reinforced by the international human rights system (supported by international human rights law). In particular, the monograph analyses the ways in which international treaties, case law, and authoritative international standard-setting reinforce and support the idea of the capability to achieve a standard of living adequate for survival and development—including adequate nutrition, safe water and sanitation, shelter and housing, access to basic health and social services, and education—as a basic human right that governments have individual and collective obligations to respect, protect, and promote. Eight key correspondences and analogues between the 'capability approach' and evolving standards in international human rights law and jurisprudence are set out in Box 1.2. The monograph highlights these correspondences and considers their implications for the development of an integrated cross-disciplinary framework for analysing poverty as a human rights issue that draws on ethics, economics, and international human rights law.

Influence on the emerging body of international standards and jurisprudence in the field of poverty and human rights

Sen's work has itself become an important influence on the emerging body of international standards and jurisprudence in the field of poverty and human rights. Whilst Sen's influence on international organizations such as the UNDP is well-known, the direct influence of Sen's work on international efforts to deepen and expand international legal obligation in the field of poverty and human rights is less appreciated. Yet the idea of a multidimensional approach to poverty focusing on 'capability failure' rather than income has been critical to international efforts to strengthen the international recognition of poverty as a human rights issue over the last decade. Other elements of Sen's research agenda (including the notion of entitlements, meta-rights, and 'imperfect obligation') are also reflected in emerging international jurisprudence and standard-setting in the field of poverty and human rights, and have become important influences on the establishment and expansion of international obligation in this field.

Box 1.2 KEY CORRESPONDENCES BETWEEN THE 'CAPABILITY APPROACH' AND EVOLVING STANDARDS IN INTERNATIONAL HUMAN RIGHTS LAW AND JURISPRUDENCE

---

1. The ways in which the international human rights system, supported by international law, provides authoritative recognition of a broad class of fundamental freedoms and human rights that takes account of global poverty.
2. The ways in which the international human rights system, supported by international law, provides authoritative grounds for rejecting 'absolutism' and the view that 'resource constraints' represent a 'theoretical obstacle' to the establishment of international legal obligation in the field of global poverty and human rights.
3. The ways in which the international human rights system, supported by international law, provides authoritative recognition of positive obligations of protection and promotion (as well as negative obligations of omission and restraint).
4. The ways in which the international human rights system, supported by international law, provides authoritative recognition of general goals (as well as specific actions) as the object of human rights.
5. The ways in which the international human rights system, supported by international law, provides an authoritative evaluative framework for assessing the 'reasonableness' of state actions in the field of global poverty and human rights.
6. The ways in which the international human rights system, supported by international law, provides authoritative recognition of the importance of rights to policies and programmes (or 'meta-rights') when resource constraints are binding.
7. The ways in which the international human rights system, supported by international law, recognizes collective international obligations of cooperation, assistance, and aid.
8. The ways in which the international human rights system, supported by international law, provides authoritative recognition of the importance of outcomes and results to the evaluation of human rights.

Significance of fundamental freedoms and human rights for the understanding of Sen's research project

Finally, the monograph establishes that the idea of fundamental freedoms and human rights is itself a useful gateway to understanding the nature and significance of Sen's work. Sen's research contributions in ethics and economics over a period of more than thirty year cover a vast and complex terrain and can at times seem technical and fragmented. The idea of fundamental human freedoms and human rights provides an important unifying theme. Viewing Sen's research contributions through this lens promotes understanding by providing a means of orientation through the complexities and technicalities. The monograph establishes the ways in which the idea of fundamental freedoms and human rights is key to understanding the nature, scope, and coherence of Sen's research contributions and provides an overarching framework for thinking about the influence of his work on international policies and debates.

1.6 Chapter Overview

Following this 'Introduction and Overview' there are six chapters. Chapter 2 provides a point of departure for the analysis of Sen's contributions by setting out the key ways in which influential discourses in ethics and political theory in both the libertarian and liberal traditions have often excluded basic forms of deprivation and impoverishment, including hunger and starvation, premature mortality and 'excess' morbidity, and illiteracy and inadequate lack of educational attainment, from the domain of fundamental freedoms and human rights—or provide an inadequate basis for conceptualizing authoritatively recognized international standards in this field. This includes frameworks that focus exclusively on negative freedom, negative rights, and negative obligations, and that fail to take adequate account of basic states of deprivation and impoverishment associated with income poverty and shortfalls in other goods, services, and resources necessary for human survival and development as 'freedom-restricting' conditions, including those developed by Hayek and Nozick (Section 2.1), and frameworks that allow for a more sensitive handling of poverty issues but nevertheless fail to provide an adequate basis for emerging international standards in this field, including Berlin and Pogge (Section 2.2), Rawls (Section 2.3), and O'Neill (Section 2.4). The chapter reviews the key paradigmatic positions and clarifies the important ways in which these theories provide a point of departure for assessing Sen's contributions to the debate.

Chapter 3 examines the ways in which Sen's research agenda has contributed to international debates through the development of an ethical framework in which freedom from basic forms of deprivation and impoverishment, including hunger and starvation, premature mortality and 'excess morbidity', and illiteracy and inadequate educational achievement, can be meaningfully and coherently conceptualized as fundamental human rights that governments have obligations to respect, protect, and promote. Sen's contributions are shown to have moved debates about poverty and human rights in five critical ways, by providing: support for a sub-class of fundamental freedoms and human rights that focuses directly on the valuable things that people can do and be (Section 3.1); support for systems of ethical evaluation that are sensitive to consequences, outcomes, and results (Section 3.2); support for positive obligations of assistance and aid (as well as negative obligations of omission and restraint) including the relaxation of the condition of 'co-possibility' and support for the general class of 'meta-rights' (Section 3.3); support for human rights in the context of 'imperfect obligations' (including support for obligations that are associated with 'reasonable action' rather than 'compulsory action') (Section 3.4); support for universalism against the relativist and culture-based critiques (Section 3.5). It also examines Sen's work in these areas and assesses how his contributions have helped to develop a normative framework for conceptualizing poverty as a violation or denial of fundamental human rights.

Chapter 4 focuses on the ways in which Sen's research agenda has focused international attention on the critical importance of fundamental freedoms and human rights for economic analysis. In the past, the idea of fundamental freedoms and human rights has often been neglected in theoretical and empirical economics. In contrast, Sen has set out a far-reaching critique of standard frameworks that fail to take account of fundamental freedoms and human rights (Section 4.1), opening up important new lines of enquiry and pioneering the development of radical new paradigms and approaches that take account of these concerns (Sections 4.2–6). His contributions include far-reaching proposals for the incorporation of new variables and concerns into theoretical and empirical economics including individual entitlements (Section 4.2), capabilities and functionings (including gender discrimination) (Section 4.3), civil, political, economic, and social rights (Section 4.4), 'freedom of choice' and 'opportunity freedom' (Section 4.5), and 'liberty rights' and 'basic rights'

(Section 4.6). The chapter explores how these proposals have contributed to important paradigm shifts—away from an exclusive concern with income, growth, and utility, towards a range of human rights-focused variables and concerns—and provide a framework for the instrumental and intrinsic valuation of fundamental freedoms and human rights in economic assessment and empirical economic research.

Chapter 5 discusses the ways in which the development of the 'capability perspective' in ethics and economics can be reinforced and supported through the embryonic and underdeveloped—but nevertheless widening and deepening—body of international standards in the field of global poverty and human rights. It discusses the ways in which international treaties, case law, and authoritative international standard-setting reinforce and support the idea of the capability to achieve a standard of living adequate for survival and development—including adequate nutrition, safe water and sanitation, shelter and housing, access to basic health and social services, and education—as a basic human right that governments have individual and collective obligations to respect, protect, and promote. The discussion highlights the eight correspondences between the 'capability approach' and evolving standards in international human rights law and jurisprudence set out in Box 1.2. Section 5.1 examines the basis of international legal obligation in the field of global poverty and human rights. Section 5.2 discusses the nature and scope of international legal obligation in this field (with particular emphasis on the question of whether resource and feasibility constraints pose a 'theoretical obstacle' to the establishment of legally binding international obligations regulating the protection and promotion of economic and social rights). Section 5.3 examines the development of evaluative principles that facilitate judicial scrutiny of the 'reasonableness' of actions undertaken by states under conditions of resource and feasibility constraints. Section 5.4 analyses the emergence of a body of case law in the field of global poverty and human rights. Section 5.5 considers the issue of collective obligation.

Chapter 6 takes the analysis forward by exploring the ways in which formal analysis can crystallize broader conceptual debates about poverty and human rights (absolute versus non-absolute human rights, negative versus positive correlative obligations, conditions of violation versus conditions of fulfilment, etc.) and take these debates to a more rigorous level. The discussion is aimed at (*a*) identification of an appropriate analytical framework for capturing and formalizing the idea of human rights; (*b*) expansion of this framework to take account of the idea of freedom from poverty as a basic human right. Section 6.1 highlights the need for a research programme on the formal representation of human rights. Section 6.2 considers the formal representation of human rights using the 'Kanger System'. Section 6.3 sets out some of the proposals in the literature for refining and extending the 'Kanger System'. Section 6.4 analyses the formal representation of the idea of 'freedom from poverty as a basic human right'. Proposed formulations improve on past approaches by building on Sen's concepts of 'capability-rights' and 'meta-rights' and by capturing and formalizing some of the internationally recognized standards discussed in Chapter 5 (which establish a common element of 'claim' as well as a common element of 'immunity' in the field of global poverty and human rights).

The monograph concludes in Chapter 7 with an examination of how the correspondences and analogues between the 'capability approach' and the international human rights framework provide a basis for the development of cross-disciplinary 'Working Models' of international accountability and responsibility in the field of global poverty and human rights. The idea that the complementary and reinforcing elements of the 'capability approach' and the international human rights framework provide a basis for the development of integrated cross-disciplinary frameworks for analysing global poverty as a human rights issue that bridges ethics, economics, and international law is considered. The proposition that the 'capability framework' can be meaningfully extended and applied on the basis of a supplementary theory of international human rights law is then examined in the light of broader debates about the extension and application of the 'capability approach'. Finally, the notion of an 'internationally recognized capability set' is introduced.

2

Is Poverty Relevant to the Characterization of Fundamental Freedoms and Human Rights? The Broader Debates in Ethics and Political Theory

This chapter analyses the broader debates in ethics and political theory about the relevance of global poverty to the characterization of fundamental freedoms and human rights. The Universal Declaration on Human Rights (1948) establishes international standards in the field of poverty and human rights—including the human right of everyone to a standard of living adequate for health and well-being (including food, clothing, housing, medical care, and necessary social services) and to free and compulsory elementary education. This cluster of human rights has long since been codified in international treaties in legally binding form and the international recognition of global poverty as a human rights issue has been strengthened in recent years. Yet influential discourses in ethics and political theory in both the libertarian and liberal traditions have often excluded basic forms of deprivation and impoverishment, including hunger and starvation, premature mortality and 'excess' morbidity, and illiteracy and inadequate lack of educational attainment, from the domain of fundamental freedoms and human rights—or provide an inadequate basis for conceptualizing authoritatively recognized international standards in this field. This chapter discusses some of the 'theoretical obstacles' to viewing global poverty as a violation or a denial of fundamental freedoms and human rights that have been put forward in ethics and political theory, as well as identifies the key ways in which the exclusion of global poverty from the characterization of fundamental freedoms and human rights can be challenged. Emphasis is placed on the ways in which the key paradigmatic positions provide a point of departure for the analysis of Sen's contributions to the debate.

2.1 The Exclusion of Poverty, Hunger, and Starvation from Influential Discourses on Fundamental Freedoms and Human Rights

The search for objectivity in ethics has often resulted in the development of theories of fundamental freedoms and human rights that take inadequate account of global poverty and associated deprivations including hunger and starvation, other forms of avoidable morbidity and mortality, and the failure to benefit from even the most basic levels of education. In responding to the relativist critique, many influential theories in both the libertarian and liberal traditions have often adopted forms of subjectivism, pluralism, anti-rationalism, and scepticism, denying the possibility of arriving at objective foundations for ethical claims—including claims about the human good or goods. Ethical theories that are explicitly based on some underlying conception of human good or goods have often been rejected, and emphasis has been placed on theories that claim to be independent of any particular conception of the human good or goods, or of any particular view of the ends that freedom can serve. Many influential theories in both the libertarian and liberal traditions have for these reasons emphasized the development of ethical categories that are independent of 'end-state' principles—such as a particular conception of 'human good' or 'human goods' or 'human flourishing'. This emphasis is associated with theories of negative freedoms and negative rights (that focus on the absence of intentional interference by other people, and that claim to be logically independent of the valuable things that people can do or be), and theories of negative obligation (that focus on negative obligations of immunity and restraint rather than positive obligations to defend and support valuable things that people can do and be). These theories are in turn associated with the proposition that the range of fundamental freedoms is limited and that poverty is inadmissible as a 'freedom-restricting' condition (Box 2.1).

Hayek, Nozick, and the 'Outcome-Independent' Approach

The theories developed by Hayek (1960, 1982a, 1982b, 1982c) and Nozick (1974) suggest that impartiality and neutrality require the development of

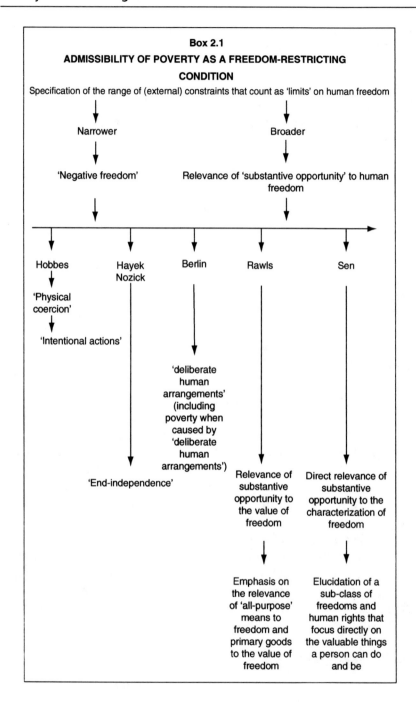

Box 2.1

ADMISSIBILITY OF POVERTY AS A FREEDOM-RESTRICTING CONDITION

Specification of the range of (external) constraints that count as 'limits' on human freedom

Narrower

Broader

'Negative freedom'

Relevance of 'substantive opportunity' to human freedom

Hobbes

Hayek Nozick

Berlin

Rawls

Sen

'Physical coercion'

'Intentional actions'

'deliberate human arrangements' (including poverty when caused by 'deliberate human arrangements')

'End-independence'

Relevance of substantive opportunity to the value of freedom

Direct relevance of substantive opportunity to the characterization of freedom

Emphasis on the relevance of 'all-purpose' means to freedom and primary goods to the value of freedom

Elucidation of a sub-class of freedoms and human rights that focus directly on the valuable things a person can do and be an 'outcome-independent' approach to ethical evaluation that focuses on the evaluation of the fairness of formal rules and procedures (e.g. in terms of their universal and equal application), rather than on the evaluation of outcomes or 'states of affairs'. At the individual level, these theories focus on immunity from deliberate interference by other people, rather than on the personal states of being and doing that are achieved (e.g. the fulfilment of a person's needs, their real opportunities and capabilities, or their wants, desires, and goals). At the societal level, they focus on the fairness of procedures and rules (e.g. the rule of law and formal equality of treatment), rather than on achieved 'social states' (e.g. socio-economic outcomes, including market outcomes).

Hayek's characterization of individual freedom as an 'essentially negative concept'

Hayek characterizes individual freedom in exclusively negative terms—as the absence of coercion, with coercion defined in terms of intentional interference by other people in a protected individual domain. According to Hayek's analysis, coercion does not include *all* influences that a person can exercise on the action of others, but only those actions that entail (*a*) the threat of harm and (*b*) the intention to cause another person or other people to act in specific ways. In this way, Hayek (1960: 134) links the characterization of individual freedom to a theory of individual responsibility that suggests that people are only responsible for states of affairs that they intentionally cause. The range of possible 'constraints' on individual freedom are specified in terms of intentional acts of coercion, rather than (*a*) the fulfilment of individual needs, opportunities, desires, and the ability or effective power to fulfil particular goals; (*b*) the outcomes of impersonal circumstances and processes (including competitive market allocations and the outcomes of socio-economic processes of development and growth). Whilst the question of the number of courses of action—or the opportunities—that are open to a person is important, this question is in Hayek's view analytically distinct from the question of whether an individual *is* or *is not* being coerced (ibid. 133–4).

[W]hether [an individual] is free or not does not depend on the range of choice but on whether he can expect to shape his course of action in accordance with his present intentions, or whether somebody else has power to so manipulate the conditions as to make him act according to that person's will other than his own. (Hayek 1960: 13)

Hayek emphasizes the distinction between the effects of *intentional human action* and the effects of *impersonal physical circumstances* and *events* in this context. He proposes that only those actions for which a distinct human agency is responsible can limit individual freedom—and that *circumstances* and *events* that are not the responsibility of a distinct personal agent fall outside of the range of possible constraints on freedom. Freedom can only be limited by *other people—circumstances* and *events* that are not the responsibility of a distinct personal agent cannot limit freedom. Even if circumstances are difficult, and an individual has to act under great pressure, he or she ought only to be characterized as acting under *coercion* if a distinct human agency is responsible for causing the circumstances through the intentional threat of harm. In this sense:

[W]hile we can legitimately say that we have been compelled by circumstances to do this or that, we presuppose a human agent if we say that we have been coerced. (Hayek 1960: 133)

'Invisible hand' explanations and the analysis of the 'constraints' on individual freedom

In taking this analysis forward, Hayek links the characterization of individual freedom to a theory of individual responsibility that combines the proposition that people are only responsible for states of affairs that they intentionally cause, with a social and economic theory that characterizes a wide range of socio-economic phenomena as 'unintended outcomes' for which nobody is responsible. Hayek builds here on empiricist approaches that identify a category of phenomena that arise as 'the result of human action but not the execution of human design'. Hayek maintains that this category of social phenomenon—described by Ferguson as 'the result of human action but not of human design'—gives rise to states of affairs for which no specific human agent is responsible. This proposition is developed in the context of a broader social and economic theory that imposes far-reaching limits on the concept of human responsibility by suggesting that:

- A wide range of human practices, values, and institutions—including customs, languages, morals, laws, and markets—are best explained not as the 'intended outcomes' of human actions (i.e. as deliberate acts of will or design), but as the 'unintended outcomes' of 'spontaneous social processes'—for which no distinct human agent is responsible.

- Phenomena which arise as the 'unintended outcomes' of human actions fall *outside* the ambit of human responsibility. They cannot be meaningfully described as 'just' or 'unjust' and ought not to be the subjects of ethical evaluation.[1]

For example, in developing Smith's theory of the 'invisible hand', Hayek emphasizes that competitive market allocations arise not as an 'intended outcome' of some foreseen purpose or plan, but as a result of the actions of millions of self-interested economic agents acting independently, in a 'self-generating' process of adaptation and cumulative growth. He argues that 'unintended outcomes' of this type (*a*) fall outside the ambit of human responsibility; (*b*) cannot be categorized as just or unjust; (*c*) fall outside the range of 'freedom-restricting' conditions (Hayek 1960: 54–70; 1982*b*: 107–32). For example, in developing Smith's theory of the 'invisible hand', Hayek suggests that a *competitive market allocation* does not arise as the *intended outcome* of some foreseen *purpose* or *plan*, but 'spontaneously'—as the *unintended outcome* of actions of millions of independent, self-interested economic agents; and that no distinct human agent can be held responsible for 'self-generating' states of affairs (or 'orders') of this type. He concludes from this analysis that competitive market outcomes are to be categorized as non-coercive—and are inadmissible as constraints on human freedom (Hayek 1982*b*: 107–32). He introduces an important distinction here between *coercion* and the *conditions or terms on which economic agents are willing to render specific services or benefits*. According to Hayek's analysis, so long as the services of a particular person are not crucial to another person's existence or preservation, the conditions exacted for rendering these services cannot properly be called 'coercion'. The only possible exception that Hayek (1960: 137) concedes relates to a situation where a monopolist withholds an indispensable supply of an essential commodity, when the actions of the monopolist entail both the threat of inflicting harm, and the intention to bring about a certain action.

---

[1] Hayek's 'evolutionary' approach builds on eighteenth-century empiricist theories that suggest the existence of a category of social and economic phenomena that arise not as the *intended outcomes* of human plans and purposes, but which emerge and prevail as the *unintended outcomes* of spontaneous processes of *adaptation, selection,* and *cumulative growth*. Hence 'order' in human affairs arises not only from rational processes, but also from spontaneous processes of evolutionary development and change. Hayek's distinction between 'self-generating' (or 'endogenous') orders and planned (or 'exogenous') orders builds on this approach (Hayek 1960: 69; 1982*a*: 84).

The focus on 'universal negative obligations'

Hayek's negative theory of freedom is complemented by a negative theory of 'universal obligation' and a negative theory of fundamental or human rights. In Hayek's view (1982b: 38–55), fundamental principles of justice take the form of 'end-independent' general and abstract rules that consistently apply to everyone equally without exception. He maintains that abstract and general rules of this type are essentially 'negative' and 'limiting' principles that are independent of particular ends and goals and establish 'universal negative obligations' of omission and restraint rather than 'universal positive obligations' of assistance and aid. This emphasis also gives rise to a principle of 'equal treatment' that focuses on the fairness of processes, rules, and transactions, rather than outcomes and results, and which according to Hayek is a defining characteristic of an equal (as opposed to privileged) and an impartial (as opposed to arbitrary) society. Significantly, Hayek maintains that this principle of equal treatment cannot take account of the results achieved by particular population groups and in this sense conflicts with the goal of material equality. Given differences in ability and needs, as well as in physical and social environments, the only means for government to ensure an *equal distribution* on the basis of need, merit, and/or desert would be to undertake actions to *compensate* for individual and environmental differences. In Hayek's view, this would involve the government in arbitrary, discretionary, and discriminatory actions that are incompatible with the principle of equality of treatment.

Equal treatment in this sense has nothing to do with the question whether the application of such general rules in a particular situation may lead to *results* which are more favourable to one group than to others: justice is not concerned with the results of the various transactions but only with whether the transactions themselves are fair. (Hayek 1982a: 141)

The negative characterization of fundamental or human rights

Hayek maintains that negative rights fall within the scope of the 'fundamental principles of justice' and can be meaningfully and coherently characterized as fundamental or human rights. Whereas he characterizes negative rights as 'end-independent', abstract and general rules, which are admissible as 'universal rights' because they apply to all people on an equal basis, he contends that positive rights are not admissible as 'universal rights'. In Hayek's conceptual framework, positive rights are viewed as rights 'to particular things' that are only possible in the context of voluntary agreements and/or special circumstances (such as tie-relationships), and that require the assignment of responsibility to particular agents (in the form of precise counterparty obligations to ensure that the benefits of the right are provided). Hayek (1982b: 101–2) further argues in this context: '[N]obody has a right to a particular state of affairs unless it is the duty of someone to secure it'. This argument reflects traditions in ethics and law that maintain that the ability of an individual to enforce the performance (or non-performance) of a specific action that should be performed or not performed is an essential characteristic of a right. In the absence of specification of counterpart duties, or if the bearers of the counterpart duties fail to be identified, there is no way of ensuring that the benefits incurred by the rights are fulfilled, rendering rights-based claims legally unenforceable and meaningless. Hayek's critique of the economic and social rights enumerated in the Universal Declaration arises in this context. According to Hayek, these 'alleged rights' have no legal meaning because they represent positive claims to particular benefits to which every human being is allegedly entitled, but for which no distinct human agent is responsible—with no precise corresponding obligation to ensure that the benefits of the rights are provided.[2]

Nozick on 'invisible hand' explanations and the 'side-constraint' model

In building on Hayek's 'outcome-independent' approach, Nozick (1974) sets out a theory of individual justice that focuses on procedural fairness (the fairness of historical rules of acquisition, transfer, and rectification) rather than the evaluation of end-states (including personal outcomes and the results for individuals groups). Although Nozick does not commit to Hayek's evolutionary social theory (ibid. 20), 'invisible-hand explanations' nevertheless play an important role in Nozick's rejection of 'end-state principles' and in his treatment of the parameters of legitimate state action (by ruling out the pursuit of 'patterned outcomes' including redistribution). According to Nozick's analysis, libertarian rights do not limit individual freedom because this set of rights is compatible with an

---

[2] Hayek further argues that claims of this type cannot be universalized within the framework of a free society (Hayek 1960: 1–22, 71–84, 133–47; 1982b: 101–6). Guaranteeing these rights would entail replacing society (a 'spontaneous order') with a planned order (or 'taxis') and this cannot be achieved within the framework of a free society. '[Such rights] could not be made universal within a system of rules of just conduct based on the conception of individual responsibility .... [T]he old

'invisible hand' explanation of the 'minimal state' and the rejection of 'end-state principles'. Fundamental or basic rights of this type are associated with prohibitions of action or courses of action and take the form: '[D]on't violate constraints C' (ibid. 29). Nozick contends that this characterization captures the fundamental moral obligation not to treat others as a means to an end (as set out in the second formulation of Kant's 'categorical imperative'). He argues that the side-constraint model captures this fundamental moral obligation through the imposition of inviolability conditions that rule out the possibility of balancing-off individual rights in an overall system of maximum rights-fulfilment for a population as a whole, or of trading-off individual rights in pursuit of *other* (non-rights related) end-state principles or goals. In a model of this type, fundamental or basic rights function to limit and constrain the domain of legitimate social choice (by fixing certain alternatives and excluding others, rather than by determining a social ordering) (ibid. 166). Nozick contrasts this model with approaches that build the side constraints (C) into the goals (G) of consequentialist ethical systems. He maintains that embedding rights-realizations in a system of overall rights-maximization, or some other goal-maximizing ethical system, results in a relaxation of the prohibition of rights-violations and a 'utilitarianism' of rights (ibid. 28–30).

The logical structure of libertarian rights

In order to preclude a need for balancing and trade-offs, and to ensure that conflicts of duties do not arise, Nozick presents the 'side-constraint' model as a 'frictionless' model in which all admissible fundamental or basic rights are viewed as being logically co-possible. The 'co-possibility' thesis seems to imply:

- Each admissible human right must be *realizable* in the sense that their complete fulfilment is feasible (the associated duties are feasible);
- The complete set of individual rights must be simultaneously feasible (the associated duties do not conflict).

Nozick's position here may be understood in terms of a logical condition (the 'condition of universalization') that relates to the admissibility of

---

civil rights and the new social and economic rights . . . are in fact incompatible . . . It is . . . meaningless to describe [these human rights] as claims on 'society' because 'society' cannot think, act, value, or 'treat' anybody in a particular way. . . . [These] rights could not be enforced by law without at the same time destroying that liberal order at which the old civil rights aim' (Hayek 1982*b*: 103–4).

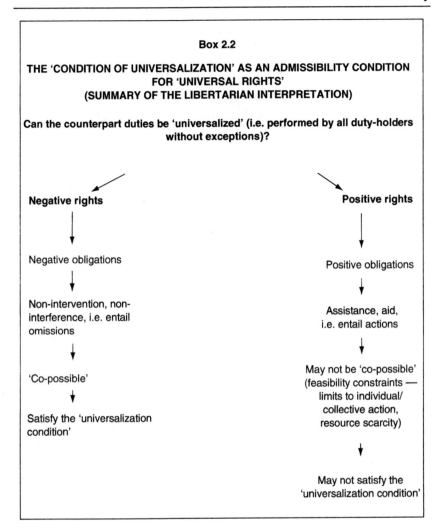

Box 2.2

THE 'CONDITION OF UNIVERSALIZATION' AS AN ADMISSIBILITY CONDITION FOR 'UNIVERSAL RIGHTS' (SUMMARY OF THE LIBERTARIAN INTERPRETATION)

Can the counterpart duties be 'universalized' (i.e. performed by all duty-holders without exceptions)?

Negative rights

Negative obligations

Non-intervention, non-interference, i.e. entail omissions

'Co-possible'

Satisfy the 'universalization condition'

Positive rights

Positive obligations

Assistance, aid, i.e. entail actions

May not be 'co-possible' (feasibility constraints — limits to individual/ collective action, resource scarcity)

May not satisfy the 'universalization condition'

obligations as 'universal obligations' (Box 2.2). The libertarian interpretation of this condition focuses on the question of whether it is logically possible for counterpart duties (in the form of actions) to be performed by all duty-holders without exception. Negative obligations of non-interference and non-intervention are viewed as being associated with duties that (*a*) involve negative actions of omission and restraint, (*b*) are not subject to feasibility and resource constraints, and (*c*) are logically *co-possible* in the sense of being individually and simultaneously feasible. For example, it is feasible for a person to refrain from undertaking a certain action (such as interfering in another person's 'private sphere' or interfering with their property) in respect of all others. In contrast, positive obligations of assistance and aid are viewed as giving rise to duties that entail positive acts of commission that may not be logically co-possible. The performance of positive duties of this type may incur costs and be limited by resource and feasibility constraints. For example, it may not be feasible for a person to perform a particular positive action (such as 'feeding those in need') in respect of all others. The 'mutual incompatibility' of positive duties of this type is taken to rule out the possibility of 'universal positive obligations' in the libertarian framework. Nozick contends that the entire set of individual rights that satisfy these conditions comprises a set of negative rights that is associated with exclusively negative duties of omission and restraint. Negative conceptions of the human rights to 'freedom from severe poverty' and to 'freedom from hunger and starvation' that focus on non-interference with the 'means of life' (e.g. with the person or property) are admissible in this framework. However, fundamental freedoms and human rights that are limited by resources and/or other feasibility constraints (such as the human rights to an adequate standard of living, food, and health) are viewed as generating 'conflicting positive obligations' and are ruled out by the model. Similarly, the Hayekian position on the non-admissibility of positive fundamental or human rights can be explained with respect to the 'condition of universalization'. Although Hayek views positive rights as having meaning and coherence in the context of tie-relationships and special relationships, as universal claims they are viewed as incoherent, indeterminate, and unenforceable—because they fail to satisfy a test of 'generalization' and do not relate to duties that can be performed systematically and consistently by all duty-holders in relation to all rights-holders without exceptions (Hayek 1982*b*: 15–17, 27–9, 38–55).

The 'side constraint model' and 'absolutism'

Nozick's 'side constraint' model is often interpreted as a paradigmatic example of an 'absolutist' model of fundamental or basic rights. In a pure 'absolutist' model, duties that flow from individual rights are viewed as being non-contingent (in the sense of applying in all circumstances), categorical (in the sense that their violation is always wrong), and irreducibly absolute (in the sense of imposing absolute limits on individual action rather than prima facie obligations to be weighed up and balanced against other considerations). Nozick's (1974: 28–30, 164–6) model 'approximates' an 'absolutist' theory of fundamental freedoms and human rights by suggesting that a neutral vantage point in ethics can be achieved by adopting deontological rather than consequential forms of reasoning—with little or no weight attributed to consequences in ethical evaluation.[3] In practice, however, Nozick fails to develop an ethical system that is entirely independent of the evaluation of end-states. For example, he concedes the possibility of a limited role for consequences in ethical evaluation in his treatment of the 'Lockean proviso', stating that: 'A process normally giving rise to a property right in a previously un-owned thing will not do so if the position of others no longer at liberty to use the thing is thereby worsened' (ibid. 178). Nozick also concedes the possibility that 'side-constraints' may be violated in order to prevent 'catastrophic moral horrors'—suggesting that the duties in his theory may after all be prima facie rather than absolute (ibid: 30).[4]

2.2 Broadening the Reach of Negative Theories of Fundamental Freedom and Human Rights

Influential theories in the liberal as well as the libertarian tradition have also suggested that impartiality in ethics requires the development of exclusively negative characterizations of fundamental freedoms and human rights. For example, Berlin (1969) defends a negative theory of human freedom and fundamental rights in the context of a background theory of value pluralism and the limits of rationalism in ethical evaluation. He contends that conceptions of the human good or human goods may conflict and that there may be no rational means of resolving ethical disputes. Given these conditions of irreducible value pluralism, Berlin suggests a characterization of the idea of freedom that relates not to the

---

[3] Deontological theories focus on the idea of intrinsically right actions, with little or no weight being given to the goodness (or badness) of resulting states of affairs. These theories are often characterized in terms of absolute, categorical constraints that ought not to be relaxed, even to maximise the fulfilment of rights over a population as a whole, or to maximize the achievement of other goods (such as utility-maximization). Deontological theories are often contrasted with consequentialist theories, which define right actions derivatively—in terms of producing the maximum good. See McNaughton (1998a, b).

[4] Do these concessions to the role of consequences in ethical evaluation imply that Nozick's theory is not truly deontological? The ongoing debate about the status of moral constraints under deontological theories—whether they must be absolute, or whether they merely provide a 'weighty reason' for non-violation—is summarized in McNaughton (1998a).

power or ability of an individual to achieve some *particular* end or goal, but rather to their freedom to exercise choices between *alternative* ends and goals—that is, to the area within which a person or group of persons is or should be left to do or be what he is able to do or be, without interference by other persons. Berlin distinguishes this 'fundamental' meaning of the term freedom ('negative freedom') from 'positive freedom' (or *freedom to*)—which he suggests relates exclusively to the realization of individual desires, powers, capacities, needs, or interests. Hence:

You lack...freedom only if you are prevented from attaining a goal by human beings.... Coercion implies the deliberate interference of other human beings within the area in which I could otherwise act. (Berlin 1969: lx, 122)

Berlin's treatment of the distinctions between freedom, needs, and opportunities

This emphasis on 'deliberate interference' is often taken to encapsulate the idea of *intentionality*, so that Berlin, like Hayek, is often interpreted as implying that only other people's *intentional actions* can constrain or limit negative freedom. Like Hayek, Berlin characterizes freedom in terms of the absence of *coercion* by others and that the characterization of negative freedom is logically independent of the fulfilment of individual desires and of the *power*, *ability*, or *capacity* of an individual to achieve desired goals in practice. For example, Berlin (1969: 122) emphasizes that 'mere incapacity to attain a goal' is not a lack of negative freedom. He also emphasizes the analytical distinction between freedom and the conditions and value of freedom (ibid. liii–iv) and insists that negative freedom is logically independent of the fulfilment of individual needs.

To provide for material needs...is not to expand liberty....The Egyptian peasant needs clothes or medicine before, and more than, personal liberty, but the minimum freedom that he needs today, and the greater degree of freedom that he may need tomorrow, is not some species of freedom peculiar to him, but identical with that of professors, artists, and millionaires. (Berlin 1969: lv, 124–5)

Yet there are significant differences between Hayek and Berlin's position. In contrast to 'objectivist approaches', Berlin contends that any assessment of individual freedom is deeply evaluative, and will be dependent on the evaluation of both the range and adequacy of the options and opportunities available.

[The extent of negative freedom depends on the] absence of obstructions on roads along which a man can decide to walk. Such freedom ultimately depends not on whether I wish to walk at all, or how far, but on how many doors are open, how open they are, upon their relative importance in my life. (Berlin 1969: xxxix–lx; cf. lxviii)

Can a concern with poverty, hunger, and starvation be accommodated within a theory of negative freedom?

Furthermore, the question of whether poverty, or deprivation in human needs, can fall within the reach of Berlin's characterization of coercion hinges on interpretation of the idea of 'deliberate human arrangements'. Berlin contends that when poverty is caused by the deliberate arrangements of other human beings, poverty can be meaningfully characterized as a limitation of negative freedom.

[I]f my poverty were a kind of disease, which prevented me from buying bread . . . as lameness prevents me from running, this inability would not naturally be described as a lack of freedom. . . . [But if] I believe that my inability to get a given thing is due to the fact that other human beings have made arrangements whereby I am, whereas others are not, prevented form having enough money with which to pay for it. . . . I think myself a victim of coercion or slavery. In other words, this use of the term depends on a particular social and economic theory about the causes of my poverty or weakness. If my lack of material means is due to my lack of mental or physical capacity, then I begin to speak of being deprived of freedom (and not simply about poverty) only if I accept that theory. (Berlin 1969: 122–3)

The debates about the interpretation of Berlin's position here have far-reaching implications for the specification and justification of a class of fundamental freedoms and human rights. According to Plant, the phrase 'human beings have made arrangements' should probably be interpreted as implying human *intentionality*. He nevertheless acknowledges that Berlin's stated position depends on the socio-economic analysis of the causes of poverty and that broader readings would result in a significantly expanded list of freedom-limiting conditions. For example, under a broader interpretation, the outcomes of social and economic processes (including market outcomes) might be characterized as 'freedom restricting' conditions if their consequences, though *unintended,* are *foreseeable* or *alterable* (Plant 1991: 235). Gray's analysis emphasizes this broader reading of Berlin's position. He maintains that the phrase 'deliberate human arrangements' accommodates a recognition that 'the reasonable attribution of human responsibility' depends on a range of factors other than intentionality. In this conceptual framework, individual freedom can be characterized as being restricted by states of affairs that are unintended, but that are, for example, remediable, alterable, foreseeable, and/or predictable (Gray 1989: 61–5; 1995a: 27).[5]

Building on Berlin's emphasis on the relevance of socio-economic analysis of the causes of poverty

The argument that the characterization of fundamental freedoms and human rights is contingent on economic and social theories about the *causes* of global poverty, hunger, and starvation provides an important link with Sen's work. Sen interprets Berlin as taking a 'demanding view of negative freedom', going well beyond the 'immunity' component of process, and taking note 'of the various parts that others play in making a person unable to do something'. He suggests that this approach is 'not incompatible' with the idea that poverty and starvation resulting from insufficient demand in the labour market could be characterized as a violation of negative freedom (Sen 1993b: 524). The reach of Berlin's framework is extended if poverty, hunger, and non-survival can be demonstrated to be the *foreseeable* or *alterable* outcomes of social and economic processes—and many of Sen's contributions in economics can be interpreted in terms of the analytical space generated by this idea. Sen's research in theoretical and empirical economics has made a major contribution to the evaluation of economic arrangements, processes, and outcomes (including processes such as development, growth, and globalization and competitive market outcomes) from the perspective of substantive human freedoms, rather than other informational perspectives (e.g. including utility or growth). His research has pushed forward understanding of the ways in which the denial and violation of human freedoms can sometimes be characterized as the foreseeable outcomes of economic processes and arrangements and provides an important body of empirical evidence establishing the ways in which economic outcomes, processes, and arrangements are alterable and remediable. For example, Sen's (1981) applications of the 'entitlement approach' establish the role of individual entitlements (rather than the overall food supply) in explaining hunger and starvation in four major famines, whilst the 'capability framework' provides an important body of empirical evidence on the

---

[5] Berlin also develops the case for collective obligations to undertake the actions that are necessary to secure the minimum conditions of negative freedom (1969: xlvi).

complementary role of different institutions (economic, political, legal, etc.) in expanding substantive freedoms and protecting and promoting human rights.

Pogge's extensions of the exclusively negative approach

Pogge (2002a, 2004) also emphasizes the ways that the reach of negative theories of fundamental freedoms and human rights can be extended by taking account of *causes* of global poverty. He contends that it is possible to go beyond the libertarian position without denying its central tenet (that human rights entail only negative obligations) by establishing that social institutions have a *causal* role in generating insecure access to the objects of human rights (ibid. 66). Given (*a*) the proposition that institutions have a *causal* role in the generation and persistence of poverty and (*b*) the proposition that individuals have responsibility (albeit collectively) for the creation and perpetuation of such institutions, he maintains that fundamental freedoms and human rights can be viewed as giving rise to negative obligations of individuals and collective agents to refrain from supporting such institutions—with failure to respect negative obligations being viewed not in terms of the failure to assist and aid those who are in desperate need, but in terms of causal responsibility for the generation and persistence of poverty. In developing this approach, Pogge emphasizes the ways in which global institutions, rules, and processes can be shown to play a causal role in generating and perpetuating severe poverty and proposes that 'any institutional order that foreseeably and avoidably produces an excess of severe poverty and of mortality from poverty-related causes manifests a human rights violation on the part of those who participate in imposing this order' (Pogge 2004: 17).

'Severe poverty as a violation of negative duties'[6]

The core of Pogge's argument is that by bringing in the issue of causality it is possible to establish severe poverty as a human rights violation under a 'minimalist normative position' that is widely acceptable—namely, that

---

[6] Pogge adopts the following interpretation: (*a*) duties are morally fundamental; (*b*) some duties are *generative* duties—that is, duties that, in conjunction with appropriate empirical circumstances, create more specific moral reasons of action: obligations (2005: 68). The sub-sections that follow reflect these terminological distinctions as much as possible.

human rights and justice involve fundamental principles of negative duty: that is, 'specific minimal constraints—more minimal in the case of human rights—on what harms persons may inflict upon others' (Pogge 2002*a*: 13; 2004). The underlying rationale is to develop a theory of severe poverty as a violation of human rights on the basis of the assumption that human rights impose not a fundamental positive duty to protect the vulnerable or to remedy urgent need, but rather a fundamental negative constraint on conduct (prohibiting conduct that causes severe poverty, and imposing an associated restriction on intuitional schemes that can be imposed). Human rights-based claims arising from severe poverty are then characterized in terms of rectification for harm done by past and present conduct (rather than on the basis of fundamental positive duties of assistance and aid).

The ethical distinction between 'active causation' and 'failure to alleviate'

In developing his theory of severe poverty as a violation of negative duties, Pogge adopts the following 'working' assumption:

[H]uman rights impose only negative duties: Human rights require that agents *not harm* human beings in certain specific ways but they do not require that agents help or protect anyone whose human rights are unfulfilled or threatened . . . [The assumption that] human rights impose only negative duties means that they require only omissions, not acts, and that they can be violated only by acts, not by omissions. Agents must refrain from (actively) causing others' human rights to be unfulfilled. (Pogge 2004: 8)

Pogge maintains that, by moving forward on the basis of this 'minimalist normative position', it is possible to construct a 'middle position' between the libertarian emphasis on negative constraints (which he rejects on the grounds that people are entirely disconnected from deprivations that they do not directly bring about) and consequential approaches (which he rejects on the grounds that people are held to have obligations in relation to *all* deprivations, regardless of their causal relation to them). He places particular emphasis in this context on the 'important ethical distinction' between the *active causation* of severe poverty and the *failure to alleviate* severe poverty emphasized by libertarians for the development of a negative theory of human rights. For example, consider the moral claim that we are responsible for any poverty deaths that we actively cause, but not for poverty deaths that we might have prevented.

Challenging [this] moral claim, one might argue that the distinction between causing poverty and failing to reduce it has little or no moral importance.... This challenge can draw support from consequentialist ideas and veil-of-ignorance reasoning à la Rawls. But I reject such a heavily recipient-oriented approach and agree, on this point, with libertarians...that the distinction between causing poverty and merely failing to reduce it is morally significant...(Pogge 2002a: 13)

The clarificatory remarks in Pogge (2005: 67) suggest that acceptance of the 'working assumption' that human rights correlate with negative duties entails neither a rejection nor an acceptance of the proposition that human rights correlate with positive duties—but rather makes no further assumptions on this issue. That is, Pogge suggests that acceptance of a theory of severe poverty as a violation of negative duties entails acceptance of the following proposition:

Proposition 1: '[T]he human rights of others impose upon us a negative duty "not to cooperate in the imposition of a coercive institutional order that avoidably leaves human rights unfulfilled without making reasonable efforts to aid its victims and to promote institutional reform" ' (ibid. 65), where scope of proposition 1 is apparently restricted by:

- A focus on negative duty (i.e. a 'minimalist normative position' that imposes a moral constraint not to cause poverty (and hence a moral constraint not to participate in or support global institutions that cause poverty));
- An emphasis on the ethical distinction between 'actively causing' and 'failing to alleviate';

without accepting (or rejecting) the following proposition:

Proposition 2: The human rights of others impose upon us a *positive duty* not to cooperate in the imposition of a coercive institutional order that avoidably leaves human rights unfulfilled without making reasonable efforts to aid its victims and to promote institutional reform (where 'positive duty' refers to 'fundamental' positive duties of assistance and aid).

The role of socio-economic theory in the ethical framework set out in Pogge (2002a, 2004)

Underpinning Pogge's position here is the proposition that it is possible to move forward in the characterization of severe poverty as a violation of human rights by challenging the (libertarian) factual claim that the existing global order is not causing poverty and harming the poor, whilst accepting the (libertarian) normative assumption that human rights correlate with a fundamental principle of negative duty but not with a fundamental principle of positive duty. The underlying rationale here is to address sceptics and to demonstrate that even on minimalist libertarian assumptions, the negative duty imposes a negative constraint with respect to the imposition of global economic and financial institutions that cause severe poverty. Pogge's analysis then turns on socio-economic theory and the ways in which global economic and financial arrangements such as those discussed in Section 1.2—including those relating to the intellectual property rights (e.g. the WTO patent rules set out in 'TRIPS' agreements), agricultural subsidies, dumping practices, restrictions on developing country market access, as well as the impact of structural adjustment, debt repayments, and other economic and development policies—can be viewed as causing foreseeable and avoidable forms of severe poverty.

The reach of Pogge's theory

What proportion of the world's cases of severe poverty will give rise to human rights-based claims by adopting this approach? Pogge maintains that 'features of the present global order cause massive severe poverty' and that many or most cases of severe poverty will therefore fall within the reach of a negative theory of human rights. However, this proposition requires far-reaching theoretical and empirical investigation. As Pogge notes, in considering the characterization of severe poverty as a human rights issue under a negative theory:

The relevant analogue to torture is ... not (actually) poverty, but rather a certain kind of impoverishment that other agents are causally and morally responsible for. (Pogge 2004: 4)

The status of two categories of cases of severe poverty within Pogge's theory requires further examination. These are:

- Cases of severe poverty included within the scope of Pogge's negative theory of human rights, but only because they fall within the reach of a contested theory of causality.
- Cases of severe poverty excluded from the scope of Pogge's theory, because they fall outside the reach of Pogge's theory of causality.

The question of the extent to which the global economic order causes harm, versus the extent to which the global economic order can be credited with the improvement in living standards, including poverty alleviation and the ground-breaking improvements in health, is widely contested. The first category of cases raises far-reaching and controversial theoretical and empirical questions concerning the evaluation of trends in global poverty and inequality; nature and scope of the underlying explanatory variables; the relative weight to be given to global institutions versus other variables such as domestic factors (including domestic economic policy, domestic political and institutional arrangements, cultural variables, climatic and environmental factors, economic endowments, and interpersonal variations); the nature of the evidential thresholds of 'causation' and the use of baseline comparisons; and the differential impact, aims, and functions of different international institutions (e.g. WHO, UNDP and FAO, the WTO, the World Bank, and the IMF).[7] In relation to the second category of cases, even if global institutions can be shown to generate and perpetuate a large proportion of the world's cases of severe and extreme poverty, other cases may nevertheless fall beyond the 'causality' threshold and therefore outside the characterization of severe poverty as a human rights issue. Examples might include cases of severe poverty attributable to interpersonal variations that cannot be attributed to socio-economic causes (e.g. inherited disability), to factors widely attributed to 'bad luck' (e.g. harsh climatic conditions or having poor factor endowments such as being landlocked), and to other contextual variables (e.g. environmentally induced disasters). Consider a poor country A in which cases of severe poverty are generated by the loss of livelihood and shelter caused by an environmentally induced tsunami, and where resource and feasibility constraints prevent an adequate domestic response. If cases of severe poverty of this type cannot be plausibly characterized as being caused by rich-country imposition of global institutions, then they apparently fall outside the reach of Pogge's theory of causation and culpability, and therefore of his negative theory of human rights.[8]

Is the position set out in Pogge (2002a, 2004) accurately characterized as a 'minimalist normative position'?

Another set of issues concerns the question of whether the normative position set out in Pogge (2002a, 2004) is as 'minimalist' as Pogge suggests.

---

[7] For further discussion of these issues, see Cruft (2005), Gilabert (2005) and Patten (2005), Risse (2005), and Barry (2005).

[8] But see the comments on pages 83–4.

Whilst claiming to accept as a 'working assumption' the central tenet of the libertarian normative position (i.e. the view that justice and human rights correlate with a negative fundamental principle of duty), Pogge's normative position in fact makes a radical departure from the libertarian framework in critical respects. For example:

- Pogge's characterization of the range of fundamental freedoms and human rights, a far-reaching departure from the libertarian list, includes liberties, political participation, and other elementary basic goods including physical integrity, subsistent supplies (of food and drink, clothing, shelter, and basic health care) as well as basic education (Pogge 2002a: 49).

- Pogge proposes a broad characterization of human rights as the universal core criterion of justice that demands that all social institutions be designed so that all human rights, in so far as reasonably possible, have secure access to the objects of their human rights. Applying this criterion of justice entails examining (*a*) whether the present system of institutional arrangements contributes to human rights deficits; (*b*) is there a feasible alternative that would not have generated such human rights deficits? This application of the human rights as a 'minimum criterion of justice' is a far-reaching departure from the 'outcome-independent' theories developed by Hayek (1960, 1982a, 1982b, 1982c) and Nozick (1974). In particular, it involves evaluating the fairness of global economic order in terms of the fairness of the outcomes achieved, as well as the fairness of procedures.

- Whilst proceeding on the assumption that human rights correlate with fundamental negative duties, Pogge maintains that under particular empirical circumstances these negative duties entail 'derived duties to perform positive actions' (in Pogge's terminology, 'positive obligations'), including an important category of 'positive derived duties' to make compensating protection and reform. In claiming that these 'positive derivate duties' fall within the scope of a negative view of human rights, Pogge maintains that these 'positive derived duties' are 'remedial duties' that follow from a fundamental principle of negative duty, rather than a fundamental principle of positive duty, and are therefore compatible with the categories of positive duties accepted by libertarians (which include the duties that arise from special and voluntary relationships such as family ties and contractual as well as remedial duties) (Pogge 2005: 68). In this way Pogge arrives at the conclusion that 'a very important source of positive obligations with regard to severe poverty in the modern world is our negative duty not to participate in the imposition of social institutions under which some lack secure access to the objects of their human rights' (Pogge 2004: 12).

Arguably Pogge's position in these respects goes beyond a 'minimalist normative assumption', with Pogge developing a broad characterization of human rights that would not be accepted by libertarians, and implicitly committing himself to what are traditionally characterized as fundamental positive duties of assistance and aid.[9] Gilabert (2005: 542) notes that Pogge's 'positive derived duties' are only compatible with the minimalist normative premises of the libertarian rectification model if the objective of the compensations is strictly to remedy the harm caused for past conduct, rather than to make the objects of human rights fully secure. In order words, human rights-based claims under Pogge's negative model might be expected to arise not from a human rights deficit per se, but rather should strictly relate to the element of non-fulfilment associated with harmful conduct in the form of 'active causation'. However, many of Pogge's applications and illustrations, based on an 'institutional understanding' of human rights, seem to go considerably beyond this position.

Does the distinction between 'active causation' and 'failure to alleviate' play a pivotal role in Pogge's 'institutional understanding' of human rights?

Certainly, the ethical distinction between causing poverty deaths and preventing poverty deaths also seems to have less of a pivotal role in Pogge's ethical framework than his discussions sometimes suggest. According to Pogge's 'institutional understanding' of human rights:

A human right to X gives rise to a moral claim against all others that they not harm you by cooperating, without compensating protection and reform efforts, in imposing upon you an institutional order in which you lack secure access to X as part of a foreseeable and avoidable human rights deficit. (Gilabert 2005: 67)

In applying and illustrating this 'institutional understanding', Pogge seems to make use of an evidential threshold regarding the establishment

---

[9] On which, see Cruft (2005), Gilabert (2005), and Patten (2005).

of human rights claims that goes significantly beyond a 'minimalist normative premise' embodying a clear ethical distinction between the 'active causation' of harm and the 'alleviation of harm'. In particular, many of Pogge's applications and illustrations seem to lower the evidential threshold necessary for the establishment of human rights-based claims from one relating to the 'active causation' of severe poverty (involving 'specific minimal constraints—more minimal in the case of human rights—on what harms persons may inflict upon others') to one that relates more broadly to the 'alleviation of severe poverty'. This is achieved by interpreting the notion of the 'avoidability' and 'foreseeability' of severe poverty in a way that takes account of the feasibility of alleviating severe poverty through preventative action. For example, the causality attributed to TRIPS agreements in Pogge (2005) suggests that the 'failure to alleviate' (reduce/prevent) avoidable and foreseeable mortality and morbidity by establishing an appropriate incentive structure that can ensure appropriate research and development, and supply, of essential medicines in poor countries meets the threshold for the establishment of human rights-based claims. That is, cases of severe poverty that are avoidable because they are preventable through alternative institutional design give rise to human rights-based claims—and the category of 'institutional failure to alleviate' is brought within the reach of Pogge's theory. Despite the emphasis on the 'important ethical distinction' between causing poverty deaths and failing to alleviate poverty deaths—and notwithstanding his scepticism vis-à-vis the question of whether the category of 'interactional omissions' can be characterized as falling within the reach of a negative theory of human rights—the distinction between 'actively causing' and 'failing to alleviate' does not seem to be critical for the establishment of human rights-based claims in Pogge's ethical framework. The 'relabelling' charge posed by Patten arises in this context.

In effect, what would traditionally have been regarded as positive duties of assistance and aid get relabelled as negative duties, via the thought that the shortfall or vulnerability that gives rise, on the traditional view, to a positive duty could be redescribed as the imposition of an institutional order in which the shortfall or vulnerability is not alleviated. (Patten 2005: 27)[10]

---

[10] For further discussions of Pogge's treatment of positive duty, see the various discussions in Pogge (forthcoming).

2.3 Towards a Sub-set of Fundamental Freedoms and Human Rights that Focuses Directly on the Valuable Things that People Can Do and Be

The approaches set out in Section 2.2 are important in demonstrating the ways in which a negative conception of 'freedom from extreme poverty as a fundamental human right' can be characterized narrowly (with negative universal obligations being construed in terms of non-interference with the means of life) or more broadly (in terms of the negative obligation to refrain from supporting institutions that cause and perpetuate extreme poverty). They establish the important links between the justification of a class of fundamental or human rights and the socio-economic analysis of the causes and foreseeability/avoidablility and remediability of poverty, hunger, starvation, and other states of deprivation such as morbidity and mortality, and the important ways in which a fundamental principle of negative obligation might be extended from a theory of non-interference and non-intervention to a theory of non-injury that covers both the obligation not to contribute to harm (including harm caused by supporting institutions that cause and perpetuate global poverty) and not to cause harm through omissions (including the harm caused by individual and collective failure to reduce and eradicate global poverty).

Can an exclusively negative theory of human rights capture and reflect internationally recognized standards in the field of global poverty and human rights?

Nevertheless, even a broadly conceived negative theory of fundamental freedoms and human rights can have important limitations. Pogge's theory is important for highlighting the ways in which an important category of 'positive derived duties' (or 'positive obligations' in Pogge's terminology) can be viewed in terms of a theory of rectification for past and present harm caused. However, as Pogge explicitly acknowledges, the adoption of a 'minimalist normative assumption' imposes limits on what an exclusively negative theory of human rights can do. Viewing human rights as imposing a negative constraint on conduct (prohibiting the causation of severe poverty, including participation in institutions that cause severe poverty) restricts the imposition of harm 'actively inflicted'; but this minimalist normative assumption does not provide a basis for the justification of 'fundamental' positive duties of assistance and aid (with no causality established). The reach of Pogge's applications and illustrations—based on his 'institutional understanding' of human rights—is only extended by introducing a broad evidential threshold that relates human rights-based claims to the 'failure to alleviate severe poverty' (through preventative measures) as well as to the 'active infliction of severe poverty'. However, the reasons for questioning how precisely this 'institutional understanding' relates to Pogge's 'minimalist working assumption' were discussed in Section 2.2. In particular, the positive duties involved seem to go beyond Pogge's elucidation of the set of 'positive derived duties'—characterized as being 'triggered' by non-compliance with a fundamental negative duty 'not to actively cause harm' and excluding positive duties of assistance and aid (with no 'active causality' established).

It is possible to give moral weight to the distinction between 'actively inflicting harm' and 'failing to alleviate harm' without making this distinction pivotal to the establishment of human rights-based claims. Arguably, internationally recognized standards in the field of global poverty and human rights can be best elucidated and justified in an ethical framework of this type. As the discussion in Chapter 5 (especially Section 5.5) will show, internationally recognized standards are widely interpreted as establishing binding positive obligations of assistance and aid on governments—including positive obligations of assistance and aid on non-national governments where resource and feasibility constraints are binding. These standards may be best elucidated in terms of an underlying normative premise that recognizes that human rights give rise to claims of 'reasonable assistance and aid'—whether or not responsibility for the 'active causation' of harm is established. Whereas Pogge's ethical framework makes analytical space for a set of 'positive derived duties' triggered by non-compliance with a fundamental principle of negative obligation, claims of 'reasonable assistance and aid' of this type are often viewed in terms of the general positive obligations to defend and support human rights on the part of those in a position to help. As will be discussed in Section 3.3, positive obligations of this type could perhaps be characterized as arising from a causal relationship of a type—with the concept of 'avoidability' being interpreted even more broadly than in Pogge's (2002*a*, 2004) framework (e.g. by incorporating the idea of an agent having the power to change a human rights-based outcome). In this sense, positive obligations of 'reasonable assistance and aid' could perhaps be incorporated into an extended scheme of 'derived' rather than 'fundamental' positive duties. However, this approach would go even further beyond the 'minimalist normative position' than Pogge's applications and illustrations; and could not be reconciled with the proposition that the ethical distinction between *active causation* and *failure to alleviate* is pivotal to the establishment of human rights-based claims.

Towards a broader theory of fundamental freedoms and human rights

Against this background, Chapter 3 will focus on the ways in which Sen's contributions in ethics have taken forward:

- Discussions relating to the justification of a broad characterization of fundamental freedoms and human rights, including the justification of a sub-set of fundamental freedoms and human rights relating to the valuable things that people can do and be;
- Discussions relating to the question of whether positive obligations of assistance and aid can be meaningfully and coherently incorporated into a theory of fundamental freedoms and human rights—including the question of how the nature and scope of positive obligations to support and defend human rights might be delimited through the development of the notion of 'reasonable' assistance and aid.

The remainder of this chapter discusses how these issues have been dealt with in the broader literature. This section deals with some of the broader debates in the literature about how the distinction between negative and positive views of fundamental freedoms and human rights can be challenged. Section 2.4 then deals with debates concerning the question of whether universal positive obligations (as well as universal negative obligations) can correlate with human rights.

Challenging the logical basis of the distinction between negative and positive freedom

The downgrading and neglect of global poverty as a human rights issue has often been associated with attempts to draw categorical distinctions between negative and positive freedoms, and negative and positive rights. Important bodies of literature in ethics and political theory challenge the underlying logical basis of these distinctions. MacCallum has, for example, argued that the concept of freedom is only intelligible as a *single complex* concept. He contends that a range of possible constraints—positive, negative, internal, or external—are relevant to a full description of freedom, which he characterizes in logical terms as being of the *triadic* form 'x is (is not) free from y to do (not do, become, not become) z', where x represents an agent or agents, y 'preventing conditions' (e.g. constraints, restrictions, interferences, and barriers), and z actions or conditions (MacCallum 1973 [1967]). Gewirth similarly suggests that all rights fall within the logic of the following formula: 'A has a right to X against B in virtue of Y' (Gewirth 1978). In another important intervention, Taylor has rejected the *end-independent* status of rights-based ethical theories on the basis that rights-based claims entail an explicit or implicit affirmation of the *value* of certain human capacities, and cannot, therefore, be independent of some underlying theory of the human good or goods. In defending and elaborating this view, Taylor contends that the claim of an agent A to moral respect in enjoying or doing X entails a recognition that A has *essential properties or capacities, E*, such that the injunction 'Don't interfere with A's doing or enjoying X' is somehow inescapable. Agent A has a right to X if doing or enjoying X is 'essentially part of manifesting E' or is 'a causally necessary condition of manifesting E'. In this way, the properties or capacities E provide an explicit or implicit basis both for identifying the substantive content of the rights (X) and for identifying the class of rights-bearers (A) (Taylor 1985*a*: 192, 195).

[A right]...has an essential conceptual background, in some notion of the moral worth of certain properties or capacities....[A] right to independent moral convictions...[implies] that the exercise of the relevant capacity is a human good. (Taylor 1985*a*: 195, 198)

Challenges to the basis of the categorical distinction between civil and political rights and economic and social rights

The basis of categorical distinctions between civil and political rights on the one hand, and economic and social rights (e.g. Cranston 1967), has also been widely challenged (e.g. Shue 1980, 1984; Plant 1991; Waldron 1993). The association of civil and political rights with negative obligations, and economic and social rights with positive obligations, has been deconstructed and the institutional requirements and resource implications of civil and political rights have been emphasized. Alternative typologies have emerged that analyse human rights in terms of complex clusters of negative and positive obligations. For example, Shue's influential work in this area characterizes human rights as providing social guarantees in respect of certain basic interests and analyses the obligations associated with human rights in terms of the following typology:

(1) To avoid depriving
(2) To protect from deprivation
    (a) By enforcing duty (1)
    (b) By designing institutions that avoid the creation of strong incentives to violate duty (1)
(3) To aid the deprived
    (a) Who are one's special responsibility;
    (b) Who are victims of social failures in the performance of duties 1, 2(a), and 2(b); and
    (c) Who are victims of natural disasters.

According to this approach, the human right not to be tortured entails (a) duties to avoid depriving (i.e. duties not to eliminate a person's liberty); (b) duties of protection (i.e. duties to protect people against torture, to investigate allegations of torture, and to remedy established cases of torture) through appropriate legislative and institutional measures. The human right to subsistence entails (a) duties to avoid depriving (i.e. duties not to eliminate a person's means of subsistence); (b) duties of protection (i.e. duties to protect people against deprivation in the means of subsistence by third parties); (c) duties of aid (to assist and provide for those deprived of the means of subsistence) (Shue 1980: 13, 60–100; 1984: 83–95). The discussion in Chapter 5 establishes the ways in which this typology underpins widely and authoritatively accepted international legal standards (c.f. Section 5.3).

'Autonomy-based approaches' and the value of positive freedom

A third body of literature emphasizes the importance of personal autonomy, as well as immunity from interference by others, to the characterization of fundamental freedoms and human rights. For example, in Raz's conceptual framework, negative freedom—freedom from coercive interferences—is valuable to the extent that it *serves* autonomy. It does this by preventing coercion and by protecting the options that are open to a person. However, in Raz's view, increasing the number of options does not necessarily increase autonomy. A person may be better off without certain options, or by being denied an option now in order to improve options in the future. Furthermore, whereas discussions of negative freedom can lead to 'a blind obsession with the avoidance of coercion', Raz contends that positive freedom, like negative freedom, has intrinsic value, because it is an essential ingredient and a necessary condition of personal autonomy. The promotion and protection of personal autonomy requires positive freedom—the 'mental abilities necessary for an autonomous life' and the 'availability of an adequate range of options' (Raz 1986: 409–10).

'Substantive opportunity' and 'primary goods'

A fourth body of literature has driven debates forward by establishing the ways that objectivity and impartiality in ethics are compatible with the idea of general, all-purpose 'means to freedom' that all people have reasons to value, whatever their conceptions of the human good or human goods, or their particular ends and goals.[11] Rawls's (1973, 1993) pioneering work in this area highlights the centrality of a person's *real opportunity* to pursue his or her objectives to ethical evaluation and characterizes primary goods as end-independent means to freedom (such as rights, liberties, opportunities, and self-respect) that rational people can be assumed to want and that constitute the core of an 'overlapping consensus' on the meaning of 'citizen's needs' (and of 'rational advantage') under conditions of value pluralism. The principles of justice as fairness aim (*a*) to equalize the basic liberties enjoyed by all people; (*b*) to maximize the value of the equal basic liberties of the least advantaged by regulating inequalities in primary goods according to the 'difference principle'.[12]

---

[11] Plant (1991: 248–51) distinguishes between 'maximalist' approaches (that characterize positive freedom in terms of the realization of particular ends and goals) and 'minimalist' approaches (based on the idea of general means to freedom that all people have reason to value). 'Minimalist' approaches avoid the need for elaborated conceptions of the human good (or goods) and only require general judgments about the needs, desires, capacities, opportunities, and resources that are of fundamental importance.

[12] Primary goods are specified as (*a*) basic rights and liberties; (*b*) freedom of movement and free choice of occupation against a background of diverse opportunities; (*c*) powers and prerogatives of offices and positions of responsibility in the political and economic institutions of the basic structure; (*d*) income and wealth; and (*e*) the social bases of self-respect (Rawls 1993: 181). The equal basic liberties in the first principle of justice are specified as: (*a*) freedom of thought and liberty of conscience; (*b*) the political liberties and freedom of association, as well as the freedoms specified by the liberty and integrity of the person; (*c*) the rights and liberties covered by the rule of law. The principles of justice as fairness are (*a*) each person has an equal right to a fully adequate scheme of equal basic liberties which is compatible with a similar scheme of liberties for all; (*b*) social and economic inequalities are to satisfy two conditions. First, they must be attached to offices and positions open to all under conditions of fair equality of opportunity; and second, they must be to the greatest benefit of the least advantaged members of society (Rawls 1993: 291).

The limitations of the Rawlsian framework from the perspective of fundamental freedoms and human rights

Whilst moving debates about opportunity and freedom forward in important ways—and supporting the relevance of discussions about poverty and inequality to the characterization of citizens' needs—the principles of justice as fairness set out in Rawls (1973, 1993) provide an inadequate basis for the conceptualization of internationally recognized human rights for two key reasons. First, the principles of justice as fairness set out in Rawls (1973, 1993) provide an inadequate basis for the development of a theory of human rights as universal benefits that all people everywhere should enjoy. The scope of the hypothetical choice situation is specified in terms of the domestic arrangements of a liberal democracy and the characterization of the principles of justice as fairness as universal principles with international scope is explicitly rejected. Second, whilst making space for the concept of primary goods, these principles provide an inadequate basis for the development of a theory of economic and social rights. The liberties incorporated in the first principle of justice focus on a limited set of civil and political rights; the lexicographic ordering of the two principles gives absolute priority to the basic liberties recognized in the first principle over all other needs when conflicts arise; and the distinction between the constituent element of liberty and the value of liberty precludes the admissibility of poverty, hunger, and starvation as freedom restricting conditions.

> The inability to take advantage of one's rights and opportunities as a result of poverty and ignorance, and a lack of means generally, is sometimes counted among the constraints definitive of liberty. I shall not, however, say this, but rather I shall be thinking of these things as affecting the worth of liberty, the value to individuals of the rights that the first principle defines. (Rawls 1973: 204)

The further modifications and extensions to the basic framework set out in Rawls (1999, 2001) address these limitations in important ways. Rawls's (1999) consideration of the normative principles of international relations provides for (*a*) direct consideration of universal human rights as the objects of rational choice behind the hypothetical 'veil of ignorance'; (*b*) an explicit acknowledgment that a list of 'basic' or 'fundamental' rights should include certain minimum economic benefits.[13] In addition, Rawls

---

[13] Shue and Vincent 'interpret subsistence as including minimum economic security, and both hold subsistence rights as basic. I agree, since the sensible and rational exercise of all liberties, of whatever kind, as well as the intelligent use of property, always implies having general all-purpose economic means' (Rawls 1999: 65, n. 1).

(2001: 48, 176) moves forward by building the idea of minimum subsistence rights to meet basic human needs, into the first principle of justice as fairness. This respecification is taken to be a logical implication of the difference principle, which will be violated 'when such a minimum is not guaranteed' (ibid. 162; see 38.3–4).[14] Rawls (ibid.) also recognizes the need to supplement a 'primary goods' index with information relating to individual outcomes (e.g. health inequalities). The Rawlsian framework moves the debate about opportunity and freedom forward in important ways but nevertheless has important limitations vis-à-vis the justification and elucidation of internationally recognized standards in the field of poverty and human rights. When evaluated from this perspective, the modified and extended Rawlsian framework remains limited in three key respects:

(1) Whereas in the domestic context the objects of choice are specified in terms of alternative principles of justice, the (1999) model limits the objects of choice to alternative interpretations of the 'Law of Peoples'. This specification fails to make analytical space for 'universal primary goods' or for a 'global difference principle' and results in a different specification of basic rights in the domestic and international context.[15]

(2) The broadening of the first principle of justice in Rawls (2001) accommodates minimum subsistence rights but not a broader list of economic and social rights. Constitutional entrenchment of the 'difference principle' is treated as 'non-essential'. Institutional conditions recognized as necessary for the regulation of inequality (e.g. access to basic health for all) are to be dealt with 'at the legislative' rather than the 'Constitutional' stage (Rawls 2001: 176; 1993: 49; 1999).[16]

(3) The list of human rights 'proper' set out in Rawls (1999: 78–85) is limited to Articles 3–18 of the Universal Declaration (and logical implications of these human rights (e.g. the rights recognized in the Conventions on Genocide and Apartheid)). This set is exclusive of Article 1 (the underlying premise of freedom and equality), Article 2 (non-discrimination), Articles 19 and 20 (freedom of opinion, expression, association, peaceful assembly, and association), and Article 21 (political participation). Not-

---

[14] The first principle deals with 'constitutional essentials' and 'a social minimum providing for the basic needs of all citizens is also a constitutional essential'. However, the difference principle is not itself taken to be a 'constitutional essential' (Rawls 2001: 48).

[15] This issue is discussed extensively in Hayden (2002).

[16] However, these inequalities are to be dealt with at the legislative rather than the constitutional stage.

withstanding the explicit acknowledgement that the right to life 'entails' the right to subsistence, Articles 22–28 (i.e. the entire cluster of social and economic rights) are also excluded.[17]

Proposals for moving beyond the Rawlsian position

There have been various attempts in the literature to modify the Rawlsian framework in order to develop a more adequate basis for conceptualizing internationally recognized standards in the field of human rights. These have ranged from earlier attempts to broaden the first principle of justice to include minimum economic and social benefits, to more recent attempts to construct a 'global' original position in which the difference principle applies. The general possibility of conceiving basic human rights as terms of agreement that rational actors would choose in the original position is analysed in Hayden (2002: 120–79). He argues that the theories set out in Rawls (1973, 1993, 1999) cannot support a genuinely universal human rights project and focuses on the necessity of types of modifications to the Rawlsian scheme. These are: (*a*) modifications of the first principle to incorporate a broader characterization of basic rights reflecting not only the civil and political rights but also clearer articulation of economic and social rights; (*b*) broadening the scope of the problem addressed in the first formulation of the original position to accommodate universal human rights in the global context. Other proposals fall within the reach of this analysis. These include proposals for (*a*) broadening the first principle of justice to include social and economic rights; (*b*) broadening the scope of the second principle of justice by (*c*) constructing a 'global' original position in which (*d*) a 'global difference principle' applies.[18] For example, Gewirth (1982, 1996) develops a theory of primary goods in terms of the *necessary conditions for moral agency* and places this idea at the centre of a broad theory of fundamental freedoms and human rights. Beitz (1999 [1979]: 125–69) contends that if social cooperation is the foundation of domestic distributive justice, then international economic interdependence is the foundation for global distributive justice, whilst Pogge (1989: 272) suggests that a 'globalized' first principle might

---

[17] Article 1 of the Universal Declaration is excluded from the set of human rights proper on the grounds that this Article is purely aspirational. Other Articles (e.g. Articles 22 and 23) are excluded on the grounds that they presuppose specific kinds of institutions.

[18] See Hayden (2002: 198–206) for fuller references to the broader literature.

require a set of basic rights and liberties 'analogous to the Universal Declaration of Human Rights'.

The link with the 'capability approach'

The 'capability approach' provides an important critique of the characterization of goods in the Rawlsian framework and the development of this perspective by both Sen and Nussbaum (1993, 1995, 1997, 1999a, 1999b, 1999c, 2000, 2003, 2004) has been an important influence both on the modifications and extensions to the original scheme set out by Rawls himself and on the broader debates. As discussed in Chapters 3 and 4, in elucidating, justifying, and applying the 'capability approach,' Sen has emphasized the central argument that focusing on 'primary goods' can result in indifference to, and neglect of, the actual things that people can and do achieve. The relationship between access to 'primary goods' and the things that people can do and be is contingent and conditional, and can vary between different families, individuals, and population goods. Therefore, in order to take adequate account of the notion of substantive opportunity, there is a need to move beyond 'primary goods' as an informational focus of evaluative exercises concerning basic human interests, and to evaluate more directly the substantive freedoms that people can and do enjoy.[19]

2.4 Can Positive Obligations of Assistance and Aid be Coherently Incorporated into a Theory of Fundamental Freedoms and Human Rights?

The arguments set out in O'Neill (1986, 1989, 1993, 1996) represent another important paradigmatic position in debates about global poverty and human rights. O'Neill departs from the libertarian position and defends the possibility of establishing far-reaching 'universal positive obligations' of assistance and aid—including far-reaching positive obligations

---

[19] Rawls accepts that capabilities are more fundamental for people than primary goods but questions the practical feasibility of information about capabilities as opposed to primary goods. He suggests that, by embedding primary goods rather than capabilities in principles of justice, 'we may come as close as we can in practice to a just distribution of Sen's effective freedoms' (Rawls 1999: 13n; 1996: 182, 185). For more general criticisms of contractarianism (individualistic/non-contextual focus, idealistic/unrealistic premises, etc.) see, for example, Sandel (1984), O'Neill (1997), and Nussbaum (2003).

to relieve poverty, hunger, and starvation. She builds here on the interpretation of the Kantian framework that challenges the libertarian focus on 'universal negative obligation' and that emphasizes the possibility of establishing 'universal positive obligations' under a 'universal moral law'. However, O'Neill disputes the idea that 'universal positive obligations' establish counterparty human rights and limits the coverage of her theory of fundamental or human rights to the domain of 'universal perfect obligation' (rather than 'universal imperfect obligation').

Kant on the distinction between 'universal perfect obligation' and 'universal imperfect obligation'

Kant's ethical framework creates analytical space for the concept of 'universal positive obligation' by emphasizing the possibility of a class of obligations that cannot be universalized in the form of specific actions or types of action, but that nevertheless constitute the object of 'universal positive obligations' to promote types of 'end-of-action' (or general policies or goals) under a 'universal moral law'. The distinction between 'universal principles of perfect obligation' (relating to the performance and non-performance of types of action) and 'universal principles of imperfect obligation' (relating to the promotion of 'ends-of-action' or general policies or goals) was introduced by Kant in *Groundwork of the Metaphysics of Morals* (Kant 1991 [1785]: 83–6) and further developed in the *Metaphysics of Morals* (Kant 1996 [1797]). For example, in his treatment of the positive obligation of beneficence, Kant maintains that since it is non-feasible for a single person to assist all needy people in a consistent way, there can be no rational (contradiction-free) principle that can prescribe the extent to which an individual should act to assist those in need in any particular situation. Hence the injunction 'assist those in need' cannot be universalized in terms of a duty to perform a particular type of action, and it is not possible to establish that *specific actions* relating to this injunction are obligatory under the 'universal law'. However, Kant argued that injunction *can* be consistently willed as an 'end-of-action' (or general policy or goal) in respect of all others, and that, in this form, the positive obligation of beneficence can be shown to be obligatory under the 'universal law'. Hence:

The maxim of common interest, of beneficence toward those in need, is a universal duty of human beings...with needs. (Kant 1996 [1797]: 202)

Do the universal obligations in Kant's ethical system conflict?

How, then, does Kant's treatment of this issue deal with the problem of conflicting positive duties? The interpretation of the 'condition of universalization' discussed in Section 2.1 was taken to rule out the admissibility of positive obligations of assistance and aid on the grounds that the performance of positive actions (such as 'assisting the needy') is limited by feasibility and cost constraints. Positive obligations of assistance and aid were taken to be not 'simultaneously feasible'. Kant's ethical framework takes the debate forward here by suggesting that it is possible to specify 'universal positive obligations' that are 'intrinsically compatible' and that do not contravene the logical principle 'ought implies can'. In Kant's ethical framework, the class of 'universal perfect obligations' constitute the grounds of duties relating to the performance and non-performance of specific types of action. Duties of this type are 'narrow' in the sense that actions of the specified type should be uniformly and consistently performed (or not performed) without exception in all relevant cases. In contrast, the class of 'universal imperfect obligation' constitute the grounds of duties that have as their object the promotion of 'ends-of-action' (general policies or goals). Kant provides here for 'permitted limitations' when there are pragmatic constraints on the promotion of obligations of a required type. In this way, he provides for the compatibility of obligations where goal-fulfilments are not mutually co-possible. Kant reasons that duties that flow from obligations of this type (*a*) cannot be specified in the form of duties to perform or not to perform specific actions or types of action on a consistent or uniform basis; and (*b*) are 'wide' in the sense that there is *latitude* for *inclination* or *choice*. Whereas 'universal perfect obligations' are associated with actions that should be performed or not performed in all relevant cases, practical action in the domain of 'universal imperfect obligations' requires the development of 'subordinate principles' of judgement:

[I]f the law can prescribe only the maxim of actions, not actions themselves, this is a sign that it leaves a playroom (*latitudo*) for free choice in following (complying with) the law, that is, that the law cannot specify precisely in what way one is to act and how much one is to do . . . (Kant 1996 [1797]: 153)

Do 'imperfect obligations' establish 'counterparty' human rights?

The Kantian framework therefore challenges the libertarian focus on negative obligation by providing a basis for the justification of positive obligations of assistance and aid. Nevertheless, in developing this framework, O'Neill disputes the idea that universal positive obligations are associated with strict duties and counterparty rights, and limits the coverage of a theory of fundamental or human rights to the domain of 'universal perfect obligation'. She contends that whereas 'universal perfect obligations' are associated with strict duties, and claimable and enforceable universal rights, there is 'systematic unclarity' in the domain of 'universal imperfect obligations' that renders human rights-based claims incoherent and unenforceable. Whereas 'perfect obligations' (relating to the performance of specific types of action) can be adequately reflected in a rights-based ethical framework, 'imperfect obligations' (relating to the promotion of general goals) will be 'unallocated' and 'neglected'—and that general obligations to relieve poverty, hunger, and starvation 'can at best have subordinate status in an ethical system in which the concept of rights is fundamental' (O'Neill 1996: 127–8). Thus the argument that positive rights are not admissible as universal human rights is central not only to libertarian theories but also to O'Neill's (1986, 1993, 1996) critique of human rights-based discourse in the context of poverty, hunger, and starvation.

The coverage of Kant's 'fundamental principles of right'

O'Neill's argument that enforceable rights-based claims are established by 'universal perfect obligations' but not by 'universal imperfect obligations' reflects Kant's treatment of the 'fundamental principles of right'. Whilst Kant's treatment of the class of 'universal imperfect obligations' makes analytical space for the concept of positive obligation—including far-reaching positive obligations to assist those in need—he limits the reach of a theory of fundamental rights to the domain of 'universal perfect obligation'. The *Metaphysics of Morals* divides the 'doctrine of duties in general' into the system of the *Doctrine of Right (Ius)* and the system of the *Doctrine of Virtue (Ethica)*. According to Kant's analysis:

- The system of the *Doctrine of Right* deals with duties for which external lawgiving is possible. Duties of this type can be enforced by external sanction and are associated with enforceable counterparty rights. The fulfilment of duties of right is mandatory and non-fulfilment is culpability.

- The system of the *Doctrine of Virtue* deals with duties for which external lawgiving is not possible. Duties of virtue must be performed voluntarily, on exclusively ethical grounds, and cannot be enforced by external sanction. The fulfilment of duties of this type is merit and non-fulfilment is not *culpability* but *deficiency in moral worth*. Kant maintains that duties of this type are not associated with counterparty rights (Kant 1996 [1797]: 23, 31–2, 152–6).

According to Kant the sub-set of 'duties of right' include 'narrow duties' and 'perfect duties'. He suggests that, in the context of 'duties to others', these duties are of an essentially 'negative' and 'limiting' nature. They are usually interpreted as (*a*) determined relatively strictly and precisely; (*b*) being suitable for judicial enforcement; (*c*) giving rise to claimable counterparty rights. It is also often interpreted as the set of negative duties of non-interference that do not conflict under any circumstances. In contrast, the set of 'duties of virtue' includes 'wide duties' and 'imperfect duties'. These (*a*) deal with the ends of action (with particular actions unspecified); (*b*) are not suitable for judicial enforcement; (*c*) are not associated with counterparty rights (Kant 1996 [1797]: 168–9). The class of 'universal imperfect obligations' is therefore characterized as falling strictly *outside* the domain for which legislative enforcement is possible. Whilst Kant's 'obligation of beneficence' can be established as a 'universal imperfect obligation' under Kant's 'universal law', duties of beneficence fall within the scope of a sub-set of duties that are ethically binding but not legally binding, and are not associated with counterparty rights:

Ethics does not give laws for *actions*, (*Ius* does that), but only for *maxims* of actions . . . [I]mperfect duties are . . . only *duties of virtue*. Fulfilment of them is *merit* but failure to fulfil them is not in itself *culpabilitiy*. (Kant 1996 [1797]: 152–3)

O'Neill on the logical structure of human rights-based claims

O'Neill cautions against a simplistic interpretation of the division of duties into the sub-classes of 'duties of right' and 'duties of virtue'. The clear distinction between a law of justice prescribing actions, and a law of virtue prescribing maxims, is blurred by the fact that both laws embody general principles and entail elements of indeterminacy that can only be resolved through judgement, agreement, and institutionalization, and that may require far-reaching judicial and administrative procedures. The object of

Table 2.1 Summary of Kant's position

Perfect duties	Imperfect duties
Duties to perform or not perform specific types of action	Duties to promote types of ends-of-action
Narrow (precise/strict) duties—no exceptions permitted	Wide (non-precise) duties with latitude for choice of actions to be performed or not performed (exceptions not permitted)
Justiciable (can be enforced by external sanction)	Non-justiciable (not suitable for external enforcement—must be undertaken as acts of 'good motive')
Associated with counterparty rights	Not associated with counterparty rights

'universal perfect obligations' should be characterized as 'act-types' rather than specific 'act-tokens':

> In each case the law prescribes only... a principle... and principles of all sorts are indeterminate. The difference between the cases lies in the type of principle at stake: principles of right prescribe *types of act*; principles of virtue prescribe *types of end*... [Both require] accounts of judgement for a view of the way in which the gap between principle and particular act, or pattern of action, is to be bridged. (O'Neill 2002: 332)

For this reason, O'Neill challenges the possibility of a strict demarcation between ethics and law on the grounds of the determinacy of action. She suggests that even Kant's 'law of justice' fails to provide a clear-cut resolution of the problem of choosing an action in particular circumstances (i.e. to resolve completely the practical question: what should I do?) and 'indeterminacy cannot distinguish clearly between perfect and imperfect obligations' (O'Neill 1989: 224; 2002: 334). Kant's treatment of 'universal imperfect obligation' provides 'latitude for choice' and the indeterminacy of 'maxims of right' should be viewed as a 'lesser form of latitude' (O'Neill 2002: 336). Nevertheless, important 'structural differences' between the class of 'universal perfect obligations' and the class of 'universal imperfect obligations' are central to O'Neill's analysis. 'Universal perfect obligations' are *relatively* precise and *relatively* specific. They are negative in form and give rise to duties that do not conflict. They are 'held by all' and 'owed to all' and are sufficiently determined to characterize a relationship between an agent and a recipient. They are associated with the class of counterparty liberty rights (O'Neill 1996: 147; 2002: 340). In contrast, 'universal imperfect obligations' are characterized by their *relative* generality and *relative* indeterminacy. They are to be viewed primarily not in terms of a rights-based relationship between an agent and a recipient, but in terms of the character of agents (as 'required virtues'). They are 'held by all' but 'owed to none'. They are 'unclaimable' in the sense that they require action but do not specify for whom or to whom action is to be directed (O'Neill 1996: 148).

'Antecedent allocation' as a condition for the establishment of counterparty human rights

Furthermore, O'Neill contends that the distinction between the principles of 'universal perfect obligation' and 'universal imperfect obligation' has far-reaching implications for the establishment of 'fundamental rights' or 'human rights'. Whereas in the domain of 'perfect obligation' the allocation of specific actions to be performed by each obligation-holder is established in the abstract, this antecedent allocation of recipients to obligation-holders is not established in the domain of 'universal imperfect obligations'. As a result, whilst 'imperfect obligations' are associated with claims from the perspective of agency, claims of this type cannot be meaningfully and coherently characterized as universal human rights, because the allocation of duties to perform or not to perform specific actions to duty-holders is not 'antecedently established'. In this way, O'Neill suggests that the establishment of fundamental or human rights follows from the prior establishment of 'allocated obligation'. Where the allocation of obligations is not 'antecedently established', there can be no fundamental or human rights.

If the obligation is breached, nobody will have been wronged, although wrong will be done. From the perspective of recipience there is no ethical claim. From the perspective of agency, however, the claim is clear enough, although its allocation is underdetermined. If there are obligations that are imperfect in this sense, a theory of rights can incorporate only part of a theory of obligations—the part that covers perfect obligations, those that are mirrored by rights. (O'Neill 1989: 225)

The argument that general obligations to relieve poverty, hunger, and starvation will have a subordinate status in ethical frameworks where the concept of rights is fundamental follows from this discussion. Rights-based ethical frameworks focus on required action in the domain of justice, but neglect required action in the domain of virtue (and therefore 'universal imperfect obligations'). Furthermore, there is in O'Neill's view a critical disanalogy between liberty rights on the one hand and welfare rights on the other. When a liberty right is violated, 'there are determinate others to whom the violated might be imputed' whether or not 'specific institutions have been established'. However, this antecedent allocation of recipients to obligation-bearers is not established in the context of positive rights to goods and services and (in the absence of institutions for distributing or allocating special obligations) 'there is systematic unclarity about whether one can speak of violators, and not just contingent uncertainty about who they might be' (O'Neill 1996: 132).

O'Neill on the class of 'distributed universal rights'

It would be inaccurate to conclude from the above that obligations in the field of poverty, hunger, and starvation are only a matter of virtue in O'Neill's conceptual framework. A negative conception of 'freedom from severe poverty as a fundamental human right' falls within the domain of 'universal perfect obligation' and of O'Neill's treatment of the principle of 'non-injury'. The arguments set out above clearly do not preclude the possibility of procedures for determining the allocation of 'imperfect obligations' to obligation-holders being instituted, and O'Neill repeatedly emphasizes the importance of the establishment of institutions for allocating and specifying obligations relating to positive rights goods and services. In making this case, O'Neill suggests that rights can be 'distributed universally' by institutions that define the numerous special relationships and specify for each right-holder those from whom the right can be claimed. Although institutional and positive rights are typically established in restricted forms (e.g. for the citizens of certain states, or within a certain community), 'certain sets of special obligations can effectively institutionalize positive rights to goods and services for each, and so for all'. However, universal rights to goods and services of this type are correctly characterized as sets of 'distributed special rights' rather than 'fundamental rights' or 'human rights'.

This is not . . . an argument to show that there can be no universal rights to goods or services. It is an argument to show that they would have to be a particular sort of right whose counterpart obligations were distributed according to one or another institutional scheme, **hence strictly speaking a special right**, and that their vindication as well as their enforcement would have to justify institutional structures as well as more abstract principles. (O'Neill 1996: 132–3, emphasis added)

The argument that universal rights to goods and services are 'institutional' or 'positive' rights rather than 'fundamental' or 'human rights' is crystallized in O'Neill's typology of obligations (1996: 152) set out below. This typology focuses on (*a*) 'universal imperfect obligations' without counterparty rights and (*b*) 'universal perfect obligations' (associated with special rights but not

Table 2.2 Summary of O'Neill's (1996: 152) typology of obligations

Universal	Perfect	Held by all, owed to all; counterpart liberty rights
	Imperfect	Held by all, owed to none; no counterpart rights; embodied above all in character
Special	Perfect	Held by some, owed to specified others; counterpart special rights; can be 'distributively universal' given appropriate institutions
	Imperfect	Held by some, owed to none; no counterpart rights; embodied in ethos of special relationships and practices and in characters

fundamental or rights). This typology supports the admissibility of fundamental negative rights and of positive special rights. However, it rules out the possibility of positive rights to goods and services being characterized as 'fundamental human rights'—that is, as abstract pre-institutional moral rights in terms of which systems of positive law and sets of post-institutional special rights can be scrutinized and on occasions rejected.[20]

Conclusion

This chapter has analysed some of the debates in ethics and liberal political theory that are raised by the proposition that global poverty is a violation or a denial of fundamental freedoms and human rights. Various 'theoretical obstacles' to viewing global poverty as a violation or a denial of fundamental freedoms and human rights that have been put forward in ethics and political theory have been discussed, and the foundations of a broader approach have been identified. Chapters 3 and 4 consider the significance of Sen's research agenda in ethics and economics for thinking about this issue. Chapter 3 analyses the ways in which Sen's work in ethics has contributed to the development of an ethical framework that justifies and elucidates a sub-set of fundamental freedoms and human rights that focuses directly on individual substantive freedoms in the form of the valuable things that people can do and be. Chapter 4 analyses how Sen's work in economics takes this approach forward, by providing a pioneering

[20] O'Neill (2000: 103) introduces a somewhat different emphasis by distinguishing the 'service delivery' aspects of positive obligations in the field of welfare from certain other aspects (e.g. those relating to the determination of a scheme of delivery, or contributing proportionally to costs). She notes that the former 'can quite well be universally held obligations'. But should these be viewed as establishing fundamental rights? If so, then the approach developed in this book seems compatible with O'Neill's position.

new economic framework that focuses on individual substantive freedoms (rather than other informational focuses such as income, growth, utility, or 'primary goods') and by establishing the complementary role of different types of institutions (economic, political, legal, etc.) in expanding the valuable states of being and doing that people can and do enjoy.

3

Poverty and Human Rights: Sen's Contributions in Ethics

This chapter analyses the ways in which Sen's work contributes to ethical debates concerning the characterization of fundamental freedoms and human rights discussed in Chapter 2. It explores in particular the ways in which Sen's development of the 'capability approach' provides a framework in which the capability to achieve a standard of living adequate for survival and development—including adequate nutrition, safe water and sanitation, shelter and housing, access to basic health and social services, and education—is characterized as a basic human right that governments and other actors have individual and collective obligations to defend and support.[1] Sen's work is shown to have moved the debates about global poverty and human rights in ethics and political theory forward by providing: support for a sub-class of fundamental freedoms and human rights that focuses directly on the valuable things that people can do and be; (Section 3.1); support for systems of ethical evaluation that are sensitive to consequences, outcomes, and results (Section 3.2); support for positive obligations of assistance and aid (as well as negative obligations of omission and restraint) including the relaxation of the condition of 'co-possibility' and support for the general class of 'meta-rights' (Section 3.3); support for human rights in the context of 'imperfect obligations' (including support for obligations that are associated with 'reasonable action' rather than 'compulsory action') (Section 3.4); support for universalism against the relativist and culture-based critiques (Section 3.5). These aspects of Sen's work provide elements of—or a partial basis for—a

[1] This chapter focuses on the elucidation of the 'capability approach' in Sen's work. Nussbaum has also made a key contribution to the philosophical development of the 'capability approach' (including the link with human rights) (e.g. Nussbaum 1993, 1995, 1997, 1999*a, b, c,* 2000, 2002, 2003, 2004, 2005). Her contributions are reviewed in Chapter 7. On the differences between Sen's and Nussbaum's positions, see Crocker (1992, 1995).

theory of human rights that includes the elimination of global poverty as a central and critical objective.

3.1 Elucidation of a Sub-class of Fundamental Freedoms and Human Rights that Focuses Directly on the Valuable Things that People Can *Do* and *Be*

The 'capability approach' departs from many other frameworks by providing direct support for a broad characterization of fundamental freedoms and human rights that takes account of forms of basic deprivation and impoverishment including hunger and starvation, premature morbidity and 'excessive' mortality, and illiteracy and inadequate educational achievement. In moving beyond the Rawlsian position, Sen has argued that individual substantive freedoms in the form of the valuable things that people can do and be can be incorporated into ethical evaluation and included among the constituent elements of human freedom without losing objectivity. This central idea supports the elucidation of a sub-class of fundamental freedoms and human rights that focuses directly on the opportunities that people have to achieve valuable personal states (such as being adequately nourished, clothed, or having the opportunity to benefit from basic health and education). It provides the basis for an expanded set of 'freedom restricting conditions' and a framework in which deprivations in the means of avoiding hunger and starvation, and basic health and literacy, can be meaningfully and coherently characterized in terms of the denial and violation of fundamental freedoms and human rights.

The general class of 'capability freedoms'

Sen (1993*a*: 31; 1993*b*; 2002: 9–13; 2002*a*, *b*, *c*; 2004*a*; 2005: 152–3) characterizes freedom as a complex and pluralist concept involving irreducible elements that relate to:

(1) The process aspect of freedom, which is concerned with whether or not a person is free to take decisions himself or herself, taking note of

- immunity from interference by others;
- the scope for autonomy in individual choices.

(2) The opportunity aspect of freedom, which focuses on the actual freedom a person has to achieve things that he or she has reasons to value and want, taking note of

- the nature and scope (or adequacy) of the opportunities offered;
- their relation to individual objectives and goals.

The 'capability approach' provides an elucidation of the opportunity aspect of freedom. The term 'capability' refers to the opportunity to achieve valuable combinations of human functionings. A person's 'capability set' represents the alternative combinations of functionings that are within a person's reach (and which are therefore feasible) and over which a person has freedom of effective choice (regardless of what he or she actually decides to choose). The term 'functioning' refers to aspects of the states of being and doing that a person achieves ranging from elementary personal states (such as achieving adequate nutrition or being literate) to complex personal states and activities (such as participation in the community and appearing without shame).[2] The class of 'capability-freedoms' focuses on a set of freedoms relating to the things that a person is able to do and be; and provides the basis in Sen's work for the elucidation of a *subclass* of fundamental freedoms and human rights. Significantly, therefore, the 'capability perspective' provides a *partial* rather than a *complete* basis for a theory of fundamental freedoms and human rights.[3]

The 'capability perspective' and 'substantive opportunity'

In clarifying the role of the capability perspective in an overall theory of fundamental freedoms and human rights, Sen (1999*a*: 74) has argued that the concept of the *capability to function* can be understood as an elucidation of the idea of the *substantive freedom* or *real opportunity* of a person to choose a life that he or she has reason to value. The 'capability perspective' is in this sense intended to provide an alternative specification of the second part of Rawls's second principle of justice, which focuses on the idea of 'primary goods', and which, Sen has argued, fails to capture the parametric variability between primary goods (viewed as means or resources) and valuable ends (in the form of combinations of valuable beings and doings that a person can achieve). For example, a disabled person or a sick person may not be able to do many things an able-bodied individual can, with the same bundle of primary goods. Other individuals and population groups may also be at a disadvantage, and Sen's empirical

---

[2] For a discussion of the Aristotelian connections with the concept of capability, see Nussbaum (1993).

[3] The process aspect can also be reflected in the 'capability approach' by taking account of the value of the freedom to choose (e.g. in a 'refined' capability set) (e.g. Sen (1993*a*: 40)).

research suggests that even such elementary freedoms as the capability to be well nourished may vary greatly, despite the consumption of same amounts of food, depending on the person's metabolic rate, body size, climatic conditions, parasitic disease, age, gender, and special needs such as pregnancy (Sen 1993*b*: 532). Sen has argued that these interpersonal differences can be taken into account in the assessment of personal states without losing objectivity (Sen 1985*c*: 23) and that if the object is to concentrate on a person's *real opportunity* to pursue her objectives (as Rawls suggests), then account should be taken not only of a person's access to primary goods but also of the capability to function (Sen 1985*a*, 1993*a*, 1999*a*: 74). The 'capability approach' therefore provides a basis for the respecification of the second half of Rawls's second principle of justice, with the 'difference principle' being elucidated in terms of capabilities and functionings, rather than in terms of access to 'primary goods' (Sen 2004*a*: 330–8).

The relevance of agency goals and objectives

Sen's treatment of both the process and opportunity aspects of freedom challenges theories that suggest that a person's freedom can be evaluated independently of agency objectives and goals. He has, for example, disputed the possibility of judging the *range of choice* independently of the assessment of the adequacy and value of the elements in that range, taking note of the nature and scope of the options involved, and their relationship to individual agency goals and objectives (Sen 1993*a*, 1996*a*, 2002*a*: 595–608; cf. Section 4.7). In addition, Sen has argued that an exclusive focus on the processes of choice without reference to a person's preferences and values can provide only a very limited understanding of the lack of freedom in situations of entrenched inequality. Exclusive concentration on individual choices can, for example, neglect the phenomenon of 'choice inhibition', whereby individuals choose not to exercise fully their rights because of social stigma or fear. For example, Sen introduces the example of a woman in a sexist society who would like to go out to the market place with watchable hair (w), rather than with her head bound and blanketed from view (b), if a certain conservative member of the family will not be in the market place (w) rather than being there (b). That is, the woman ranks (w,w) over (b,w). However, if the feared man is in the market place, the woman would prefer to blanket her hair, ranking (b,b) above (w,b). Suppose we are concerned with the woman's right to go out to the market without the blanket when she would like to do this— that is, with her right to choose (w,w) over (b,w). If the worst that the woman fears is (*w,b*), then she would not dare to go without the blanket if she follows a maximin strategy. However, if in practice the man is not at the market place when she arrives with blanketed hair, she ends up with (*b,w*), whereas she would have preferred (*w,w*). Whereas it is sometimes argued that liberty has nothing to do with a person's ability to get chosen or preferred outcomes, but only of having right procedures, Sen maintains that individual agency objectives and goals are critically relevant to the characterization of this woman's lack of freedom (Sen 1992*b*: 149–55; 1993*a*: 34–5).

The analytical validity of expressions such as 'freedom from hunger'

Sen has emphasized in this context the need to develop a *broad* view of preferences reflecting a person's *counterfactual* ends—that is, those valuable ends that an individual *would choose*, given the choice (Sen 1992*a*: 66) and meta-preference rankings (Sen 2002*a*: 587–90). He has suggested that this approach has important implications for the analytical validity of expressions such as 'freedom from hunger', 'freedom from malaria', and 'freedom from epidemics'. It is sometimes suggested that expressions of this type represent a misuse of the concept of freedom, and are of purely rhetorical value. In contrast, if the assessment of freedom takes into account counterfactual preferences and meta-preference rankings, then the elimination of hunger, malaria, and epidemics may be of direct relevance to the assessment of individual freedom. If people have *reasons to value* a life without hunger, malaria or epidemics, if they *desire* such a life, and, if given the choice, they *would choose* such a life, then the absence of these maladies enhances their 'liberty to choose to live as they desire'; and Sen has argued that expressions such as 'freedom from hunger' and 'freedom from malaria' can be understood and made cogent in this framework (Sen 1992*a*: 66–7). Significantly, the critical variable in assessing individual freedom here is *not* the *number of options* (e.g. the elimination of malaria does not necessarily increase the number of options that an individual person has, as far as having or not having malaria) or the exercise of direct control (e.g. the feasibility of an individual living a hunger-, malaria-, or epidemic-free life may for example depend entirely on choices and actions of other people), but on the *relation of results to individual counterfactual choices*—that is, of the results to what one would have chosen (and would have had reasons to choose) given the choice. This analysis reflects Sen's distinction between the process and the opportunity aspects of freedom. Whereas the process aspect of freedom reflects the intrinsic value of a person's procedural or formal freedom to choose and attributes value to direct personal control over mechanisms of decision-making and to the ability of a person to choose for themselves (the act of choice), the opportunity aspect reflects the intrinsic value of the *substantive* or *real opportunities* to achieve valuable combinations of human functionings, rather than the numbers of options, or the mechanisms of control (Sen 1982c, 1983b, 1985b: 208–12; 1992a: 64–9; 1993a: 44–6; 2002a: 595–608).[4]

The general class of 'capability-rights'

The class of 'capability-freedoms' is associated in Sen's conceptual framework with derivate classes of 'capability-rights' and obligations that have as their object the protection and promotion of valuable states of being and doing. In this way, the tripartite relationship between freedoms, rights, and obligations that characterizes many ethical and political theories (Box 3.1: diagrams *a*, *b*, *c*) is mediated in Sen's conceptual framework by the idea of capability (diagram *d*). This approach supports the valuation of both negative and positive freedoms (diagram *e*) and the elucidation of a class of fundamental freedoms and human rights that focuses on the valuable things that people can *do* and *be* (diagram *f*), and provides direct support for the characterization of personal states of basic deprivation and impoverishment (e.g. hunger, ill-health, starvation and other forms of premature mortality, ill-health, and illiteracy) as 'freedom-restricting' conditions. For example, if a person (*x*) has reasons to value a life without hunger and would choose such a life, then the capability of this person to achieve adequate nutrition is directly relevant to her real opportunity to promote her objectives and expand her freedom. Conversely, deprivation in the capability to achieve adequate nutrition restricts *x*'s real opportunity to promote her objectives, and is admissible as a 'freedom restricting' condition. In this way: 'Minimal demands of well-being (in the form of basic functionings, e.g. not to be hungry), and of well-being freedom (in the form of minimal capabilities, e.g. having the means of avoiding hunger)' can be conceptualized as rights that 'command attention and call for support' (Sen 1982a: 4–7, 15–19; 1985a: 217; 1985b: 21–4; 1992a: 66–8; 1993a; 1999a: 13–35, 54–86).[5]

---

[4] Sen adopts both the term 'effective freedom' and the term 'power' to refer to '... a person's ability to get systematically what he would choose 'no matter who actually controls the levers ...'. For example, see Sen (1992a: 65, n. 13; 1982c).

[5] For a different emphasis on the interpretation of Sen's position here, see Osmani (2005: 215–16), who argues that it is only when the causes of poverty directly relate to command over resources that 'capability failure' is to be characterized as a denial of human rights.

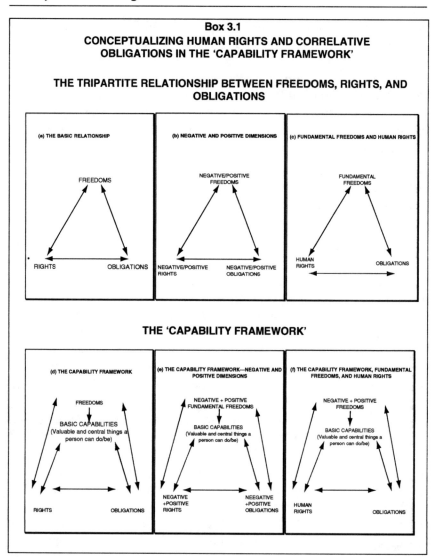

Box 3.1
CONCEPTUALIZING HUMAN RIGHTS AND CORRELATIVE OBLIGATIONS IN THE 'CAPABILITY FRAMEWORK'

THE TRIPARTITE RELATIONSHIP BETWEEN FREEDOMS, RIGHTS, AND OBLIGATIONS

THE 'CAPABILITY FRAMEWORK'

3.2 'Consequence-sensitive' Ethical Systems and the Importance of a Broad Informational Base that Takes Account of Outcomes and Results

Sen's treatment of fundamental freedoms and human rights departs from many other influential theories by emphasizing the importance of 'consequence-sensitive' systems of ethical evaluation that are sensitive to outcomes and results. Even with a broad specification of fundamental freedoms and human rights, there is in Sen's view a need to develop 'consequence-sensitive' systems that take account of outcomes and results (including the realization of fundamental freedoms and human rights).

'Outcome-independence' and the phenomena of hunger and starvation

'Outcome-independent' models attribute little or no role to consequences in ethical evaluation and suggest that fundamental freedoms and human rights should always take strict priority over other goals when there are conflicts. For example, in the Nozickian model, the set of libertarian rights (including rights to life, liberty, and property) takes strict priority over other goals, with individual rights being characterized as constraints on individual action that are non-contingent (in the sense of applying in all circumstances), unqualified (in the sense that their violation is always wrong), and absolute (in the sense of being independent of the evaluation of consequences).[6] Sen has set out a far-reaching critique of this approach in the context of poverty, hunger, and famines. For example, Sen (1984: 310–315) poses the following question: *Can famines plausibly occur in a system of rights of the kind often defended in deontological theory, including that of Nozick?* In Sen's view, the moral system of 'ownership, transfer, and rectification' outlined by Nozick is, in many respects, quite close to such a legal system of property rights and market exchange. However, evidence from the economic literature on starvation and famines establishes that it is possible for large-scale famines to occur without violating anyone's libertarian rights and without departing from the operation of a free market mechanism. Hunger, starvation, and famines can be caused, for example, by insufficient entitlements of substantial sections of the population, without any violation of libertarian rights and with freedom of ownership and exchange. Furthermore, where the condition of trade-independent security is not satisfied, these phenomena can arise under competitive market arrangements (see Section 4.6).

'Complex multilateral interdependences' and generalized relevance of consequences in ethical analysis

In taking this analysis forward, Sen poses a second question. If results such as starvation and famines were demonstrated to be the consequence of a particular distribution of holdings, would the distribution of holdings still

---

[6] But see Chapter 1; fn. 5.

be ethically acceptable? The pure 'outcome-independent' model focus suggests that ethical evaluation is entirely independent of consequences and rules out limitations and trade-offs. Limited modifications of the pure 'outcome-independent' model (e.g. with permitted exceptions for 'catastrophic moral horrors') would permit entitlements based on rights of ownership and transfer to be compromised in extreme cases such as starvation and famine. However, Sen's critique of 'outcome approach' rejects both the pure deontological position and limited modifications of this position. In Sen's view, the claim that consequences in the form of life or death, starvation or nourishment, are intrinsically matters of ethical indifference, or have only very weak intrinsic ethical relevance is 'implausible'. Even if the libertarian specification of fundamental or basic rights were to be accepted, this would not eliminate the need for 'consequence-sensitive' ethical evaluation—because even intrinsically important activities can have instrumental roles in influencing other intrinsically important things. Systems of ethical evaluation should incorporate not only an assessment of the intrinsic value of an activity, but also an assessment of 'the various intrinsically valuable or disvaluable consequences that this activity may have' (Sen 1987*b*: 75). 'Constraint-based' deontology is 'fundamentally defective' because it is unable to deal with 'complex', 'pervasive', and 'inescapable' problems of 'multilateral interdependence' involved 'in valuing rights in a society'. Whereas the constraint-based deontological view approximates an 'absolutist' model (with rights being viewed as side-constraints that cannot be justifiably violated under any circumstances), the introduction of consequence-sensitive reasoning raises the possibility of justified limitations on fundamental freedoms and human rights when there are sufficiently strong reasons. For example, in Sen's view, it might be justifiable to violate the property rights of some people on the grounds that a famine could be prevented (Sen 1985*b*: 217; cf. 1982*a*: 4–7, 15–19, 38–9; 1983*a*; 1984: 310–15; 1985*a*: 212–21; 1985*b*; 1987*b*: 70–8; 2000; 2002*b*: 632–52).[7]

---

[7] The Rawlsian framework narrows the set of individual rights that take absolute priority over the fulfilment of basic needs to the set of basic liberties and weakens the 'absolutism' of the libertarian model in a number of important respects. For example, Rawls does not characterize the basic liberties themselves in absolutist terms. He acknowledges that the basic liberties might conflict with one another and distinguishes between the 'restriction' of the basic liberties from 'regulation' when combined into a coherent scheme (Rawls 1993: 294–5). In addition, despite emphasizing the lexicographic principle, Rawls (1999: 297) concedes that the priority of liberty is not required under all conditions, depending, for example, on the level of economic development. Finally, although the right to property is included in the list of basic liberties, Rawls rejects broad interpretations, suggesting that the role of this liberty is 'to allow a sufficient material basis for a sense of personal independence and self-respect' (Rawls 1993: 298).

Support for a broad evaluative framework that takes account of outcomes and results

Against this background, Sen has argued that fundamental freedoms and human rights should be evaluated in 'consequence-sensitive' ethical s tems that take account of the 'complex multilateral interdependenc involved in valuing freedoms and rights in a society. He suggests that 1 methodological insights of economics (interdependence and interconnℴ tions) may be highly relevant here:

'[G]eneral interdependence' calls for internalisation of external accounting in a way that is better dealt with by incorporating the value of right fulfilment and the disvalue of right violation in the assessment of resulting states of affairs. The framework of consequential reasoning and pursuit of interdependences exten-sively developed in economics in many different contexts (including that of gen-eral equilibrium analysis...) provide many insights into pursuing the inescapable problems of interdependence involved in valuing rights in society. (Sen 1987b: 73)

The case for 'consequence-sensitivity' is not in Sen's view contingent on a narrow specification of fundamental freedoms and human rights (as in the libertarian model). Even with a broad specification of fundamental freedoms and human rights, the case for 'consequence-sensitivity' is not disestablished. For example, the specification of systems of derived rights is often based on consequential analysis, taking into account direct and indirect effects and the existence of complex interdependences. Thus a *general prohibition* on smoking might be introduced as a means of avoiding a particular *outcome*—that is, passive smoking (Sen 1992b: 36). In general, the introduction of 'consequence-sensitive' reasoning supports a depart-ure from theories that focus on formal guarantees of fundamental free-doms and human rights—whilst failing to take account of outcomes and results. By focusing attention on the correspondence between the valuable states of being and doing that are formally guaranteed in the domain of fundamental freedoms and human rights, and the things that people can and do achieve in practice, the 'capability-approach' supports the analysis of (*a*) individual preferences—broadly defined, taking account of values, meta-rankings, and counterfactual desires and choices; (*b*) the results that people *can* actually achieve (i.e. the capabilities that are within a person's reach); and (*c*) the results that people *do* actually achieve (i.e. a person's realized functionings). This provides recognition that the valuable states of affairs reflected in formal guarantees of fundamental freedoms and human rights may not be realized in practice. For example, formal guar-antees of the human right to education may be systematically unrealized in countries where customary practice, choice inhibition, and/or adaptive expectations militate against school attendance by girls (Sen 2002*b*: 632–51; Nussbaum 2000: 135–47).

Sen's defence of 'consequence-sensitive' frameworks

In taking this analysis forward, Sen has argued that a 'consequence-sensitive' ethical system can provide a sensitive and robust structure for evaluating fundamental freedoms and rights, combining the advantages of consequential reasoning (including the accommodation of interdependences, trade-offs, and instrumental accounting) with intrinsic valuation, agent sensitivity, and position relativity in ethical assessment (Sen 1987*b*: 74–8). In particular, he has argued that 'consequence-sensitive' ethical reasoning is adopted without the additional limitations imposed by 'full consequentialism' and 'welfarist consequentialism' (i.e. with recognition of the intrinsic value of fundamental freedoms and human rights) then the fulfilment of basic freedoms and human rights can be included among the fundamental objectives of a goal-based ethical system, and can be adequately reflected in the evaluation of states of affairs (Sen 1982*a*: 6; 1982*d*; 1984: 310–15; 1985*a*; 1985*c*: 15; 1987*b*: 70–8).

Sen's defence of this position also addressed a number of the traditional concerns regarding consequential ethical systems and intrinsic valuation. For example, 'consequentialist' systems have been widely criticized in the literature for failing to accommodate the agent-relative values associated with the importance of tie- and special-relationships and personal autonomy, integrity, and responsibility (including a person's special concern and responsibility for his or her own actions and/or for states of affairs that incorporate these actions) in processes of moral reasoning. Whereas deontological theories are often characterized in 'agent-relative terms', 'consequentialist' systems have been criticized for being specified in an 'agent-neutral' way—in terms of goals that are independent of the identity of the individual agent concerned—with 'act-consequentialism' suggesting that the 'best action' is the action that will cause the best consequences, and is independent of the identity of moral agents concerned. This approach has been widely criticized for failing to reflect an individual's sense of integrity and personal responsibility in bringing consequences about (e.g. by failing to distinguish between a person's evaluations of (*a*) a social state in which a murder occurs (*b*) a social state in which a murder that is brought about by a person's own actions). Furthermore, whilst tie-relationships might be included among the fundamental goals of a consequence-sensitive ethical system (e.g. with friendship being characterized as a fundamental goal of the system), it has been argued that the general duty of a consequentialist would be to promote friendship in general between persons—rather than requiring an agent to give special attention to his or her friends (McNaughton 1998b).

In responding to these arguments, Sen (1982a: 19–32; 1983a; 1993d) has challenged the idea that there is a fundamental conflict between consequential evaluation on the one hand, and agent-relativity on the other. Rejecting the contention (attributed to Nagel) that 'certain ethical positions, those sometimes called consequentialist, admit only agent-neutral values', Sen has argued that some forms of agent-relativity can be incorporated within a consequentialist framework. His analysis here distinguishes between different types of agent-relativity (including *doer*-relativity, *viewer*-relativity, and *self-evaluation* relativity). He has argued that doer-relativity and viewer-relativity can both be accommodated within consequentialist frameworks by adopting a broad characterization of states of affairs. For example, if consequences are defined in a manner that excludes the action that brings states about, then agent-relativity of the *doer*-relative kind cannot be accommodated within a consequentialist framework. In contrast, a broader characterization of consequentialism that incorporates actions that bring about consequences can accommodate *doer*-relativity of action judgements. In addition, it is often assumed that consequences (other than identity of the agent doing the act) depend only on whether or not the action is performed and are independent of the question of whether an action has been prevented by third-party intevention. The relaxation of this assumption provides increased scope for *viewer*-relativity within consequentialist ethical systems. Furthermore, Sen's analysis suggests that even those agent-relative values that are inconsistent with 'full consequentialism' can be accommodated in 'consequence–based evaluation'—that is, 'broad consequentialism with the feature of evaluator relativity being explicitly permitted'. In elaborating this argument, Sen has contrasted an evaluator-neutral outcome evaluation function ($G_i(x) = G_j(x)$ for all i, j and all x) with an outcome evaluation function $G_i(.)$ in a 'separable' form, related to the evaluation of the goodness of the actions a and the evaluation of the goodness of the 'rest of the state of affairs' b brought about by those actions: $G_i(x) = V(z_i(a), y_i(b))$, when $x = (a,b)$. An outcome evaluation function of this type permits evaluator-relative outcome of the same morality—with evaluator-relativity being admitted in the evaluation of consequences themselves—and can broaden the scope for agent-relative evaluation. For example, it can yield the *doer*-relativity and *viewer*-relativity of action judgements suggested by deontological concerns, but operating through consequence-based reasoning. Sen concludes:

[A]ctions and their effects are among the *constitutive* elements of a state of affairs ... consequential reasoning can certainly accommodate ... [important] deontological concerns. ... There is no basic conflict between consequential ethics and agent-relativity in judging states and actions. (Sen 1993*d*: 144–5)

3.3 Strengthened Support for Positive Obligations to Income-poverty and Other Forms of Basic Deprivation and Impoverishment Including Hunger and Starvation, Ill-health, and Illiteracy

The traditional distinction between acts and omissions

Does an act of commission (e.g. killing someone) have the same moral weight as an act of omission (e.g. failing to prevent a death)? Does a murder carry the same moral blame as the failure to intervene to rescue a drowning person, or failing to take actions that would prevent starvation? The conventional treatment of these questions ('the doctrine of acts and omissions') suggests that people are responsible for the harm caused by their positive acts, but not for the harm caused by their omissions. This approach results in the delineation of a relatively narrow sphere of strict human responsibility—with a broader sphere of benevolence, charity, and supererogatory action. However, the moral distinction between acts and omissions is blurred if account is taken of the harm caused by intentional omissions; by *foreseeable* as well as *intentional* acts; and by double-effects and other consequences (e.g. Glover 1990; Reeder 1996). Furthermore, the moral distinction between acts and omissions has been criticized in the literature for legitimizing 'moral indifference' towards harm and suffering and a 'casual approach' to deprivation, malnutrition, and the lack of access to medical care (Glover 1990: 108). The analysis of these limitations has given rise to increased support for the concept of positive obligation in relation to preventive action and the provision of life-saving assistance and aid, at both the individual and the societal levels.

Positive obligation and the characterization of human rights as 'goals'

The implications of the characterization of human responsibility and culpability for the development of a theory of fundamental freedoms and human rights were a central theme in Chapter 2. Sen's elucidation of the 'capability approach' has made an important and distinctive contribution to ethical debates about negative and positive obligation. The 'capability framework' supports the approaches discussed above by suggesting that the valuation of 'capability freedoms' provides the grounds for far-reaching positive obligations of assistance and aid, as well as negative obligations of omission and restraint. The valuation of a state of being or doing (that is, of a 'capability freedom') gives rise to claims on others to *respect* the 'capability freedom' (through non-interference) and to *defend* and *support* the 'capability freedom' (through positive acts of assistance and aid).

Why should it be important that I should not be hindered or stopped by others from doing something and—at the same time—unimportant whether or not I can in fact do that thing? Further, in deciding, for example, whether one is under an obligation to help a starving person, should one say 'yes' if the person has been robbed (with her negative freedom being violated), but remain free to say 'no' if she has suffered from flooding or drought (without any violation of negative freedom)? (Sen 1984: 314–15; 1987*b*: 56–7, 70–8)

In taking this approach forward, Sen has argued that the greatest scope for establishing moral obligations to relieve income poverty and other forms of basic deprivation and impoverishment, including hunger and starvation, premature mortality and 'excess' morbidity, and ill-health and illiteracy, may arise in rights-based ethical systems that are 'consequentialist but not welfarist' (Sen 1982*d*: 358). His argument here suggests that if rights are purely instrumental (e.g. as in the utilitarian moral approach) then there is no case for including the realization of rights in the specification of the fundamental objectives of a system. If on the other hand rights are viewed as fundamental, but are characterized in terms of negative libertarian constraints (as in the Nozickian framework), then individuals can pursue their self-interest within the system of negative constraints, but are not under positive obligations to pursue the goal of the maximization of rights-fulfilments or the rights-violations. This framework provides a basis for linking the objective of 'goal-realizations' to moral obligations through 'consequence-sensitive' links—strengthening the role of ethical considerations in individual behaviour, and providing support for far-reaching obligations on third parties 'who can help' (Sen 1981*b*; 1982*a*: 2–20, 38–9; 1984: 310–5; 1985*a*: 212–21; 1985*b*: 14–19; 1987*b*: 56–7, 70–8; 2000*a*; 2000*b*).

Relaxation of the condition of 'co-possibility' and elucidation of the general class of 'meta-rights'

Sen's conceptual framework also relaxes certain conditions that absolutist models impose on the admissibility of human rights-based claims. As discussed in Section 2.1, 'absolutism' suggests a 'frictionless' model of fundamental freedoms and human rights that rules out conflicts and incompatibilities. Models of this type necessarily focus on a narrow class of fundamental freedoms and human rights that in logical terms are mutually 'co-possible'. The possibility of the 'complete realization' of a human right is made a condition of the admissibility of a human rights-based claim—ruling out the possibility of human rights that are limited by resource and feasibility constraints. In contrast, the 'capability approach' recognizes the possibility of mutual conflicts and incompatibilities and supports the admissibility of fundamental freedoms and human rights that are limited by resources and other cost and feasibility constraints. Sen has argued that feasibility cannot be a condition of coherence, and that fundamental freedoms and human rights can be coherent and meaningful when the immediate and complete realization of human rights is not feasible. He has reasoned that where there are resource constraints, the positive obligations associated with 'capability-freedoms' and 'capability-rights' may not relate directly to valuable states of being and doing (x) (that may be currently unachievable) but to policies and programmes $p(x)$ that promote the achievement of (x) as an immediate or cumulative outcome. The violation of obligations of this type involves the *absence* and *inadequacy* of policies and programmes $p(x)$—rather than the *non-fulfilment of (x)* per se (Sen 1982*d*, 2000*a*).

Correspondences between 'meta-rights' and the establishment of international legal obligation in the field of global poverty and human rights

Sen's general class of 'meta-rights' encapsulates a critical element in the establishment and development of international legal obligation in the field of poverty and human rights. For example, as will be discussed in Section 5.4, Articles 26–29 of the Bill of Rights attached to the South African Constitution (1996) entrenches a cluster of socio-economic rights essential for an adequate standard of living—including the human rights to housing, access to health care, sufficient food and water, social security, and education. The justiciability and legal enforceability of these human rights has been put beyond question by the jurisprudence of the South African Constitutional Court, which has upheld claims for the violation of socio-economic rights in a series of landmark judgements. These cases establish that resource constraints do not relieve the government of the positive obligation to fulfil the socio-economic rights established in Articles 26–29 of the constitution by taking positive measures to eliminate or reduce the large areas of severe deprivation that afflict South Africa. However, the Court has also sought to delimit the nature and scope of the duties that flow from this positive obligation, reasoning that the responsibilities of the state under these Articles can be discharged through the adoption of policies and programmes that aim at the achievement of human rights over time rather than their immediate and/or complete fulfilment. When resource constraints are binding, and the government is not able to secure even minimum levels of economic and social rights as immediate entitlements, the social and economic rights recognized in the South African Constitution can nevertheless be viewed as 'legal meta-rights'.[8]

Sen versus Pogge on the establishment of 'general positive obligations of those in a position to help'

Sen's emphasis on a broad theory of obligation that incorporates positive obligations of assistance and aid (as well as negative obligations of omission and restraint) contrasts with the apparent emphasis in Pogge (2002*a*; 2004). As discussed in Chapter 2, Pogge's theory is important in demonstrating the ways in which a negative conception of 'freedom from extreme poverty as a fundamental human right' can be characterized narrowly (with negative universal obligations being construed in terms of non-interference with the means of life) or more broadly (in terms of the negative obligation to refrain from supporting institutions that cause and perpetuate extreme poverty). Like Berlin and Sen, Pogge emphasizes the important links between the justification of a class of fundamental or human rights and the socio-economic analysis of the causes and foreseeability/avoidablility and remediability of income poverty and other forms of basic deprivation and impoverishment, such as hunger and starvation, premature mortality and 'excess' morbidity, and illiteracy and inadequate educational achievement.

---

[8] Full references to the South African cases are given in Section 5.4.

As was suggested in Section 2.3, one way of interpreting Pogge's theory is in terms of the way a fundamental principle of negative obligation might be extended from a theory of non-interference and non-intervention to a theory of non-injury that covers the duty not to contribute to harm (including harm caused by supporting institutions that cause and perpetuate global poverty) and the duty not to cause harm through omissions (including the harm caused by individual and collective failure to reduce and eradicate global poverty). However, Pogge calls in to doubt this interpretation by placing emphasis on the importance of the ethical distinction between the 'active causation' of severe poverty and the 'failure to alleviate' severe poverty. Furthermore, whilst Pogge maintains that he neither denies nor affirms the proposition that human rights can correlate with fundamental positive duties—but rather makes no further assumptions on this issue—he nevertheless calls into question the possibility and plausibility of a satisfactory theory of fundamental positive duty. In particular, he contends that positive conceptions of 'freedom from poverty as a basic human right' based on the general obligations of those 'in a position to help' can fall foul of a 'plausibility thesis' (Pogge 2004: 7–8). His scepticism here is based on two central charges:

(1) The charge that consequential ethical systems fail to give moral weight to the distinction between acts and omissions;
(2) The charge that positive obligations of assistance and aid can be open-ended and implausible.

These charges are not specifically directed at the development of the 'capability approach' as a (partial) basis for a theory of fundamental freedoms and human rights. However, they relate to Pogge's (2002*b*) critique of the 'capability approach' as a theory of justice in important ways. Focusing on the central question of whether a criterion of public justice should incorporate compensation for different rates at which individuals convert resources into valuable functionings, Pogge contends that Sen fails to establish that resources rather than capabilities should be the focal variable of a theory of justice on the following grounds:

- As a metric used as a part of a public criterion of social justice, for the comparative evaluation of individual advantage, the 'resourcist' metric can in principle take account of differences attributable to the effects of personal heterogeneities (e.g. disability) and to the effects of contextual variables (natural disasters, climatic variables, etc.).

- As a criterion of social justice, 'resourcism' 'has every reason' to take account of personal heterogeneities caused by past inequalities in access to resources, and to compensate for the effects of past wrong-doing, as well as ensuring that the current institutional order neither produces nor reinforces such inequalities. In addition, resourcism can also take account of the ways in which social rules exacerbate the effects of adverse contextual variables (e.g. the ways in which adverse environmental events might be exacerbated by social rules that result in population groups living in mud huts).

- A 'plausible' and widely shared criterion of social justice is unlikely to compensate for the effects of personal heterogeneities and contextual variables per se, rather than for the effects of personal heterogeneities and contextual variables that can be attributable to past and current inequalities in access to resources. There might nevertheless be other reasons than justice (e.g. duties arising from charity and/or solidarity) for support compensations of this type.

The significance of Pogge's charges for the development of the 'capability approach' as a basis for a theory of fundamental freedoms and human rights

To what extent does Pogge's defence of this position pose a challenge to Sen's treatment of the idea of fundamental freedoms and human rights? A general point to make here is that the 'general positive obligations of those in a position to help' could perhaps be viewed as arising from a type of causal relationship—with the concept of 'avoidability' being inter-preted even more broadly than in Pogge's (2002a, 2004) framework (e.g. by incorporating the idea of an agent having the power to change a human rights-based outcome). In this sense, positive obligations of assist-ance and aid could perhaps be incorporated into an extended scheme of 'derived' rather than 'fundamental' positive duties. This would of course go significantly beyond a 'minimalist normative position' and could not be reconciled with the proposition that the ethical distinction between *active causation* and *failure to alleviate* is pivotal to the establishment of human rights-based claims. However, the ways in which Pogge's applica-tions and illustrations of his 'institutional understanding' of human rights go beyond a 'minimalist normative position'—and the reasons to doubt whether the ethical distinction between 'active causation' and 'failure to alleviate' plays as pivotal a role in Pogge's theory of human rights as he at times suggests—were discussed in Section 2.2. In particular, the positive duties involved seem to go beyond Pogge's elucidation of the set of 'posi-tive derived duties'—characterized as being 'triggered' by non-compliance with a fundamental negative duty 'not to actively cause harm' and excluding positive duties of assistance and aid (with no 'active causality' established). Furthermore, it is an interpretation that Pogge (2004a: 7–8) seems explicitly to reject.

In relation to the charge that consequential theories fail to give moral weight to the distinction between acts and omissions, it is of course possible to give moral weight to this distinction without making it pivotal to the establishment of human rights-based claims. The ways in which Sen's framework makes analytical space for the particular responsibility that agents have for human rights violations they cause is clearly built into Sen's ethical framework. His suggestions for moving forward on this issue—through the development of 'consequence-sensitive' ethical frameworks that can accommodate agent-relative values (including special ties and deontic concerns such as causal responsibility)—were discussed in Section 3.2 above. As Pogge acknowledges, Sen has emphasized that the importance of the overall freedom to achieve cannot eliminate the special significance of negative freedom and the particularly negative role of intentional actions in causing violations of negative freedom. He notes, for example, that a person's capability may be reduced because of (*a*) a violation of liberty through intentional interference in a personal domain or (*b*) through some 'internal debilitation'. 'Capability space' cannot adequately distinguish between these two cases and in this sense provides only *partial* basis for a theory of justice and human rights (cf. Section 3.1). In relation to Pogge's 'charge two', the ways in which Sen has attempted to avoid the problem of 'open-ended' and 'implausible' positive obligations will be discussed in the context of Sen's treatment of 'imperfect obligation' in Section 3.4 below. It will be argued that Sen's theory of human rights avoids the charge of 'implausibility' by recognizing the need to develop subordinate criteria for delimiting the nature and scope of the positive obligation to assist and aid human rights fulfilments, based on the notion of 'reasonableness'.

3.4 Support for the Validity of a Theory of Fundamental or Human Rights in the Context of 'Imperfect Obligation'

Sen's position represents an important departure from theories in the liberal tradition that make analytical space for the concept of positive obligation—but that maintain that, in the context of income poverty and other forms of basic deprivation and impoverishment such as hunger and starvation, ill-health, and illiteracy, positive obligations are not associated with counterparty human rights. As discussed in Chapter 2, O'Neill (1986, 1989, 1993, 1996) departs from the libertarian position and argues that it is possible to establish far-reaching 'universal positive obligations' of assistance and aid—including obligations to relieve income poverty and other forms of basic deprivation and impoverishment. However, she disputes the idea that positive obligations of this type are associated with strict duties and enforceable counterparty rights. This argument is based on the view that whereas 'perfect obligations' (relating to the performance of specific actions) can be adequately reflected in a rights-based ethical framework, 'imperfect obligations' (relating to the promotion of 'maxims' or 'ends of action') will be 'unallocated' and 'neglected'; and that general obligations to relieve poverty, hunger, and starvation 'can at best have subordinate status in an ethical system in which the concept of rights is fundamental' (O'Neill 1996: 127–8). In responding to O'Neill, Sen has argued that the introduction of 'consequence-sensitive' reasoning provides a framework in which the value of human rights achievements and the disvalue of non-realizations can be reflected in the evaluation of states of affairs. This evaluation is *not* contingent on the precise specification duties or on legal codification, and in Sen's view, the 'consequence-sensitive' approach provides a basis for the conceptualization of human rights that correspond to 'imperfect' as well as 'perfect' obligations (Sen 1981*b*; 1982*a*: 2–20, 38–9; 1984: 310–15; 1985*a*: 212–21; 1985*b*: 14–19; 1987*b*: 56–7, 70–8; 2000*a*).

Table 3.1 Human rights and perfect and imperfect obligations

Type of obligation	Object of obligation	O'Neill	Sen
Perfect obligation	Action	Human rights possible (domain of justice)	Human rights possible
Imperfect obligation	Maxim ('end of action')	Human rights not possible (domain of virtue)	Human rights possible

Sen versus O'Neill on the treatment of 'unallocated claims'

A key distinction here relates to the question of the status of 'unallocated claims'. O'Neill maintains that 'imperfect obligations' are associated with claims from the perspective of agency, but that claims of this type cannot be meaningfully and coherently characterized as universal human rights, because the allocation of duties to perform or not to perform specific actions to duty-holders is not 'antecedently established'.

> If the obligation is breached, nobody will have been wronged, although wrong will be done. From the perspective of recipience there is no ethical claim. From the perspective of agency, however, the claim is clear enough, although its allocation is underdetermined. If there are obligations that are imperfect in this sense, a theory of rights can only incorporate part of a theory of obligations—the part that covers perfect obligations, those that are mirrored by rights. (O'Neill 1989: 225)

In contrast, Sen's approach suggests that general obligations that are 'established' but not 'allocated' in the form of specific actions that should be performed or not performed by duty-holders can be meaningfully and coherently captured by a theory of human rights. This critical distinction relates to the difference in 'perspective' in the theories set out by O'Neill and Sen. O'Neill addresses the central question *What should I do?* and suggests that the establishment of fundamental or human rights follows from the prior establishment of 'allocated obligation'. In contrast, Sen places primary emphasis on the fundamental importance of the freedom being protected and fulfilled, and only derivate emphasis on the allocation of specific actions that should be performed or not performed by duty-holders. In Sen's conceptual framework, human rights protect and promote fundamental freedoms, and the associated obligations can take the form of allocated action (i.e. of obligations to perform or not to perform specific actions) or of more general obligations to help. These distinctions have relevance for the logical structure of human rights-based claims. In O'Neill's conceptual framework, there is an identity between the conditions under which a human right is completely fulfilled, and the performance or non-performance of a specific action or actions by duty-holders. In contrast, a goal-rights system breaks down the emphasis on a binary correspondence between the complete fulfilment of a human right and the performance or non-performance of specific duties or actions, and focuses instead on a tripartite relationship between outcomes, human rights, and associated obligations (Sen 1982*a*: 38; 1982*d*: 347; 1985*c*; 2002*b*: 644–6).[9] This conceptual framework accommodates a possible dichotomy between the conditions under which a human right is completely fulfilled and the performance or non-performance of specific actions by duty-holders. Human rights can be characterized as valid and

---

[9] The general class of rights that focus on outcomes rather than on permissions and obligations to act (or not to act) is discussed in Sen (2002*b*: 645) and referred to as the class of 'contingent rights to "states of affairs"'.

meaningful from the perspective of recipience—whether or not actions or courses of action that would result in the complete realization of the human rights have been 'antecedently allocated' to duty-holders. Arguably, in a situation of this type, the non-fulfilment of human rights might be usefully characterized in terms of 'denial' rather than 'violation'.

Evaluating the fulfilment of 'imperfect obligations': the concept of 'reasonable action'

In defending the validity of a theory of fundamental freedoms and human rights in the context of 'imperfect obligation', Sen has suggested that the concept of 'reasonable action' provides a basis for delimiting positive obligations of assistance and hence a means of avoiding 'open-ended' positive obligations that are 'implausible'. The concept of positive obligation is in this sense elucidated by Sen in terms of a domain of 'compulsory action' (involving 'perfect obligations' to perform or not to perform specific actions) and a domain of 'reasonable action' (involving 'imperfect obligations' to take reasonable actions towards specified objectives or 'ends'). The notion of 'reasonable action' addresses the problems of 'open-ended' and 'implausible' positive obligation by qualifying and limiting the nature and scope of the actions to be performed by obligation-holders in the field of imperfect obligation. Sen does not provide a complete/specific 'list' of subordinate principles on the basis of which considerations of this type are to be balanced or a full account of the procedures by which such principles might be developed. His treatment of the concept of 'reasonableness'—including his treatment of the basis on which actions might be evaluated as reasonable or unreasonable—is in this sense underdeveloped. Nevertheless, his discussion suggests the balancing of the following considerations:

- The fundamental importance of human rights being protected and promoted
- Special concern with actions and causal responsibility for violations
- Commitments, values, and special relationships
- The extent to which actions of the agent can make a difference (either singly or in conjunction with others)
- The pragmatic constraints on the fulfilment of the maxim
- The alternative actions or courses of action that might have been performed
- Whether the range of pragmatic constraints could be altered by collective action and institutions

'Reasonable Action' and the interpretation of the Kantian framework

Sen's emphasis on the need for 'subordinate principles' reflects the Kantian argument that the evaluation of practical action in the domain of 'universal imperfect obligation' requires the development of 'subordinate principles' of judgement.

[T]he doctrine of right has to do only with narrow duties, whereas ethics has to do with wide duties. Hence the doctrine of right, which by its nature must determine duties strictly (precisely), has no more need of general directions (a method) as to how to proceed in judging ... but ethics, because of the latitude it allows limits imperfect duties, unavoidably leads into question that call upon judgement to decide how a maxim is to be applied in particular cases, and indeed in such a way that judgement provides another (subordinate) maxim. (Kant 1996 [1797]: 168)

Does this position entail moral indifference to the actions or courses of action chosen by agents in relation to 'imperfect obligation'? Or is there scope for impartial evaluation of the reasonableness of actions or courses of action, given commitment to material maxims? As discussed in Section 2.4, Kant introduces a mapping between 'imperfect duties' and 'wide duties' that provide latitude for choices in relation to actions and/or courses of action that agents should perform or not perform. This provides recognition that, in the realm of 'imperfect obligation', it is not possible to specify precisely 'in what way one is to act and how much one is to do by the action' (Kant 1996 [1797]: 390). This latitude for choice of action or courses of action is related to pragmatic considerations and judgements, and to nature and scope of feasibility constraints. It does not provide a license for exceptions, but rather a means of making obligations compatible where goal-fulfilments are not mutually co-possible:

... but a wide duty is not to be taken as permission to make exceptions ... but only as permission to limit one maxim of duty by another (e.g. love of ones neighbour in general by love of ones parents). (Kant 1996 [1797]: 153)

Can there be impartial evaluation of the reasonableness of practical action taken to promote particular material maxims? Various responses to this question have been articulated in the secondary literature. Sullivan maintains that '[s]ince we are rarely in a position to know all the factors that may go into others' decisions, we are also rarely, if ever, in a position to judge how well or badly they are fulfilling their positive obligations' (Sullivan 1996: xix). Wood suggests that Kant's position implies moral indifference with the exception of cases where the actions or courses of action performed entail 'general abandonment of the required end'

(Wood 2002: 5). O'Neill questions whether Kant should be interpreted as implying indifference between any acts or courses of action of the required type, and raises the need for an account of practical judgement in the Kantian framework (Wood 2002: 336). Sen's emphasis on the concept of 'reasonable action' takes forward this debate by focusing attention on the following question: *Does the action or actions performed demonstrate a genuine commitment to the material maxim in question?* This question focuses attention on the need for a framework for the development of ethical, social, and legal norms with respect to the evaluation of reasonable action to protect and promote human rights. If this approach is accepted, then the concept of 'reasonable action' arguably restores the coherence and validity of a theory of human rights in the domain of 'imperfect obligation'. Whereas O'Neill suggests that a theory of fundamental or human rights can only apply in the context of 'universal perfect obligations' that are 'antecedently allocated', the concept of 'universal imperfect obligation' can be interpreted as requiring agents to take 'reasonable actions' to protect and promote human rights, with practical action that fails to satisfy a 'reasonableness' threshold being interpreted in terms of non-fulfilment or violation.

Table 3.2 Sen on the admissibility of human rights

Universal perfect obligations	Human rights established in relation to compulsory action
Universal imperfect obligations	Human rights established in relation to reasonable action

Can the concept of 'imperfect obligation' have validity beyond the ethical domain?

The mapping between 'imperfect duties' and 'duties of virtue' in the Kantian Framework was discussed in Section 2.4. This mapping is often taken to imply that the Kantian concept of 'imperfect obligation' cannot be meaningfully and coherently invoked as a basis for the conceptualization of human rights-based claims that are (*a*) determinate, (*b*) justiciable, and (*c*) enforceable, and that the Kantian notion of 'imperfect obligation' cannot have meaning beyond the ethical domain. Furthermore, the discussion in Chapter 5 (especially Section 5.3) will demonstrate the ways in which debates about the legal validity of economic and social rights in international human rights law have also often focused on the argument that obligations in this field relate to the promotion of general goals rather than to the performance and non-performance of specific actions. Sceptics have argued that obligations specified in this form have an ethical and programmatic rather than a legal character, on the grounds that specific actions that duty-holders should or should not perform cannot be directly derived from the relevant legal texts.

Evolving evidentiary thresholds in the field of global poverty and human rights: the significance of judicial scrutiny of 'reasonableness'

Whilst Sen's work in ethics has emphasized the important role of the idea of human rights outside the legal domain, and suggests that the justification and elucidation of this idea is not contingent on the degree of precision necessary for codification and judicial enforcement (e.g. Sen 2000*a*), his emphasis on 'reasonable action' nevertheless encapsulates a critical element in the establishment and development of international legal obligation in the field of global poverty and human rights. For example, as discussed above (and as will be further discussed in Section 5.4), the South African Constitutional Court has established in a series of landmark judgements that resource constraints do not relieve the government of the positive obligation to fulfil the socio-economic rights established in Articles 26–29 of the constitution by taking positive measures to eliminate or reduce the large areas of severe deprivation that afflict South Africa. In making the case for justiciability, the Court has emphasized judicial scrutiny of the *reasonableness* of actions performed. The South African government has been viewed as being under a positive obligation under Articles 26–29 of the constitution to act reasonably to ensure the progressive realization of these rights over time. Programmes or policies that exclude a significant segment of society, or that do not take adequate account of immediate crisis needs, cannot be said to be reasonable. In the two landmark cases to be discussed in Section 5.4, the policies and programmes adopted by the government failed to comply with a reasonableness criterion and the government was held to be in violation of the positive obligations established in the constitution.

Possible analogues of the concept of 'imperfect obligation' in international human rights law

This analysis seems to point towards the possibility of direct analogues of the concept of 'imperfect obligation' in international human rights law and jurisprudence. In his discussion of this issue, Marks (2003: 16–23) highlights the possible analogy between the ethical distinction between 'perfect obligations' and 'imperfect obligation', and the international legal distinction between obligations to 'respect' human rights on the one hand, and to 'promote', 'fulfil', and 'provide' human rights on the other. His analysis departs from the standard Kantian framework by supporting the legal significance of 'imperfect obligations' but nevertheless suggests that 'imperfect obligations' are 'typically non-justiciable'—with accountability *not* taking the form of enforceable remedies. However, this analysis falls short of emerging standards in international jurisprudence, which establishes that even in poor countries where resource constraints are binding, positive obligations can be enforced through the courts in a meaningful and coherent way. An alternative approach would be to focus on the analogy between the ethical distinction between 'perfect obligation' and 'imperfect obligation' and the legal distinction between 'international obligations of conduct' (requiring the performance or non-performance of specific actions) and 'international obligations of result' (requiring the evaluation of the achievement or non-achievement of a particular situation or result, without determining the specific means by which this situation or result is to be achieved). As discussed in Chapter 5 (especially Section 5.3), Article 2 of the ICESCR has been widely interpreted as codifying 'obligations of result' as well as 'obligations of conduct', with states being required to undertake actions or courses of action to bring about certain results, as well as duties to perform or not perform specific actions. This application to Article 2 of the ICESCR suggests that the concept of 'obligation of result' extends to cases where the achievement of the specified result (i.e. the full realization of the human rights set out in the Covenant) may not be immediately feasible. The jurisprudence of the South African Court affirms the application of the concept of 'obligation of result' to cases where resource and feasibility constraints are binding and it is not possible to apply even the 'Minimum Threshold Approach' discussed in Section 5.3. The Court has reasoned that in cases of this type, compliance is to be evaluated in terms of the 'adequacy' and the 'reasonableness' of the actions that duty-holders perform in the light of the results achieved.

3.5 Support for Universalism in the Context of the Relativist and Culture-based Critiques

In addressing the relativist and culture-based critiques, Sen has defended the idea of human rights as a 'universal category' whilst making allowance for an 'appropriately contingent, or parametric, specification of the exact demands of human rights' (Sen 2004*a*: 351). His work in this area includes conceptual development relating to cross-cultural elements of a contemporary human rights project and the consideration of the nature of universality and objectivity under conditions of diversity and difference.

Responding to the relativist and culture-based critiques

Sen's defence of the idea of universal human rights emphasizes the heterogeneous elements of different cultures and societies and suggests that the historical roots of contemporary ideas about fundamental freedoms and human rights 'be sought in terms of constitutive elements, rather than as a whole' (Sen 1997: 35). His work in this area contributes to attempts in the broader literature to challenge assumptions about 'shared values' that underlie the culture-based and relativist critiques. For example, Barry (1995: 4–5) argues that the view of culture that sustains the anti-universalist programme is an inaccurate one, in which societies and cultures are characterized in terms of bounded, homogeneous, and coherent sets of values—with underlying power structures, heterogeneities, and conflicts being neglected, and conclusions being inferred from inaccurate assumptions about the allegedly shared values in different cultures and societies. Sen contributes to the further development of this argument by setting out the ways in which elements within Western societies, cultures, and philosophies that are consistent with and supportive of contemporary ideas about universal human rights have coexisted with other elements that are neither supportive nor consistent with the idea of human rights (e.g. slavery, sexism, racism, and fascism). His analysis challenges the tendency to locate the historical antecedents of contemporary ideas about fundamental freedoms and human rights in Western philosophical traditions and suggests that that the ideas from which contemporary concepts of human rights emerged—ideas of universalism, tolerance, and respect for human dignity and worth, traditions of freedom, traditions of concern for the poor, needy, and exploited, and traditions of interpersonal obligation and government responsibility—have broad historical antecedents in diverse cultures, religions, and philosophies that are not regionally constrained. For example, the historical antecedents of the ideas of freedom, democracy, and equality are often located in exclusively Western traditions of natural law and natural rights that have their roots in Ancient Greek philosophy. Yet slavery was common in Ancient Greece and justified by many Ancient Greek philosophers (with Aristotle reasoning: 'the condition of slavery is both beneficial and just' (1995 [350 BC]:

13–14, 17)). Sen infers the general methodological principle that the presence of elements in different cultures from around the world that are incompatible with contemporary human rights-standards should not obscure the presence of other elements that are supportive of such standards. His work subjects the idea of a monolithic Asian culture that is opposed to fundamental freedoms and human rights to critical scrutiny, and reappraises the contributions of non-Western thinkers (including Ashoka, Kautilya, and Akbar) in the light of this principle (Sen 1997*c*: 35–40; 1999*a*: 227–40; 1999*b*).[10]

Objectivity, variability, and 'positional-dependency'

This attempt to move *beyond* the universalism–relativism dichotomy by defending the possibility of universal category of human rights that can accommodate variations over time and cultures is reflective of a broader emphasis in Sen's work on the question of how to preserve a role for the development of universal ethical categories (capabilities, freedoms, human rights, etc.) whilst recognizing the importance of diversity and difference in human affairs. This emphasis on the possibility of universal ethical categories under conditions of diversity and difference is a repeated and recurring theme in Sen's work. For example, in defending the proposition that 'irreducible absolutist core' in the idea of poverty against the view that relativism 'dissolves' the concept of absolute need, Sen has argued that a *relativist* characterization of poverty in commodity-space may correspond to *absolutist* characterization in the space of capabilities and functionings—because there may be more variation in the commodity requirements of capabilities than in capabilities themselves. The 'commodity-basis' of the 'capability to be adequately nourished' may vary greatly across communities—giving the poverty line in commodity-space a relative character. Similarly, the commodity requirements of the 'capability to appear in public without shame' will vary in different societies with different social and cultural norms, income levels, modes of production, and so on (Sen 1984 [1983*c*]: 325–45; 1987*a*: 17).

This underlying concern with the reconciliation of universalism on the one hand, and diversity and difference on the other, is also central to Sen's contributions to theoretical thinking about the nature of moral objectivity (in the argument that universal values can be compatible with variances

---

[10] Also see Vizard (2000*b*).

associated with positional characteristics). Here Sen challenges the characterization of objectivity as a form of invariance with respect to individual observers and their positions (with standard-neutrality conditions requiring that different persons, irrespective of their positions, must evaluate the same state of affairs in exactly the same way). Approaches of this type view interpersonal variations associated with positional variables as an 'inevitable source of subjectivity'. In contrast, Sen has argued that, whilst objectivity may require interpersonal invariance when the observational position is fixed, this requirement is compatible with position-relativity when the observational position is variable. Indeed, in Sen's view, interpersonal variances associated with informational constraints and a wide range of positional variables (including location, social and cultural position, and other key aspects of a person's situation) may be an inevitable feature of objective evaluation. Parametric dependence on positional variables may be 'inescapably relevant' for observations, knowledge, beliefs, practical reason, decisions, and choices and can be reflected in the evaluation of states of affairs without compromising objectivity (e.g. by building positional variables into an 'evaluative-relative outcome morality' of the type discussed in Section 3.2) (Sen 1982a: 19–38; 1983a; 1993d).[11]

Objectivity, variability, and 'trans-positional agreement'

Anderson (2003) suggests that Sen's work takes the agenda forward here by providing a 'trans-positional' view of moral objectivity that entails a 'constructed view from nowhere' (based on a synthesis of different views from distinct positions) rather than on 'non-positional detachment' (e.g. Nagel's 'view from nowhere'). This contrasts with other approaches by (a) suggesting that moral objectivity *requires* the acceptance and use of the variability of observations in order to arrive at an integrated and coherent picture; (b) reconciling the proposition that value judgements are situated in particular positions with an acknowledgement that certain values may become widely shared; (c) affirming the 'universal value of democracy' in assimilating and integrating decentralized local information derived from particular positional perspectives. Local information is viewed in this framework not as a source of error or conflict, but as a critical informational resource for constructing more global points of

---

[11] Sen's approach is further discussed in Anderson (2003).

view. The critical role of deliberative democracy and public scrutiny in constructing more global understandings from local points is, for example, central to Sen's discussions about the conceptualization of needs and the derivation of a list of central and basic capabilities. In both contexts, Sen emphasizes the critical importance of public debate and of open-ended, revisionist frameworks rather than fixed lists. Furthermore, in addressing the question of the conditions under which convergence and agreement are more likely to be achieved, Sen has highlighted the critical importance of (*a*) information; (*b*) the opportunity for pubic discussion and critical scrutiny; (*c*) interactions (including interactions across borders). In contrast to postmodernist approaches that suggest that human rights are simply 'what people agree' and/or 'struggle for', Sen has finally emphasized the importance of 'reflected valuation' (as well as stated preferences) and of free and fair underlying conditions. Sen builds here on the Rawlsian concept of 'public reasoning' and its role in 'ethical objectivity'. The implication is that, whilst agreement over a complete ordering of values is not required, the development of an adequate theory of human rights nevertheless involves open public discussion, critical scrutiny, and reflection based on some minimal understanding of the requirements of objectivity for 'limited political purposes'.

[The distinction between] (1) the values that are dominantly favoured in a society (no matter how repressive it is), and (2) the values that could be expected to gain wider adherence and support when open discussion is allowed, when information about other societies becomes more freely available, and when disagreements with the established views an be expressed and defended without suppression and fear.... The viability and universality of human rights are dependent on their ability to survive open critical scrutiny in public reasoning. The methodology of public scrutiny draws on Rawlsian understanding of 'objectivity' in ethics, but the impartiality that is needed cannot be confined within the borders of a nation. (Sen 2004*a*: 355–6)[12]

---

[12] Rawls lists six 'essential elements of a conception of objectivity' for limited political purposes. These are:

(1) The conception of objectivity must establish a framework of thought sufficient for the concept of judgement to apply and for conclusions to be reached on the basis of reasons and evidence after discussion and due reflection.

(2) The conception of objectivity must specify a concept of a correct judgement (e.g. Rawls's political constructivism views a correct judgement as reasonable 'that is, supported by preponderance of reasons specified by the principles of right and justice issuing from a procedure that correctly formulates the principles of practical reason in union with an appropriate conception of society and person').

Conclusion

This chapter has analysed the ways in which Sen's contributions in ethics have challenged the exclusion of forms of basic deprivation and impoverishment (reflected in income poverty, hunger, ill-health, starvation and other forms of premature mortality, ill-health, and illiteracy) from the characterization of fundamental freedoms and human rights, and contributed to the development of a framework in which authoritatively recognized international standards in the field of poverty and human rights can be meaningfully conceptualized and coherently understood. Sen's work has been shown to have moved debates about global poverty and human rights forward by providing: support for a sub-class of fundamental freedoms and human rights that focuses directly on the valuable things that people can do and be (Section 3.1); support for systems of ethical evaluation that are sensitive to consequences, outcomes, and results (Section 3.2); support for positive obligations of assistance and aid (as well as negative obligations of omission and restraint) including the relaxation of the condition of 'co-possibility' and support for the general class of 'meta-rights' (Section 3.3); support for human rights in the context of 'imperfect obligations' (including support for obligations that are associated with 'reasonable action' rather than 'compulsory action') (Section 3.4); support for universalism against the relativist and culture-based critiques (Section 3.5). Chapter 4 moves on to discuss Sen's research agenda that has resulted in interdisciplinary cross-fertilization and theoretical integration on issues around global poverty and human rights with theoretical and empirical economics.

(3) The conception of objectivity must specify an order of reasons as given by its principles and criteria and assign these reasons to agents (with the possibility that assigned reasons may override the reasons agents have or think they have from their own point of view).

(4) The conception of objectivity must distinguish the objective point of view (as given, say, by the point of view of certain appropriately defined and reasonable and rational agents) from the point of view of any particular agent or group at any particular point in time.

(5) The conception of objectivity must have an account of how agreement in judgement is to be reached among reasonable agents (e.g. Rawls's political constructivism assumes that people will reach similar conclusions if they apply the concepts and principles of practical reason as well as the principles of right and justice that issue from the procedure of construction and that, given the same information, they will reach the same or similar conclusions).

(6) The conception of objectivity must account for divergence of agreement in terms of the difficulties of surveying and assessing evidence and of balancing up competing reasons.

4

Poverty and Human Rights: Sen's Contributions in Economics

This chapter examines the ways in which Sen's research agenda has focused international attention on the critical importance of fundamental freedoms and human rights for economic analysis. In the past, the idea of fundamental freedoms and human rights has often been neglected in theoretical and empirical economics. Dominant approaches have evaluated the adequacy of economic processes and arrangements in terms of income expansion, whilst standard frameworks in welfare economics have evaluated interpersonal advantage and the efficiency and fairness of competitive market outcomes in terms of utility—with no explicit recognition of instrumental and intrinsic value of fundamental freedoms and human rights (see Box 4.1). In contrast, Sen has set out a far-reaching critique of standard frameworks that fail to take account of fundamental freedoms and human rights (Section 4.1), opening up important new lines of enquiry in the broader literature, and pioneering the development of radical new paradigms and approaches that take account of these concerns (Sections 4.2–6). His contributions include far-reaching proposals for the incorporation of new variables and concerns into theoretical and empirical economics including individual entitlements (Section 4.2), capabilities and functionings (Section 4.3), civil, political, economic, and social rights (Section 4.4), 'freedom of choice' and 'opportunity freedom' (Section 4.5), and 'liberty rights' and 'basic rights' (Section 4.6). These proposals have contributed to important paradigm shifts—away from an exclusive concern with income, growth, and utility, towards a range of human rights-focused variables and concerns—and provide a framework for the instrumental and intrinsic valuation of fundamental freedoms and human rights in economic assessment and empirical economic research.

Box 4.1

NEGLECT OF THE INSTRUMENTAL AND INTRINSIC ROLE OF FUNDAMENTAL FREEDOMS AND HUMAN RIGHTS IN 'STANDARD' ECONOMIC ANALYSIS

Focus on income and utility

↓

Overly narrow informational base

↓

Overly narrow characterization of the means and ends of development and growth

↓

Neglect of the instrumental and intrinsic role of fundamental freedoms and human rights in economic evaluation

↙ ↘

Neglect of the instrumental role of fundamental freedoms and human rights in achieving effective development and growth	Neglect of the intrinsic role of fundamental freedoms and human rights in evaluating the benefits of development and growth for individuals, populations, and groups

---

4.1 Towards a Human Rights-based Critique of Standard Economic Frameworks

The failure of standard frameworks in economics to take adequate account of the instrumental and intrinsic value of fundamental freedoms and human rights is a central and recurring theme in Sen's work. His research agenda over more than forty years has highlighted the limitations of dominant income-focused and utility-focused paradigms in theoretical and empirical economics from the perspective of fundamental freedoms and human rights. These frameworks concentrate on an overly narrow informational base and an overly narrow view of the *means* and the *ends* of development and growth. Both the *instrumental* role of fundamental freedoms and human rights (in influencing the effectiveness of development and growth) and the *intrinsic* value of fundamental freedoms and human rights (in assessing the benefits of trajectories of development and growth for individuals, groups, and populations) are neglected.

The critique of 'income-focused' and 'utility-focused' frameworks

Sen's critique of income-focused frameworks has emphasized the finding that competitive market economies and trajectories of development and growth can generate many different outcomes and that non-income variables (including institutional conditions and respect for fundamental freedoms and human rights) are among the variables that can affect these results. For example, effective development and growth may critically depend on a wide range of non-income variables such as the presence or absence of pro-poor public policies related to basic education, health care, and employment generation, and the institutional context in which markets function, including respect for fundamental freedoms and human rights (see Section 1.5). Income-focused approaches concentrate on a particular means (or instrument), resulting in the neglect of the intrinsic value of ultimate objectives and goals (including the intrinsic value of fundamental freedoms and human rights), as well the neglect of the instrumental value of other (non-income) instruments. An exclusive focus on income can therefore result in systematic bias and policy failure because of (*a*) the focus on a single instrument when many may be relevant; (*b*) the focus on the 'wrong' policy target (Drèze and Sen (1989) and Sen (1999*a*; 2001*b*)). In welfare economics, individual well-being is often characterized in terms of the concept of utility (understood in terms of individual 'pleasures and pains', happiness, and/or desire-fulfilment) and operationalized in terms of revealed preferences and actual choices. Sen has developed a far-reaching critique of 'welfarist' frameworks for concentrating on an overly narrow view of human rationality and well-being. His work has 'unpacked' the 'welfarist' foundations of a wide range of conceptual and technical apparatus and has analysed the limitations of this informational base from the perspective of fundamental freedoms and human rights—for the prediction of individual behaviour, the characterization of interpersonal advantage, and the evaluation of the efficiency and fairness of competitive market outcomes. Key limitations include:

(1) **Neglect of the relevance of fundamental freedoms and human rights to the characterization of human motivation and rationality and the prediction of individual behaviour.** Standard frameworks assume (*a*) that individual utility can be interpreted in terms of the real representation of individual preferences (via the utility function); (*b*) that individual preferences are motivated by 'self-interested utility maximisation'; (*c*) that individual preferences can be deduced from individual choices (the theory of revealed preference); (*d*) that 'maximal choices' can be equated with 'optimal choices'. Sen has argued that these assumptions result in an overly narrow view of human motivation and rationality and can result in wrong predictions. The objective of individual behaviour is not necessarily 'self-interested utility maximisation', and other motivations and objectives may be important determinants of preferences and choices. These include identity, loyalties, commitments, agency, and the pursuit of goals and values such as fundamental freedoms and human rights.

(2) **Neglect of the relevance of fundamental freedoms and human rights to the characterization of personal and interpersonal advantage.** Sen has argued that 'welfarism' is an overly narrow informational base for characterizing personal interests because it focuses on the *well-being* aspect of a person (relating to his or her own personal physical and mental interests), whilst neglecting the *agency* aspect (relating to the goals that a person values, desires, and has reasons to pursue); on a single dimension of human well-being (utility), whilst neglecting other dimensions (including entitlements, capabilities and functionings, opportunity, freedom, and human rights); and on outcomes, whilst neglecting process-sensitivity and the intrinsic value of individual freedom of choice and participation. Furthermore, interpersonal comparisons based on individual 'mental states' such as happiness and desire-fulfilment may be systematically biased because of the phenomenon of 'adaptive expectations'. This phenomenon may be particularly common in the context of inequality, poverty, and oppressive cultural traditions—with the expectations and desires of vulnerable groups including the poor, and women in traditional and sexist societies, being particularly affected—whilst the limitations of utility-based frameworks in the context of 'adaptive expectations' are exacerbated by the use of choice information as a proxy for utility (through the theory of revealed preference).[1]

---

[1] See, for example, Sen (1985*a*: 15; 1987*b*: 45–6; 1984: 309) and Nussbaum (2001).

(3) **Neglect of the relevance of fundamental freedoms and human rights to the evaluation of the efficiency and fairness of competitive market outcomes.** Standard approaches in welfare economics adopt utility-based interpretations of Pareto optimality as a necessary condition for economic efficiency and distributional fairness. Sen has critiqued this concept on the grounds that it is 'supremely unconcerned with distributional issues'. A state can be Pareto optimal 'with some people in extreme misery and others rolling in luxury, so long as the miserable cannot be made better off without cutting into the luxury of the rich' (Sen 1987b: 31–2; 1997 [1973]: 7). Furthermore, the concept of Pareto optimality is insensitive to the possibility of entitlement failure and starvation, and can conflict with respect for individual liberty-rights. These limitations feed into judgements about the efficiency and fairness of competitive market outcomes through the Fundamental Theorems of Welfare Economics.[2]

The need to expand theoretical and empirical economics to take account of fundamental freedoms and human rights

Against this background, Sen's research agenda has moved both theoretical and empirical economics forward by highlighting the importance of fundamental freedoms and human rights for the analysis of economic processes and arrangements including the evaluation of (*a*) personal advantage; (*b*) the efficiency and fairness of market outcomes; (*c*) poverty and inequality; (*d*) the adequacy of public policy and institutional arrangements; (*e*) the nature of development and growth. His work has

---

[2] The concept of Pareto optimality suggests that a situation is optimal if no non-conflicting improvements can be made (i.e. if no one's situation can be improved without worsening the situation of someone else). Utility-based interpretations suggest that a situation is optimal if no one's utility can be improved without worsening the utility of someone else. The First Theorem of Welfare Economics establishes that under certain assumptions (e.g. no externalities) all competitive market equilibria are Pareto optimal. That is, no one's situation (utility) can be improved without worsening the situation (utility) of someone else, starting from any competitive market equilibrium. The Second Theorem establishes that given certain additional conditions (e.g. no convexities) every Pareto optimal outcome is a competitive equilibrium with respect to some set of prices and some initial distribution of resources. Therefore, every Pareto optimal outcome can be decentralized using the competitive market mechanism (with an appropriate initial allocation and price vector). Although more radical interpretations are possible, these Theorems are often interpreted as implying that, under certain assumptions and conditions, competitive market outcomes are not improvable in ways that would increase the utility of at least one person without reducing the utility of somebody else. For further discussion, see Sen (1993b) and, for example, Mas-Colell et al. (1995: 556–7).

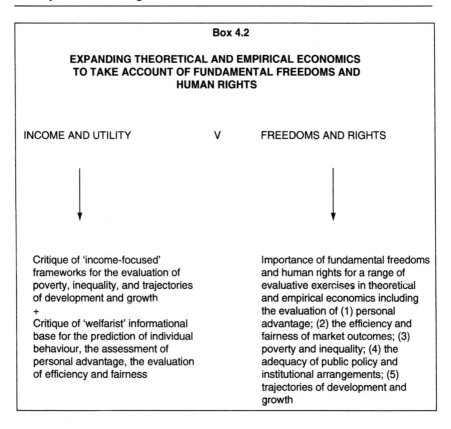

Box 4.2

EXPANDING THEORETICAL AND EMPIRICAL ECONOMICS
TO TAKE ACCOUNT OF FUNDAMENTAL FREEDOMS AND
HUMAN RIGHTS

INCOME AND UTILITY　　　　　V　　　FREEDOMS AND RIGHTS

Critique of 'income-focused' frameworks for the evaluation of poverty, inequality, and trajectories of development and growth
+
Critique of 'welfarist' informational base for the prediction of individual behaviour, the assessment of personal advantage, the evaluation of efficiency and fairness

Importance of fundamental freedoms and human rights for a range of evaluative exercises in theoretical and empirical economics including the evaluation of (1) personal advantage; (2) the efficiency and fairness of market outcomes; (3) poverty and inequality; (4) the adequacy of public policy and institutional arrangements; (5) trajectories of development and growth

emphasized the development of new frameworks and approaches in theoretical and empirical economics that take account of both the *instrumental* role of fundamental freedoms and human rights in influencing competitive market outcomes and trajectories of development and growth; and of frameworks in welfare economics that take more account of the *intrinsic* value of fundamental freedoms and human rights in assessing the impact of economic arrangements and processes on individuals, groups, and populations. 'Post-welfarist' frameworks of this type include:

(1) Frameworks that adopt a pluralistic informational base, taking account of both well-being and agency; frameworks that take account

of the non-utility features of human motivation and personal well-being;

(2) Frameworks that are sensitive to process as well as to outcomes, reflecting the intrinsic value of freedom of choice, agency, and participation;

(3) Frameworks that go beyond the view of individual preferences as 'self-interested utility maximisation' by adopting a broader view of agency and things that people *would* choose to do (given the choice);

(4) Frameworks that give a central and constitutive role to the value of freedoms and rights in economic analysis and evaluation.

Hence: 'the assessment of "value" has to take us well beyond utilities.... [T]he evaluation of consequences [should take] explicit note of the violation and fulfilment of [freedoms and] rights ... by incorporating the value of right fulfilment and the disvalue of rights violation into the assessment of resulting states of affairs' (Sen 1987b: 73; 1996a: 26).[3]

Proposals for moving forward

Sections 4.2–7 analyse the key ways in which Sen's proposals have moved theoretical and empirical economics forward by incorporating new variables and concerns that reflect the intrinsic and instrumental value of fundamental freedoms and human rights. These contributions include far-reaching proposals for the incorporation of individual entitlements, capabilities and functionings, civil and political rights, 'freedom of choice', 'liberty-rights', and 'basic-rights' into economic analysis and evaluation. These proposals have contributed to important paradigm shifts—away from an exclusive concern with income, growth, and utility, towards a range of human rights-focused variables and concerns. They have opened up important new lines of enquiry and provide a framework for the instrumental and intrinsic valuation of fundamental freedoms and human rights in economic assessment and in empirical economic research.

---

[3] The criticisms of utilitarianism highlighted in the literature include (a) focus on utility information; (b) failure to give adequate weight to agent-relative values; (c) failure to give adequate weight to intrinsically good and bad actions; (d) failure to give intrinsic weight to the violation and fulfilment of individual rights (including internationally recognized human rights). These and other limitations are discussed in Sen and Williams (1982). In responding to (c), Sen has argued that the proposition that rights are instruments to ultimate objectives be split into the propositions that (a) rights do not have intrinsic importance (only a derivate role, ideally in promoting utility), and (b) any acknowledgement of rights—legally or morally—has consequential implications which must be examined. He maintains that even when (a) is rejected, the relevance of (b) is not disestablished. See, for example, Sen (1996b: 156).

Box 4.3 SUMMARY OF SEN'S PROPOSALS FOR THE INCLUSION OF HUMAN RIGHTS-BASED CONCERNS AND VARIABLES INTO THEORETICAL AND EMPIRICAL ECONOMICS

- **Individual Entitlements (Section 4.2).** Analytical framework for assessing the sensitivity of the 'rights-structure' prevailing in a particular society to poverty, hunger, and starvation; empirical evidence of the importance of variables other than aggregate food supply as determinants of individual access to food.
- **Capabilities and Functionings (Section 4.3).** Conceptualization of substantive freedoms as the primary objectives of social and economic arrangements; empirical evidence of the dissonance between the expansion of individual income and the expansion of capability achievement; evaluation of trajectories of development and growth in terms of capability expansion (e.g. 'development and freedom' and 'human development'); development of approaches to poverty and inequality that focus on capability deprivation (e.g. poverty as 'capability deprivation' and analysis of inequalities in capability achievement by different population groups (e.g. by gender, ethnicity, nationality, etc.)).
- **Civil and Political Rights (Section 4.4).** Analysis of the instrumental role of political freedoms in promoting effective development and growth (e.g. role of civil and political rights in preventing socio-economic disasters, promoting transparency, and providing incentives for the satisfaction of basic needs).
- **Economic and Social Rights (Section 4.4).** Analysis of the instrumental role of economic and social rights in promoting effective development and growth (e.g. the role of economic and social rights in improving access to information, reducing corruption, strengthening the incentives on governments to respond to the needs of subordinate groups, and achieving long-term changes in population expectations and choices).
- **'Freedom of Choice' and 'Opportunity Freedom' (Section 4.5).** Proposals for capturing and formalizing the idea of the right to choose and nature and scope of individual choices and constraints in economics.
- **'Liberty-Rights' and 'Basic Rights' (Section 4.6).** Proposals for incorporating the ideas of 'liberty-rights' into the theory of social choice and for extended game-theoretic approaches that take account of 'basic' or 'fundamental' rights.

4.2 Individual Entitlements

The 'entitlement approach' provides a framework for assessing the impact of the 'rights-structure' that prevails in a particular society on poverty, hunger, and starvation. Whereas the concept of *rights* focuses on the relationship between two agents (two individuals, an individual and the state, etc.), the concept of *entitlement* focuses on a person's 'command over things', given the complete specification of the rights and obligations that an agent has vis-à-vis others, and the rights and obligations that others have vis-à-vis him. A person's 'entitlement set' identifies the different bundles of things to which he or she has access, given the specification of (*a*) the rights-structure; (*b*) initial endowments, transfers, and opportunities for transforming endowments into entitlements via exchange. In economies characterized by production for own consumption (e.g. peasant economies), the exchange mapping depends on the exchange relationship with nature (i.e. agricultural productivity), whereas in economies where a significant proportion of the population acquires food by exchanging labour power for a wage, markets are a crucial determinant of a person's 'entitlement set'. Hunger and starvation are captured and formalized in this model in terms of the failure to access an 'entitlement set' that includes a commodity bundle satisfying minimum food requirements. If a set of commodity bundles F_i satisfies the minimum food requirements of person i, then i will starve if he or she is not entitled to any member of F_i (given (*a*) the rights-structure; (*b*) endowments, transfers, and exchange entitlement mappings). The 'starvation set' S_i identifies allocations of endowments that are associated with inadequate exchange entitlements, and facilitates the distinction between systems of rights that give rise to legal entitlements to adequate food, and systems of rights that do not (e.g. Sen 1981; 1982*d*: 347–51).

Empirical applications of the 'entitlement approach'

Sen's empirical applications of the 'entitlement approach' have moved the economics and human rights agenda forward by providing new insights into the nature and causation of deprivation and by focusing international attention on the range of variables other than aggregate food supply that can help to explain hunger and starvation. Sen has hypothesized that '[m]ost cases of starvation and famines across the world arise not from people being deprived of things to which they are entitled, but from people not being entitled, in the prevailing legal system of institutional rights, to adequate means for survival' (Sen 1982*d*: 349). His groundbreaking study of four major famines (Sen 1981) challenged conventional wisdom by questioning the widespread assumption that starvation deaths during periods of famine can be explained by a simple relationship between population and food supply. Empirical analysis of the evidence relating to four major famines (Bengal 1943–4; Ethiopia 1972–4; Sahel 1968–73; and Bangladesh 1974) suggested a tenuous relationship between starvation deaths and food supply, and established the range of other variables that are critical determinants of a person's entitlement to food. Indeed, empirical applications of the 'entitlement approach' suggest that starvation deaths can sometimes arise when there is no overall decline in food availability, with entitlement failure arising, for example, when particular population groups were unable to trade their labour power or skills (Sen 1981; also see Drèze and Sen (1989)). These research findings have helped to focus international attention on the importance of food security policies that take into account the determinants of the differential ability of individuals, groups, and classes to command food in practice, and have had a far-reaching international impact in the field of human rights. Thus the UN Special Rapporteur on the Human Right to Food has recommended that the first step in a national food security strategy is to map the situation for different population groups, taking into account a range of variables including occupation, gender, ethnicity, race, and rural/urban location. This approach reflects the complex causes of starvation and hunger and importance of the *precise identification* of the food-insecure—who they are, where they are located, and the particular causes underlying their vulnerability (Eide 1998, 1999).

The human right to freedom from hunger and competitive market outcomes

The 'entitlement approach' has also generated debates about whether famines can occur under conditions of perfect competition with rational behaviour. This debate is important for assessing what markets can and cannot achieve under the idealized conditions of perfect competition from the perspective of fundamental freedoms and human rights. Sen's analysis suggests that there is a possibility of a situation in which competitive markets *clear*, but in which not everyone gets an adequate food entitlement to guarantee survival. Where individuals and groups have no direct food entitlements there may be non-survival, with insecure food entitlements arising not as a result of market failure (as this is standardly understood), but when markets *work*. This analysis challenges approaches that rule out the possibility of starvation death due to an inability to buy sufficient food through production or exchange, and/or that maintain that if all economic agents are rational, there will be an appropriate behavioural response to famines that can be anticipated (e.g. insuring against food insecurity by storing grain or expanding food production). The assumption of universal survival is embodied in the principle of *trade-independent security* which implies that 'each consumer can, if necessary, survive on the basis of the resources he holds and the direct use of his own labour, without engaging in exchange and still have something to spare of some type of labour which is sure to meet with a positive price in any equilibrium' (Koopman, as cited in Sen 1981: 172). Desai suggests that this assumption comes about both for reasons of mathematical simplicity (since introducing minimum subsistence for consumers as a necessary condition for equilibrium would introduce discontinuities that make mathematical proof difficult) and because of standard assumptions about scarcity in mainstream economics. The proposition that famines—a form of systematic and pervasive scarcity—can occur (and have historically occurred) without there necessarily being a shortage of food, and in the face of available food stocks, is analogous to the claim that involuntary unemployment can occur in the face of excess capacity and unsold commodity surpluses. Just as involuntary unemployment does not arise in the pure model of competitive markets, and is standardly explained in terms of departures from the assumptions of the pure model, so the pure model of competitive markets must rule out involuntary hunger and starvation (Desai 1995 [1987]: 120–33).

Some economists have concluded that Sen's empirical findings must be explainable in terms of insufficient initial endowments, market failure caused by the violation of the initial conditions, and/or broader political conditions (e.g. restrictions on access to food and/or freedom of movement or food transportation resulting from government policy, violence, war, etc.). Others have emphasized that freedom from starvation cannot be guaranteed under the idealized conditions of competition and have developed models that support the prediction of entitlement failures in economies in which competitive markets 'work'. For example, Desai (1995 [1990]: 136–47) takes up the question of how entitlement failures in food can arise if there is no decline in food availability and/or no rise in the price of food. He develops a two individual, two goods model covering the markets for rice and fish, with an asymmetric preference structure and specialization, and demonstrates that famine conditions can occur without invoking market failure. Coles and Hammond (1995) demonstrate that standard results relating to the existence and efficiency of general market equilibria are valid even when the assumption of universal survival is relaxed. Competitive equilibria with non-survivors exist and are Pareto optimal because the survival of the non-survivors would require 'sacrifices' from survivors. 'Core equivalence' also holds, with non-survivors lacking the resources they need to block the achievement of a 'Walrasian' equilibrium and to ensure their own survival. Various modifications of the standard framework are required to establish the proofs (e.g. assumptions to deal with the distribution of 'needs' on the margin of survival and non-convexities in consumption set as an individual passes between survival and death). Coles and Hammond conclude that entitlement failures 'do nothing to create any Pareto inefficiencies' and 'cannot be market failures in any normal sense'.

[T]he tragedy of starvation can arise in economies characterized by perfect competition. Then starvation is not a result of market failure.... [Like] involuntary unemployment ... it is not the result either of unnecessary institutional rigidities in the labour market. Instead, it is an entirely natural phenomenon of a neoclassical economy with surplus labour. Only after excess labour has been removed through starvation can general equilibrium arise. (Coles and Hammond 1995: 60)

4.3 Capabilities and Functionings

Sen's contributions to the development of a cross-disciplinary bridge between economics and human rights have been driven forward by the argument that economic processes and arrangements should be evaluated from the perspective of individual substantive freedoms (rather than other informational focuses such as income and utility). This argument is reflected in a series of influential proposals for evaluating individual advantage, the efficiency and fairness of competitive market equilibria, the adequacy of public policy and institutional arrangements, poverty and inequality, and the nature of development and growth, in terms of the capabilities and functionings that people can and do achieve.

From 'entitlements' to 'capabilities'

Sen's proposals for capturing and formalizing individual substantive freedoms in the form of the valuable 'beings' and 'doings' in 'capability space' build on the 'entitlement approach' but recognize that the mapping between a person's entitlements (i.e. their command over commodities) on the one hand, and a person's *capability to achieve valuable functionings* on the other, depends on personal features (such as bodyweight, health status, and aspects of a person's situation reflected in 'environmental conditions'). 'Capability space' takes account of this parametric dependence on personal features by introducing a 'characteristics function' (that governs the conversion of commodity consumption into valuable characteristics) and a 'personal utilisation function' (that governs the conversion of characteristics into valuable things that a person can do and be). The concept of capabilities is defined derivatively in functionings space. For person i, any *point* in functionings space represents a n-tuple of functionings—that is, a particular combination of that person's doings and beings, such as being nourished, clothed, mobile, taking part in the life of the community, and so on. Whereas a *point* in functionings space represents an n-tuple of functionings, the capability set is defined as a *collection* of such points (i.e. a *collection* of functioning n-tuples) and represents the various alternative combinations of beings and doings that are *feasible* for person *i*. Since *i* is *able* or *has the capability* to choose a functioning n-tuple from the set of feasible functioning n-tuples, the capability set might be interpreted as a *possibility* or *opportunity* set for *i*. Alternatively, the capability set might be conceptualized as representing *i*'s *options* or the extent or range of his or her *freedom of choice*.

Real representation of the 'capability approach'

On the assumption that the value of functionings and capabilities can be represented in real number space (R^n) (with the extent of a person's enjoyment of functionings, and his or her evaluation or ranking of alternative combinations of functionings, represented by real numbers), different combinations of beings and doing that *i* can achieve (such as being nourished, clothed, mobile, or taking part in the life of the community) are captured and formalized as 'functioning vectors' in 'capability space'. Given *i*'s command over commodities (or entitlements) and his or her personal features (such as bodyweight, health status, and aspects of their personal situation reflected in 'environmental conditions'), the 'capability set' $Q_i(X_i)$ is defined derivatively as the set of feasible 'functioning vectors' for person *i*, and represents the freedom that a person has in terms of the choice of functionings (i.e. the various combinations of doings and beings that he or she can feasibly achieve):

$$Q_i(X_i) = [b_i | b_i = f_i(c(x_i)), \text{ for some } f_i() \in F_i \text{ and for some } x_i \in X_i],$$

where x_i is a vector of commodities possessed by *i*,

X_i is the set of feasible commodity vectors for *i*,

$c(.)$ is a function converting a commodity vector x_i into a vector of characteristics,

$f_i(.)$ is a personal 'utilisation function' for *i* (representing the conversion of a commodities vector x_i into a functionings vector by *i*),

F_i is the set of feasible 'utilisation functionings' f_i, for *i*,

and $b_i = f_i(c(x_i))$ is a vector of achieved functionings for person *i* (given a commodity vector x_i and the choice of a utilization function f_i).

Since i is *able* or *has the capability* to choose a functioning vector from the set of feasible functioning vectors, the capability set might be interpreted as a *possibility* or *opportunity* set for i. Alternatively, the capability set might be conceptualized as representing i's *options* or the extent or range of his or her *freedom of choice*. The *value* attributed to a vector of functionings is analytically distinct from the happiness (u_i) that person i derives from the vector of functionings b_i, and is given by $v_i = v_i(f_i(c(x_i)))$, where $v_i()$ is the valuation function of person i (Sen 1985c: 6–11).

Methods of 'capability set' evaluation

The method of 'elementary evaluation' is often adopted as a means of attributing a value to sets (e.g. consumption sets) and involves equating the value of a set with the value of a particular element of a set. In applying this method, it is commonly assumed that the value of a set can be equated with the value of the 'best' element available (the maximal) defined in terms of some criterion of goodness; that individual choice reflects a process of maximization according to this criterion of goodness; and that the 'chosen' or 'achieved' element from a set can be equated with the maximal element in set. This standard methodology suggests a procedure for capability set evaluation whereby the value of a capability set is equated with the value of the 'chosen' or 'achieved' functioning vector, which is taken to be the best element in the set (the maximal), defined in terms of the maximization of personal functionings (i.e. [$V(S) = \max v(x), x \in S$]). Sen has challenged the basis of the application of this standard methodology to the evaluation of capability sets on two central grounds. First, the behavioural assumptions relating to the choice of a maximal element in a given set of alternatives may be inappropriate. An individual may not seek to maximize personal well-being and individual choice may be motivated by broader objectives (e.g. other people's well-being) and other objectives (including obligations and commitments to others). Second, personal well-being may not be independent of freedom of the range and adequacy of choices available. If autonomy and freedom of choice affect personal well-being, then the possibility of choice and the number of alternatives in a set (intrinsic valuation of the freedom to choose) as well as, perhaps, the range (or diversity) and the quality (or adequacy) of these alternatives (Sen 1985a: 37–43; 1985b: 9–10; 1991; 1992b; 1993a: 33–5; 1993b; 1997a) (see Section 4.6). Furthermore, Sen does not exclusively equate 'capability set' evaluation with personal valuation by person i. The evaluative exercise may be extended to incorporate the critical scrutiny of the reasons underlying personal choice, and social or ethical valuation of the substantive freedoms that a person enjoys. For example, Sen (2001) emphasizes the sub-class of 'capability freedoms' *that people have reasons to value*. He suggests that the specification and justification of this sub-class should take account of both individual agency goals and of contextual influences (e.g. interpersonal variations associated with 'adaptive preferences' and 'positional dependences') and accommodate (*a*) reflective evaluation of capability achievement (taking account of individual counterfactual choices and meta-preferences); (*b*) external critical scrutiny of the 'reasons' underlying values, preference, and choice.

The specification of the valuation function v_i (.)

Sen has further emphasized that the valuation function v_i (.) may relate to a partial ordering of capabilities that is substantially incomplete. This argument is best understood in the context of Sen's broader contributions to the analysis of measurement and comparability in the context of informational constraints and value conflicts. Given the possibility of both pragmatic incompleteness (e.g. due to informational constraints) and fundamental incompleteness (i.e. unresolvable value conflicts), how can measurement proceed? Sen's proposals for moving forward emphasize measurement systems that allow for incompleteness and ambiguity by relaxing the standard that orderings be substantially complete. These include influential proposals for the use of quasi-orderings in the measurement of inequality (e.g. Sen 1997 [1973]) and for the development of a technical apparatus suitable for identifying relative weights-based rank order rather than full cardinal interpersonal comparability in the context of poverty measurement (e.g. Sen 1982*f* [1976]: 373–87). In the current context, Sen has emphasized the advantages of adopting 'capability space' as an evaluative space for assessing the achievement of substantive human freedoms before agreeing on the relative weights of different capabilities and functionings. In the absence of a complete agreement about relative weights, a focus on the 'intrinsic relevance and centrality of functionings and capabilities' can have 'substantial discriminatory power'. For example, a pragmatic consensus concerning the relative importance of a small number of central and highly valuable capabilities provides a basis for 'capability set' ranking using dominance reasoning and the 'partial order approach' (Sen 1985*a*; 1985*b*; 1987*a*: 34; 1992*a*: 46–9, 133–4; 1993*a*: 31–5, 48–9; 1997 [1973]: 203–9).

Empirical applications of the 'capability approach'

Sen's empirical applications of the 'capability approach' have opened up new lines of enquiry and resulted in an important body of statistical evidence on human rights-focused concerns. His research has focused international attention on the possibility and implications of divergences between the expansion of economic growth and income on the one hand, and the expansion of valuable human capabilities on the other. They establish that economic growth and income can be poor predictors of the capability to live to a mature age (without succumbing to premature mortality) in different countries (e.g. India, China, Sri Lanka, Costa Rica, Jamaica) and for different population groups (e.g. black men versus other groups in the USA; the population in the Indian state of Kerala versus populations in other states). As well as addressing the successes and limitations of market processes in securing the expansion of human capabilities and functionings, Sen's empirical research provides important insights into the critical role of public policy in securing the human rights to freedom from hunger and starvation (e.g. Drèze and Sen 1989). The idea that capabilities and functionings may be the most appropriate focal variables for a range of evaluative exercises concerning human interests has resulted in important new approaches to the analysis of poverty and inequality (e.g. Drèze and Sen 1989; Sen 1993*a*: 31–41; 1999*a*: 22–3, 74–110) and has had a major impact on international efforts to characterize and measure poverty and well-being and to evaluate the nature and adequacy of development. The UNDP's Human Poverty Index captures deprivations in living standards (where 'living standard' is characterized in terms of access to safe water, health services, and birth-weight), whilst the *Human Development Index* captures the importance of three crucially important and highly valuable human capabilities—the capability to achieve knowledge, longevity, and a decent standard of living. These indices rival income-focused measures and provide critical statistical information about the achievements and non-achievements of populations and groups.

The 'capability approach' and gender discrimination

The proposal that human equalities and inequalities be characterized and evaluated in capability space has moved the economic analysis of gender discrimination forward in innovative and important ways. Sen's critique of utility as an informational base for the characterization and evaluation of individual advantage is partly motivated by concern with the impact of the conditioning of women's preferences on individual choices and actions. The 'capability approach' was in turn partly motivated by the need for a more adequate analytical space for the characterization and evaluation of gender disparities in situations of power asymmetries, discrimination, and entrenched disadvantage. Furthermore, Sen's empirical research has opened up important new lines of investigation into the statistical relationships between gender discrimination and capability inequality. For example, Sen's analysis of the phenomenon of excess mortality and lower survival rates of women in many parts of the world (resulting in a sharp 'deficit' in women—the phenomenon of 'Missing Women') suggested that although excess mortality in women of a child-bearing age could be partly explained by maternal mortality, no such explanation was possible for female disadvantage in survival in infancy and childhood. Evidence of lower female–male ratios in countries in Asia and North Africa is indicative of the influence of social factors resulting in gender inequality including gender discrimination and the comparative neglect of female health and nutrition (Sen 1999a: 104–7). For example, in India and Pakistan, the female–male ratio is among the lowest in the world—about 0.93 in both cases, compared to average ratios of 1.05 in Europe and North America. Statistical analysis of the female–male ratio in India suggests that the patterns are cannot be explained by excess mortality before the age of one (including the practice of infanticide), but rather reflects the preferential treatment of boys and the neglect of female children in intra-household allocation—including the relative neglect in terms of health care, nutrition, and related needs, particularly in north India. Furthermore, when the figures for the female–male ratio are disaggregated by region, the regional patterns are consistent with what is known about the character of gender relations in different parts of India. North-western states, characterized by unequal gender relations, are also characterized by low female–male ratios (e.g. 0.86 in Haryana and 0.87 in Punjab). In contrast, in Kerala, which is characterized in important respects by a stronger social status of women (reflected, for example, in relatively high female literacy rates, stronger representation of women in influential social and professional activities, and traditions of matriliny), the female–male ratio is around 1.06 (Drèze and Sen 2002: 230–45). Other contributions in the field of gender discrimination also include the analysis of underlying power asymmetries on the intra-household allocation bargaining situation (including the analysis of unequal gains in situations of 'co-operative conflict' and the use of 'bargaining thresholds' to improve 'allocative outcomes' (e.g. Sen 1990).[4]

4.4 Human Rights

Is there an inevitable conflict between human rights and economic growth?

Sen's work has moved the economics and human rights agenda forward by challenging the idea that there is an inevitable conflict between the protection and promotion of human rights on the one hand, and effective development and growth on the other. The idea of a core of so-called 'Asian values' that are in some ways opposed to civil and political rights—together with high growth rates in parts of east Asia during the 1980s and the 1990s, and China's recent record of development and poverty reduction—are sometimes invoked as evidence of the positive impact of authoritarianism on economic growth. High rates of economic growth in relatively authoritarian states in parts of east Asia during the 1980s and the 1990s, together with China's record of economic growth and poverty reduction, are seen as evidence of a positive association between authoritarian forms of government and economic success. This view was reflected, for example, at the World Conference on Human Rights in Vienna in 1993, where the negotiating platform of some countries suggested that democracy and civil and political rights can mitigate or hamper economic growth and development. In challenging this thesis Sen suggests that selective and anecdotal evidence from east Asia is balanced by contrary evidence from other regions. For example, even when Singapore and South Korea were growing faster than any other country in Asia, the fastest growing economy in Africa was Botswana—'a major defender of democracy'. In Sen's view, the statistics go in contrary directions and do not yield a clear and unambiguous relationship:

[S]ystematic statistical studies give no real support to the claim that here is a general conflict between political rights and economic performance. That relationship seems conditional on many other circumstances, and indeed the hypothesis that there is no relation between them in either direction is very hard to reject on

---

[4] The use of the capability framework for the analysis of gender is discussed and further developed by Nussbaum (especially in Nussbaum 1995, 2000). The analysis of Sen's 'Missing Women' is further discussed in Corell (2001) and Klasen and Wink (2003). The question of whether or not the capability approach adequately addresses issues of power imbalances is discussed in Agarwal et al. (2003).

the basis of the empirical evidence that exists. Indeed, the case for democracy and civil rights cannot be based on their likely *positive* impact on economic growth, nor can that case be demolished by their likely *negative* effect on economic growth. If these rights have value on their own, then this value, it appears, can be obtained at little or no cost to economic growth. (Sen 1999*b*: 91)

The instrumental role of human rights in promoting effective development and growth

Indeed, Sen's empirical research findings suggest that democratic political institutions and broader democratic practices (including human rights guarantees) can often play a key role in the promotion of sustainable and equitable development and growth (including the promotion of capability expansion and the fulfilment of basic needs). His work has made an important contribution to the growing body of literature on economics and institutional conditions by establishing the ways in which democratic forms of government and civil and political rights can provide critical incentives to governments—by strengthening access to information, by facilitating public scrutiny and debate, by building up political opposition, by strengthening the responsiveness of governments to subordinate groups, and ultimately by precipitating more effective public policy. Sen's empirical work explores these incentive and informational effects in relation to the prevention and management of a wide range of social and economic shocks (ranging from famine prevention to the management of the risks and effects of financial downturns), as well as in relation to the allocation of the positive benefits of development and growth. In addition, the case studies discussed in Drèze and Sen (2002) suggest that, like civil and political rights, economic and social rights can be instrumentally important for both efficiency and equity.[5]

---

[5] There is a growing body of literature analysing the instrumental role of democracy and civil and political rights in promoting effective development and economic growth. World Bank (1998) discusses the importance of a range of variables including personal freedoms and liberties (e.g. from slavery and from forced and bonded labour), property rights, freedom of economic transactions, women's equality (e.g. freedom from labour market exclusion and nondiscrimination in relation to property rights); 'good governance' and institutional conditions (e.g. access to justice); and civil society and stake-holder participation in the design and implementation of development projects and policies. Stiglitz (1999) analyses the adverse economic effects of the failure to respect the right to freedom of information (with informational asymmetries resulting in barriers to entry that advantage 'insiders' over 'outsiders', often resulting in corruption and inefficient resource allocation); whilst Stiglitz (2002) emphasizes the participatory process as a 'public good'—with an effective civil society functioning as a check on abuses of power and influence and a source of 'countervailing

Democracy and Famine Prevention

In building up a general picture of an association between democracy and famine prevention, Sen (1981; 1982; 1984; 1999*a*: 180–8; 1999*b*: 90–3; and, with Drèze 1989, 2002) has argued that no substantial famine has ever occurred in an independent and democratic country where government tolerates opposition, accepts the electoral press, and can be publicly criticized. He suggests that this statement applies not only to the affluent countries of Europe and America, but also to the poor but broadly democratic countries such as India. For example, the incidence of famines in India until independence in 1947 (for example, the Bengal famine in 1943 killed between 2 and 3 million people) contrasts with the post-independence experience following establishment of a multiparty democratic system, where timely public action has helped to affect public policy responses to the threat of famine (e.g. through food for work schemes and public food distribution) and has successfully avoided significant and widespread excess mortality through famine deaths. Drèze (2004: 1727) cites public action during the Rajasthan drought of 2002–3 provides a recent exemplar of this phenomenon. With close to 4 million labourers employed on relief works and related programmes in rural Rajasthan in June 2003, public employment programmes on a massive scale were a key factor in averting widespread excess mortality among drought-affected people. This record of public action to prevent famine deaths in India contrasts with the history of famine in China, where, when the 'Great Leap Forward' proved to be a mistake, disastrous policies were not corrected for three full years (1958–61)—while 23–30 million people died. Although evidence relating to a number of different causal factors is relevant here, Drèze and Sen suggest that the failure of public policy to respond effectively to a famine situation fits into a more general pattern of failures of public policy in times of socio-economic crisis. Furthermore, the excesses of the Cultural Revolution in China provide an important exemplar of the ways in which the absence of civil and political rights can contribute to efficiency losses through informational failure. Assumptions at the centre regarding food stocks during this period were considerably

power'. Besley and Burgess (2002) develop a model of the determinants of government responsiveness to the needs of vulnerable citizens. Their empirical findings suggest that, in the Indian context, electoral turnout, political competition, and mass media can affect government activism vis-à-vis calamity relief and food distribution. In addition, a growing body of cross-country comparisons and empirical case studies focus on the role of democratic institutions and transparency in achieving effective and sustainable economic growth (especially in relation to the guarantee of an appropriately stable political and economic environment and the management of shocks). For an overview and further references, see UNDP (2002: Box 2.4) and McKay and Vizard (2005).

greater than food stocks in practice turned out to be—and civil and political rights can have an important informational role in the 'corrections of errors' and of 'mistaken assumptions'.

The role of democracy and human rights in preventing and managing other forms of social and economic shock

Sen's research also examines the more general role of democratic political institutions and practices in the prevention and management of other types of social and economic shock. For example, Sen (1999a: 147–59; 1999b) maintains that risks of financial and economic crisis can be increased by the absence or lack of democratic structures, accountability, and transparency in business arrangements, whilst governmental responses to economic and financial crises, and the chances of effective restructuring and reform, can be critically affected by the absence or presence of broader democratic practices such as public scrutiny and participation, media scrutiny and human rights protections. Drèze and Sen (2002) suggest that the limitations of pursuing economic growth without democratic institutions and practices were demonstrated by the effects of the crashes of financial markets in the late 1990s. There is a need for 'downturn with security' as well as 'growth with equity' and the South-east Asian crashes illustrate the ways in which rights-allocations can be of critical importance in achieving this goal.

Political freedom and the determination of distributive shares

Drèze and Sen (2002) also focus attention on the importance of the rights-structure that prevails in a particular society for the determination of distributive shares. When civil and political rights and democratic institutions are not in place, the systematic exclusion from, and disparities in, the benefits of development and growth may be more likely to arise and less likely to be scrutinized and reversed. For example, in their discussions of the linkages between political freedom and social and economic achievements, Drèze and Sen raise the example of endemic illiteracy in the Tibet province of China. On the basis of census data, they report adult male and female literacy rates in Tibet in 1990–1 as being about 45 per cent and 20 per cent respectively, significantly below the average rates of about 90 per cent and 60 per cent in China as a whole, and lower not only than the Indian national averages of just over 60 per cent and 30 per cent, but also lower than the disaggregated rates reported in the 'educationally backward' north Indian states. Since the Chinese census counts persons who are able to read and write in any local language or script as literate, these high disparities in population disaggregated literacy rates cannot be interpreted in terms of a lack of command over Chinese language.

Does China's recent record of growth and poverty reduction establish the case for growth without human rights-protections?

Drèze and Sen conclude from this evidence that China's recent record of growth and poverty reduction fails to establish the case for growth without human rights-protections. They also question the extent to which increased levels of per capita income in China are explained by coercive population policies. Fertility rates in China have fallen significantly and this decline has had a critical role in achieving increased levels of per capita income. Drèze and Sen report the low fertility rate of 1.9 in China, significantly below the 'replacement' rate of 2.1, and comparing favourably with a rate of 3.1 in India, and a combined average of 4.3 in low-income countries other than China and India. However, to what extent have the coercive measures such as the 'one child policy', tried in many parts of China after 1979, driven the reductions in fertility rates and the associated increases in per capita income? Drèze and Sen raise three issues here. First, the lack of reproductive freedom for women inherent in coercive systems of population control itself represents an intrinsic loss. Second, coercive population policies can exacerbate existing tendencies towards the relative neglect of female children in countries. This phenomenon may be present on a fairly wide scale in China, as reflected in a significant decline in the female–male ratio at birth in China (reflecting asymmetries in gender-specific abortion rates), and in gender specific infant mortality rates (with the female infant mortality rate 30 per cent higher than the male infant mortality rate). Third, the 'value added' of coercive population policy over other explanatory variables (e.g. particularly the expansion of female literacy, women's labour market participation, and increased life expectancy) in achieving reduced fertility rates in China can be questioned. The comparison with positive experiences of voluntary fertility reduction in the Kerala and Tamil Nadu regions of India is instructive here. For example, Kerala's fertility rate of 1.8 is just below China, and this has been achieved on the basis of voluntary changes in behaviour without compulsion by the state and points towards the important role of other causal factors (including reduction of population mortality and morbidity risks, access to health care, female education, and labour market participation) in achieving voluntary reductions in fertility rates.

Public sector reform and accountability

Drèze and Sen (2002: 363) address the role of extensions of democratic processes in strengthening accountability and empowering beneficiaries vis-à-vis providers in programmes of public sector reform. Their analysis highlights the ways in which public sector inefficiency has resulted in systematic public policy failures in education, health, and food security. Drawing on case studies, they find evidence that persistent public sector inefficiency is associated with a lack of public sector accountability, often reflected in the most extreme forms of public policy failure (such as public health centres being closed on a work day, or systematic absenteeism by teachers in public schools, with low accountability in the schooling system playing a role in depriving millions of children of basic education). Their recommendations for a major programme of accountability-based public sector reform in India highlight the important role of 'countervailing power structures' in asymmetric power situations—with the possibility of concentrations of power in one domain being checked and restrained by a countervailing configuration of forces in another domain. They raise the need for public participation and scrutiny, audits, complaints mechanisms, electoral procedures, and legal action in this context. In addition, Drèze and Sen (2002) and Drèze (2004) link discussions about public sector accountability to discussions about human rights. They suggest that invoking human rights, including economic and social rights, can increase 'voice' and provide an additional source of 'countervailing power', with human rights functioning to promote efficient resource allocation by strengthening accountability, improving access to information, and ensuring that appropriate 'democratic control mechanisms' are in place. For example, Drèze (2004: 1726) also discusses the important role that freedom of information can play in extending public accountability and efficiency. The 'Right to Information Movement' in India, which calls for a blanket right to access to all public records at all times by all citizens, has already led to concrete results in relation to the reduction of corruption in public life. In Rajasthan, for example, the 'Right to Information Movement' has contributed to important steps forward regarding the eradication of corrupt practices in relief works.

Strengthening the influence of subordinate groups

The analysis in Drèze and Sen (2002) and Drèze (2004) also highlights the ways in which the recognition of human rights (including economic and social rights) can function to increase the influence of subordinate groups in collective decision-making. An important theme in the literature on public choice and new institutional economics relates to the ways in which the influence of vulnerable groups on public policy might be strengthened in order to prevent 'capture' by elites and more dominant social groups—including the positive role that extensions of democratic practice can play in increasing the 'voice' of vulnerable groups in electoral democracies. The Right to Food campaign in India illustrates the important role that the legal enforcement of human rights can play in building up pressure on governments to increase both equity and efficiency in food security policy by strengthening the influence of subordinate groups. Drèze and Sen (2002: vii, 336–9) and Drèze (2004: 1723) link the roots of 'nutritional crisis' in India to the influence of organized agricultural interests on food security policy. High 'minimum support prices' for food grains, fixed by government under pressure for influential farmers lobbies, have boosted production and resulted in food buffer stocks increasing to well above official levels amid 'continuation of the severest incidence of undernourishment in the world'. The human right to food (derived from the human right to life, which is legally protected under the Indian Constitution) has been invoked as a basis for challenging this policy—functioning to increase the 'voice' and to strengthen the influence of vulnerable groups vis-à-vis organized agricultural interests in public decision-making.[6]

Human rights and social norms

Drèze and Sen (2000: 42) also address the broader role of human rights beyond the legal domain—in helping to precipitate population level changes in individual expectations, behaviour, and choices. Their discussion of the treatment of the role of 'social norms' in individual decision-making in economics is instructive here. Social norms are a key influence on individual expectations, behaviour, and choices, and the analysis of their impact has received increased attention in the economics literature in recent years. However, the focus of research so far has typically been on how social norms can emerge, or sustain themselves, in a framework of 'repeated games'—where individual decisions remain driven by well-defined exogenous preferences—with the possibility of influencing social norms through public discussion and social intervention receiving less

---

[6] It has been argued that various economic and social rights, including shelter, an adequate standard of living, and medical care, are derivable from the right to life under the Indian Constitution. The right to food is arguably derivable from the right to life under Article 21, supported by directive principles. For details of cases before the Indian Supreme Court, see Section 5.4.

attention. In contrast, Drèze and Sen's research highlights the possibility of influencing social norms through public discussion and social intervention—including through the recognition of new and strengthened rights. For example, a case study of the successful expansion of education in Himachal Pradesh region in India highlights the critical role of the emergence of consensual norms on educational matters in achieving social transformations in this field. The recognition of elementary education as a fundamental right can facilitate acceptance of the view that schooling is an essential part of every child's upbringing (girls as well as boys, and for children in all population groups)—a critical element of achieving emergence of a social consensus on the achievement of universal education (Drèze and Sen 2002: 179–85). Against a general background of structural adjustment and general disengagement of the state, growing and broad-based recognition of elementary education as a fundamental right (as reflected in political campaigns and in recent amendments to the Indian Constitution) has contributed to the relatively rapid expansion of schooling facilities and school participation in India in the 1990s (Drèze 2004:1725).

Women's right to education as an instrument of broader social change

The empirical findings reported in Drèze and Sen (2002) also suggest that the expansion of women's rights to education might play an important role in promoting other aspects of social change. Cross-sectional evidence from the different regions of India suggests that various aspects of women's agency, including higher female literacy rates and labour force participation, are associated with lower levels of female disadvantage in survival. In contrast, rates of urbanization, male literacy, the availability of medical facilities, and the level of poverty were not found to be statistically significant. Female literacy was also found to have a significant negative impact on under-five mortality, compared with comparatively ineffective roles of male literacy or general poverty reduction as instruments of child mortality reduction. Keeping other variables constant, increasing the crude female literacy rate from 22 per cent to 75 per cent was found to reduce the predicted value of under-five mortality for males and females combined from 156 per thousand to 110 per thousand. Drèze and Sen conclude that variables relating to women's agency can play a much more important role in promoting social well-being, including child survival and the nature and extent of female disadvantage in child survival, than variables relating to the general level of opulence or overall economic growth in the society.

121

4.5 'Freedom of Choice' and 'Opportunity Freedom'

Sen's formal proposals for incorporating the ideas of 'freedom of choice' and 'opportunity freedom' into mathematical and welfare economics also reflect an underlying concern with the idea of fundamental freedoms and human rights. His contributions in this area have focussed attention on the importance of process for economic assessment and evaluation—especially the opportunities that people have to choose and participate—and provide a basis of a recharacterization of the First Welfare Theorem in terms of 'opportunity-freedom' rather than utility.

Incorporating the possibility and adequacy of choice into the analysis of individual behaviour

Sen has criticized standard frameworks in economics for their lack of emphasis on agency and participation. In moving the economics agenda forward in this area, he has challanged standard conditions imposed on the rationality and consistency of choice, developing a series of technical proposals for incorporating the *possibility of choosing* and the *range and adequacy of opportunities available* into preference relations ('chooser dependence' and 'menu dependence') and for the formal representation of *constraints on choice* (e.g. by distinguishing between (*a*) 'optimizing' choice functions requiring a best choice and (*b*) 'maximizing' choice functions requiring the choice of an alternative that is not judged to be worse than any other (e.g. Sen 1997*a*, 1993*c*).

The development of formal axioms to represent the distinction between 'process freedom' and 'opportunity freedom'

In addition, Sen's proposals for capturing and formalizing the importance of process and agency include the development of formal axioms for capturing and formalizing the distinction between 'process freedom' and 'opportunity-freedom' (e.g. 1991, 1993*b*, 2002*a*, *b*, *c*; Section 3.1). The formal representation of the idea of 'process freedom' focuses as the formalization of the ability to choose, whilst possible axioms for capturing and formalizing the idea of 'opportunity freedom'—the opportunity a person has to achieve the things that he or she has reasons to value and want—are given in Box 4.4. Sen has supported the relative merits of preference–based axioms (1.1–2) over preference-independent axioms and cardinality–based axioms (2.1–4) on the grounds that an assessment of a range of choice cannot be entirely

---

Box 4.4 AXIOMATICS OF OPPORTUNITY FREEDOM (EXPOSITION IN SEN [1991])

X: Universal set of alternative social states, with elements x, y, z, etc. (taken to be finite)

Y: Power set of X (i.e. the set of all non-empty sub-sets of X, denoted by 2^x -∅). The elements of Y (i.e. the sub-sets of X) are A, B, C, etc.

R: The preference ordering of the person whose freedom is being judged over the set of social states x. R stands for weak preference ('preferred than' or 'indifferent to')

P: Strict preference ('strictly preferred than')

I: Indifference

R^*: 'Offers at least as much freedom' (defined over Y)

P^*: 'Offers strictly more freedom' (defined over Y)

I^*: 'Offers exactly as much freedom' (defined over Y)

$\#S$: The number of elements in set S (i.e. the cardinality of set S)

$\supseteq$: Weak set inclusion

$\supset$: Strict (asymmetric) set inclusion

No uncertainty is admitted

Preference dominance relations over the subsets of X

Weak preference dominance: AD^WB if and only if there is a subset A' of A such that $\#A'=\#B$., and if further there is a one-to-one correspondence $k(.)$ between A' and B such that for all x in A', we have $xRk(x)$. *Strict preference dominance*: AD^sB if and only if AD^WB holds, and further, for all x in A', we have $xPk(x)$.

Three classes of axioms for the comparisons of freedoms

1. Preference-based Axioms

1.1 *Weak preference dominance*: $AD^WB \Rightarrow AR^*B$.

1.2 *Strong preference dominance*: 1.1 holds and $AD^sB \Rightarrow AP^*B$.

2. Preference-independent Axioms (PIA)

2.1 *Weak set dominance*: $A \supseteq B \Rightarrow AR^*B$.

2.2 *Strong set dominance*: 2.1 holds and $A \supset B \Rightarrow AP^*B$.

2.3 *Weak cardinality ranking*: $A \geq B \Rightarrow AR^*B$.

2.4 *Strong cardinality ranking*: 2.3 holds and $A > B \Rightarrow AP^*B$.

3. Constructive Axioms (relating freedom judgements in some cases to freedom judgements in other—related—cases, in the absence of uncertainty)

3.1 *Identical expansion*: If x belongs to neither A nor to B, then: $AR^*B \Rightarrow (A \cup \{x\})R^*(B \cup \{x\})$

3.2 *Weak composition*: If $A \cap C = B \cap D = \emptyset$, then: $[AR^*B \ \& \ CR^*D] \Rightarrow [(A \cup C)R^*(B \cup D)]$.

4. Additional axioms for dealing with unit sets

4.1 For all x, y in X: if xPy then $\{x\}\ P^*\{y\}$.

4.2 For all x, y in X: $\{x\}\ I^*\{y\}$

5. Cardinality based indifference axiom

$\#A = \#B \Rightarrow AI^*B$.

independent of the evaluation of the nature, scope, and adequacy of the elements in that range—and therefore of the things that a person has reasons to value and want. Both the weak and the strict cardinality axioms ignore the *nature* of the alternatives on a menu of options—implying that the choice between 'a nasty life', 'a terrible life', and 'an unspeakable life' is constitutive of the same freedom as the choice between 'a fine life', 'an excellent life', and 'a wonderful life', simply because each set has three elements. Similarly, Sen rejects the idea that the extent of the opportunity-freedom enjoyed can be judged in a preference-independent way. The feasibility of options such as 'having malaria' or 'having small-pox' on the one hand, and 'living in a world in which malaria or smallpox cannot be escaped' on the other, cannot be evaluated independently of people's values and preferences—including counterfactual preferences, such as 'freedom to live as we would like'.

Implications of Sen's formal axioms for the characterization of freedom in economics

In relating the assessment of freedom to the evaluation of the nature and scope of the options available, and to the preferences and values of the individuals concerned, Sen's approach challenges (*a*) cardinality-based formulations that characterize individual freedom purely in terms of the number of options available (Pattanaik and Xu 1990); (*b*) 'flexibility-based' formulations that suggest that uncertainty about future tastes is a reason for valuing current time freedom of choice in economics (Arrow 1995). Sen rejects (*a*) on the grounds that it fails to give weight to the value of the options available to the individual concerned; and (*b*) on the grounds that it represents a purely 'instrumental approach' that fails to reflect the intrinsic value of freedom of choice. In cases where there is no uncertainty, a set of options would still be evaluated in terms of the value of the maximal (most preferred/chosen) element or elements in the choice set—with the other elements of the menu not being taken into account. In contrast, Sen argues that if the focus of evaluation is on what a person can effectively do, then a person's *best opportunity* can be invoked as a *necessary*—but not a *sufficient*—condition for improving or maintaining freedom. If the focus of the evaluative exercise is a person's best opportunity, then being sure of an expansion of opportunity-freedom involves relaxing Axiom 1.2, so that Set *A* is characterized as offering strictly more opportunity than Set *B* if (*a*) *A* offers at least as much opportunity-freedom as *B* (defined in terms of Axiom 1.1), and (*b*) *some element* of *A* is preferred to every element of Set *B*. According to this approach, a necessary condition for being sure that set *A* has at least as much opportunity-freedom as B may be taken as the requirement that some element of A is at least as good as every element in B, and to be sure of an expansion of opportunity-freedom requires in addition that some element of A is preferred to every element in B. These requirements give rise to the following Axiom:

Relevance of Preferred Opportunity Axiom: To be sure that set A offers more opportunity-freedom than set B (alternatively, at least as much as B), there must be an element of A that is preferred to (alternatively, regarded at least as good as) all the elements of B.

Sen emphasizes that this Axiom is a *necessity* rather than a *sufficiency* condition. The requirement for strictly 'more' freedom in this axiom corresponds to condition (*b*) above, without demanding (*a*). This implies that to be sure that a set of alternatives gives a person more opportunity-freedom, the set must give the person an opportunity to get to a better (more preferred) alternative. However, the converse is not claimed. That is, the presence of a better (more preferred) alternative does not necessarily guarantee an enhancement of freedom—for example, if his or her other significant options are curtailed. The possible *insufficiency* of this condition brings out the important distinction between the *Relevance of Preferred Opportunity Axiom* and a 'purely instrumental view of freedom' in the special case of no uncertainty.

From welfarist efficiency to the efficiency of opportunity-freedoms as a criterion for evaluating competitive market equilibria

The formal axioms discussed above also provide the basis of a recharacterization of the First Theorem of Welfare Economics in terms of 'opportunity-freedom' rather than utility. This proposal relies on an extension of the weak form of the *Relevance of Preferred Opportunity Axiom* given above to a corresponding weak efficiency concept:

Weak efficiency of opportunity-freedom: A state of affairs is weakly efficient in terms of opportunity-freedom if there is no alternative feasible state in which everyone's opportunity-freedom is surely unworsened and at least one person's opportunity-freedom is surely expanded.

Standard frameworks equate economic efficiency with the efficiency of utilities and assume that (*a*) preferences are determined by choices; (*b*) choices are motivated by self-interested welfare maximization. Sen has argued that the basic analytical results of the 'Arrow–Debreu' Theorem are independent of assumption (*b*), and that the proposition that competitive market outcomes are efficient under certain conditions (such as the absence of externalities) will hold if some interpretation of individual advantage *other* than utility is adopted (with the utility-based interpretation of Pareto optimality loosing its status as *necessary condition* for social optimality). For example, his results establish that the basic efficiency results reflected in the 'Direct Theorem' can be carried over from the 'space' of utilities to the 'space' of individual substantive opportunity-freedoms (both in terms of freedom to choose commodity baskets and in terms of capabilities to function). This proposal takes forward thinking about the evaluation of the competitive market equilibria from the perspective of the substantive freedoms that people enjoy freedom (rather than in terms of the maximization of personal utility though self-interested behaviour). Sen has called for reassessment of the achievement and limitations of the market mechanisms in promoting individual freedoms, and for a reinterpretation of what mechanisms of competitive markets are supposed to do—and what they can be expected to achieve—from this perspective (Sen 1993*b*; also see 1991, 1999*a*).

4.6 'Liberty-Rights' and 'Basic-Rights'

Sen has finally moved human rights-based discourse in economics forward by developing a series of influential proposals for incorporating the ideas of 'liberty-rights' and 'basic-rights' into the theory of social choice. His contributions in this area provide a framework for the social-choice theoretical representation of individual rights; formalize the tension between the Pareto criterion and the notion of a 'protected private sphere'; and provide a framework for the future development of the formal representation of basic (fundamental or human) rights in economics and social choice.

Sen's 'social-choice' theoretic formulation of 'liberty-rights'

The proposals set out in Sen (1970*a*; 1970*b*; 1983*b*; 1992*b*; 1995; 1996*a*; 1996*b*, 2002: *a, b, c*) modify and extend Arrow's (1963 [1951]) framework for social choice by introducing an explicit condition that captured the idea that social choice procedure should respect individual liberty-rights. Whereas the framework for social choice developed by Arrow required that the social choice procedure should respect the condition of *non-dictatorship*, Sen (1970*b*) strengthened this condition by introducing the stronger requirement that the social choice procedure should respect the condition of 'minimal liberalism' (ML)—the condition that the preferences of each of at least two individuals are 'decisive' for social preference in relation to at least one pair-wise choice. The implication of this proposal is that if an

---

Box 4.5 THE SOCIAL CHOICE-THEORETIC REPRESENTATION OF THE IDEA OF INDIVIDUAL LIBERTY-RIGHTS (EXPOSITION IN SEN [1970B])

Let:

- R_i be the preference ordering of the ith individual over the set X of all possible social states, each social state being a complete description of society;
- n be the number of individuals in the society;
- R be the social preference relation that is to be determined.

Def 1: A collective choice rule is a functional relationship that specifies one and only one social preference relation R for any set of n individual preference orderings (one ordering for each individual).

Def 2: A social welfare function is a collective choice rule, the range of which is restricted to orderings.

Def 3: A social decision function is a collective rule, the range of which is restricted to social preference relations that generate a choice function.

Conditions

Unrestricted Domain (U). Every logically possible set of individual orderings is included in the domain of the collective choice rule.

Weak Pareto principle (P). If every individual prefers any alternative x to another alternative y, then society must prefer x to y.

Liberalism (L). For each individual i, there is at least one pair of alternatives, say (x,y), such that if this individual prefers x to y, then society should prefer x to y, and if this individual prefers y to x, then society should prefer y to x.

Minimal liberalism (ML). There are at least two individuals such that for each of them there is at least one pair of alternatives over which he is decisive, that is, there is a pair of x,y, such that if he prefers x (respectively y) to y (respectively x), the society should prefer x (respectively y) to y (respectively x).

Theorems (Weak and Strong forms of the 'Impossibility of a Paretian Liberal')
- There is no social decision function that can simultaneously satisfy conditions U,P, and L.

- There is no social decision function that can simultaneously satisfy conditions U,P, and ML.

individual prefers x to y—and if the alternative x, y is reasonably characterized as falling within his or her personal domain—then this individual preference should determine the social preference relation in this respect and be reflected in social choice and judgement. Social states that fail to respect individual liberty-rights are then evaluated as 'worse' than social states in which individual liberty-rights are respected and fulfilled.

Understanding Sen's social choice-theoretic formulation of liberty results in a critique of the Pareto principle and of the narrow characterization of preferences in ethics and social choice

Sen's 'Impossibility of a Paretian Liberal' result captures and formalizes a potential conflict between the principle of Pareto optimality (asserting the priority of unanimous preference rankings) and individual liberty (conceptualized as freedom of choice within a private domain). The result crystallizes his critique of welfarism by demonstrating the existence of a theoretical tension between a commitment to the Pareto principle on the one hand, and a commitment to liberalism on the other. Sen's result establishes that if at least two individuals are guaranteed that their preference will be decisive for social preference in relation to at least one pairwise choice that is reasonably characterized as falling within the personal domain, then contradictory cycles may result (e.g. x socially preferred to y, y to z, and z, to x) for some set of preferences. Therefore, if the ML condition is met, and at least two individuals are guaranteed that their preference will count for social preference in relation to at least one pair-wise choice, then pair-wise choice based on the Pareto principle can conflict with pair-wise choice based on the principle of individual freedom of choice within a personal sphere. If a social choice procedure satisfies the Pareto principle, it may sometimes fail to satisfy even a minimal expression of liberal values (Sen 1982*e* [1976]: 314–15).[7]

Should the preferences that count for social evaluation be restricted?

Arguably, a possible response to the possible conflict between the Pareto principle and individual rights would be to *restrain* the Pareto principle by restricting the preferences that 'count' for the purposes of social evaluation and social choice. Given a prior commitment to the Pareto principle, society cannot 'let more than one individual be free to read what they like, sleep the way they prefer, dress as they care to, etc., *irrespective* of the preferences of others in the community'. For example, a person could be described as respecting the rights of others if and only if he or she wants only a part of his total preference to count such that it can be combined with everyone's preferences over *their* 'protected spheres'. However, whereas the Pareto principle is constructed on 'my preference and yours for *a* over *b*', the idea that individuals may not want their preferences over certain pair-wise choices to 'count' for the purposes of social choice could

---

[7] Sen (1970*b*, 1983*b*, 1986, 1992*b*); Pattanaik and Suzumura (1994, 1996); Suzumura (1999); Anonymous (1998). Explanation, proofs, and extensive citations to the literature exploring, extending, challenging, and attempting to resolve this result can be found in these references.

give rise to a *conditional* version of the (weak) Pareto principle—whereby if everyone in a community prefers *x* to *y* and wants that preference to count, then *x* must be socially preferred to *y*. Unlike the traditional Pareto principle, this *conditional* version may not conflict with individual rights. Sen concludes that whilst it may seem intuitively that preferences that are unanimously held by members of a community ought not to be rejected, rather than simply taking preferences as given, it may be necessary to examine the *motivations* and *reasons* that underlie preferences in order to judge whether a person's preferences should count for social evaluation and choice (Sen 1982e [1976]: 314–15).

Does Sen's formulation falsely imply the violation of individual rights?

Sen's social choice-theoretic model has generated an important body of literature on the formal modelling of individual rights. Critics of Sen's social choice-theoretic formulation have argued that the idea of individual rights cannot be captured in terms of individual 'decisiveness' over social outcomes, and have highlighted the relevance of game-theoretic frameworks for capturing and formalizing the idea of individual rights. For example, Gaertner et al. (1992) contend that the social choice-theoretic approach to the idea of individual rights fails to capture and reflect the 'intuitive' concept of individual rights defended and elaborated in Nozick (1974). According to Nozick, the implication of a person having a right is that, by exercising a choice, that person *fixes* or *determines* some particular *aspect* or *feature* of a state of affairs. He suggests that the need for a social aggregation procedure—and therefore a procedure for relating *individual preferences* to *social preferences*—only arises if choices remain undetermined *after* individuals have exercised their rights (cf. Section 2.1). Gaertner et al. (1992) propose that this characterization gives rise to an 'intuitive conception' of individual rights, whereby an individual can fix *aspects* or *features* of a social state that fall within his or her personal domain, with his or her choices imposing a restriction on this aspect or feature of the final social outcome (with that particular aspect or feature being as he or she chooses).

[T]he individual enjoys the power to determine a particular *aspect* or *feature* . . . of the social alternative, and when he makes his choice with respect to this particular aspect, his choice imposes restriction on the final social outcome . . . [and that] particular aspect must be exactly as he chose it to be. (Gaertner et al. 1992: 167)

If a person has more than one right, then each right *fixes* or *determines* some *feature*. Gaertner et al. (1992) contend that Sen's social choice-theoretic formulation (ML) fails to capture and reflect this 'intuition'. In particular, the 'decisiveness' concept fails to capture and reflect the intuition of an individual determining a particular *aspect* or *feature* of a social alternative and instead links constraints on *social preference* (and hence on social choice and social evaluation) to 'an individual's preference over some pair(s) of social states or complete descriptions of all aspects of the society'. Furthermore, they suggest that tensions can arise between the 'intuitive conception' (articulated in terms of the ability of an individual to fix an *aspect* or *feature* of a state of affairs) and Sen's social choice-theoretic formulation (ML) (articulated in terms of individual preferences over social states). Under the 'intuitive conception', having the power to determine *aspects* or *features* of a state of affairs does *not* entail the power to determine the social outcome. Therefore, a social outcome that fails to reflect an individual's preference relation over 'residual' *aspects* or *features* that fall outside of the scope of his or her 'personal domain' does *not* entail a violation of individual rights. However, Garterner et al. contend that Sen's social choice-theoretic formulation can falsely imply a violation of individual rights under these conditions. For example, consider the following scenario. Each of two individuals has two shirts—white (w) and blue (b)—and each individual has the right to choose the colour of his own shirt. With everything else fixed, there are four possible social outcomes [(w,w), (w,b), (b,w), (b,b)]. Suppose that the preference orderings of each individual is as follows:

1	2
(w,w)	(b,w)
(b,b)	(w,b)
(b,w)	(w,w)
(w,b)	(b,b)

With the two individuals freely choosing their shirts without knowing anything about the other individual's choice and preferences, one possible rule of choice under uncertainty is the maximum rule, with 1 choosing b and 2 choosing w, and (b,w) emerging as the social outcome. According to Gaertner et al., there is no violation of the rights here. Both individuals have exercised freedom of choice in the absence of external constraints, and the social outcome (b,w) has emerged from the process of free individual choice; the rights of both individuals have been respected. However, Gaertner et al. suggest that Sen's social choice-theoretic formulation can falsely imply a *violation* of individual rights in this situation. Since Sen's social choice-theoretic formulation implies that for every individual i, there exist distinct social alternatives x and y such that i is decisive over (x,y), and, if the right of each individual to choose his shirt is formulated in

Sen's social choice-framework, this condition must hold for $i=1,2$. Suppose that this condition holds in a form such that individual 1 is decisive over social states $\{(w,w), (b,w)\}$. It has just been established that (b,w) can emerge as a social outcome from a process of free individual choices. Gaertner et al.'s interpretation is that, in Sen's conceptual framework, the fact that the social outcome (b,w) is inconsistent with the condition that 1 is decisive over $\{(w,w), (b,w)\}$ implies that a *violation* of individual rights has occurred. However, according to Gaertner et al. (1992), if individual 1 was free to choose the colour of his shirt, then 1's rights could not have been violated in any way. Others have articulated support for this position. For example, Van Hees (1995) suggests that the failure of a social outcome to reflect a person's desired choice, rather than the choice that they make in practice, establishes the need to take into account other non-rights considerations (such as autonomy) in social evaluation rather than the violation of individual rights.

The modelling of individual rights as 'admissible strategies' in a game-form

Against this background, Gaertner et al. (1992) propose that the idea of individual rights would be more adequately represented as a *game-form*. In a game-theoretic framework, individuals are conceptualized as having sets of possible acts or strategies, with individual rights and duties conceptualized in terms of the permission of each agent to choose admissible strategies, and the obligation not to choose a non-admissible strategy. Given a specification of individual liberties and rights, sub-sets of *admissible* or *permissible strategies* from the set of *all possible strategies* can be specified for each and every agent. This specification of *admissible* or *permissible strategies* can entail either a prohibition on certain strategies or an obligation to adopt certain strategies (or both). The sub-set of permissible strategies for an individual i is then conceptualized as a 'recognized personal sphere' within the limits of which individuals have complete freedom of choice. Each individual has a preference ranking and, given the specification of liberties and rights, an individual i is conceptualized as being *free to choose* combinations of strategies from his or her sub-set of permissible strategies. When the game is played, individual preferences are revealed. Each person is free to choose to exercise their rights, subject to the constraints of the permissible sub-sets, and the outcome of a game depends on the n-tuples of acts or strategies chosen by each player. In this conceptual framework, individuals have the power to determine an *aspect* or *feature* of any *possible* social state that could emerge from the game, so that individuals are free to make choices within the constraints of their permissible sub-sets *irrespective* of the choices of others. For example, Pattanaik and Suzumura (1996: 196) suggest that if individual 1 is endowed with the right to practice the religion of his own choice, the power of choosing whatever religion 1 likes will be reflected in the set of permissible strategies that relate to person 1. However, the right of individual 1 to practice the religion of his or her choice also implies that other individuals are under an obligation not to harass him or her on account of religious beliefs and practices. In a game-form, this will be captured by the fact that harassing 1 for his religious beliefs and acts will not be a permissible strategy of any other individual. A formal outline of this proposal is given in Box 4.6.

Box 4.6 THE GAME-THEORETIC FORMULATION OF INDIVIDUAL RIGHTS (BASED ON EXPOSITIONS IN GAERTNER ET AL. (1992) AND PATTANAIK AND SUZUMURA (1994))

Conceptualization of a game

A *game-form* is a specification of:

(a) A set N of players;
(b) A set S_i of *permissible* (or *admissible*) actions (or strategies) for each player $i \in N$;
(c) A set $A \in X$ of feasible outcomes;
(d) An outcome function g that maps each strategy n-tuple $s = \{s_i\} \in S = X_{i \in N} S_i$ into a social outcome $g(s) \in A$.

A *game* arises when the preferences of players are specified for some *game-form*. Given a game-form $G = (N,\{S_i\},g)$, if a profile $R \in ?(X)$ of preferences of the players is specified, a game (G, R) ensues.

Conceptualization of individual rights

Individual rights are conceptualized in a game-theoretic framework in terms of:

(a) The specification of *permissible* or *admissible* strategies for each player;
(b) The freedom of each player to choose from admissible strategies and the obligation not to choose a non-admissible strategy.

Sen's defence of the importance of values, preferences, and consequences in the formal modelling of individual rights

Sen (1991; 1992b; 1996a, b, c; 2002a, b, c) has in turn highlighted the limitations of formulations that focus on formal permissions and obligations to act or not to act in terms of the critique of 'consequence-independence' set out in Section 3.2. In Sen's view the idea that individual rights and liberty are *exclusively* about a person having free choices within a personal sphere on the grounds that this idea is inconsistent with society *valuing* liberty and individual rights, and resisting their *violation*. He invokes the example discussed earlier of a woman in a deeply sexist society governed by rules about how women should dress, who lacks the courage to appear in public without her head being covered, even though she would prefer to go out without it. In Sen's view, in cases of this type, where choice-inhibition plays a central role in decision-making, there is a case for relating social outcomes to what a person really wants or desires, rather than concentrating only on what was or not chosen. The failure to take into account influences that may induce a person not to choose what he or she would really like into social evaluation can result in political neglect, and *formal permission to act* can provide an inadequate basis for thinking about liberty and individual rights. Sen concludes that if society cares about individual liberty and rights, then society may also attribute value to the *exercise* and the *fulfilment* of individual rights. Whether or not a person exercises his or individual rights should be taken into account in social evaluation and may have consequential relevance for the specification (and respecification) of sets of basic rights.

Sen (1992*b*) has challenged the proposition that the social choice-theoretic framework can falsely suggest a violation of individual rights in this context. In relation to the 'shirt counter-example' invoked by Gaertner et al. (1992), he contends that the social choice-theoretic approach does *not* suggest that person 1 does not have the *liberty* to exclude the choice of (*b,w*) in favour of (*w,w*)—but only that that person 1 *chose* not to *use* that *right*. By choosing *w*, person 1 could have guaranteed the exclusion of (*b,w*) in favour of (*w,w*), but he chose differently in trying to ensure the avoidance of a worse outcome (*w,b*). For this reason, Sen maintains that it is critical to maintain clear analytical distinctions between *having a right* and *the value of an opportunity*; and *having a right* and *exercising a right* (Sen 1992*b*: 141, 148). Sen further suggests that the 'shirt counter-example' does have the advantage of bringing out the distinction between a *choice-based interpretation* and *desire-based interpretation* of the *individual preference relation* (xP_iy)—and, by extension, of the ML condition. According to the choice-based interpretation of the individual preference relation (xP_iy), a person prefers a social state *x* to a social state *y* if the individual will not *choose y* when *x* can be chosen. In contrast, according to the desire-based interpretation, a person prefers social state *x* to a social state *y* if the individual *desires* social state *x* rather than social state *y*. Sen contends that this distinction results in a *desire-based* and a *choice-based* interpretation of the 'minimal liberty' condition; and that it is possible for a person's rights to be respected according to the choice-based interpretation, whilst being violated according to the desire-based interpretation. Further, Sen's analysis casts doubt on the extent to which game-theoretic models in the literature on welfare economics and social choice can be plausibly viewed in terms of the model of pure outcome-independence to which Nozick (1974) aspires (as set out in Section 2.1) or to the characterization of game-forms as Hayekian 'unintended outcomes' (as suggested in Sugden (1986*a*)). The advantages of taking into account preferences and results, as well as formal permissions and procedures, is not avoided by adopting a game-theoretic approach and formulations apparently based on the Hayekian–Nozickian model may implicitly take into account preferences and consequences (Sen 1995: 13–15; 1996: 31). Public regulations that do *not* make explicit reference to other people's actions are, for example, often based on consequential analysis, taking into account direct and indirect effects, and the existence of generalized interdependences. A general prohibition on smoking (e.g. banning smoking in public places irrespective of whether others are present or not, or whether others object or not) might be established as the most effective means of avoiding a particular *outcome*—that is, passive smoking (Sen 1992*b*: 36).

Sen's proposals for the extension of the game-theoretic approach

For these reasons, Sen has emphasized the advantages of game-theoretic formulations of individual rights that are explicitly rather than implicitly sensitive to preferences and consequences. Game-theoretic formulations concentrate on permissible strategies for each player, rather than directly taking into account the nature of the social state generated by a combination of strategies adopted in a game. However, social states may be taken into account *indirectly* in the game-theoretic framework, through the *specification of permissible strategies*. When a game is played, a combination of strategies results in an *outcome*—or a *social state*—whether this *outcome* or *social state* is described purely in terms of a particular combination of actions having occurred, or in terms of more complex characteristics and consequences. If the case for consequence-sensitivity is accepted, then there may be a case for *preventing* the emergence of certain *outcomes* or *social states*, and the *power* and *freedom* of people to avoid particular outcomes can be introduced into the game-theoretic framework by 'working backwards'—from *consequences* to *antecedents*—and establishing *explicit links* between the acceptability of actual events and outcomes on the one hand, and restrictions on permissible *strategies* on the other. This methodology provides a basis for *respecifying* the rules of the game in order to exclude the admissibility of game-forms that will fail to generate acceptable results. Yet:

[Working] 'backwards' from the unacceptable states of affairs to the strategy configurations that may *cause* these affairs, and to exclude them from the permissible strategy combinations . . . is, of course, consequential analysis with vengeance—only in the inverse direction (from unacceptable effects to impermissible strategy choices). (Sen 1996a: 31)

In illustrating this argument, Sen has emphasized the importance of 'invasive actions'—situations where there is incongruence between an individual's 'personal sphere' and his or her 'personal agency'. He invokes the example of a game-form that includes the right to smoke and the right not to smoke in certain public places as admissible strategies. Suppose that when preferences are revealed and the game is played, some individuals who exercise their own right not to smoke are forced to inhale other people's smoke. In order to prevent passive smoking, there may be a case for modifying the rule of the game so that smoking in public places is specified as a non-admissible strategy. Indeed, by working from consequences to antecedents—taking account of the (broadly defined) social states 'induced' by the specification of admissible strategies in a game-form—game-theoretic approaches can be conceptualized in terms of the specification of sets of 'derived' rights or rules 'for bringing about the affirmation and realization' of sets of basic rights.

[I]n deciding on what rights to protect and codify, and in determining how the underlying purpose might be most effectively achieved, there is a need to look at the likely consequences of different game-form specifications and to relate them to what people value and desire. (Sen 1995: 14)

The further development of game-theoretic models in the broader literature

The further development of game-theoretic formulations of freedoms and rights in the more recent literature seems more reflective of these concerns. Whilst earlier responses to Sen emphasized that the game-theoretic approach 'assigns no explicit role of individual preferences over social states in capturing rights' (Gaertner et al. 1992) and that individual preferences 'are in no way part of the definition of a game form', the more recent extensions of the game-theoretic approach emphasize the distinction between sets of basic (or higher order) rights (that are modelled in a preference- and consequence-sensitive way), and sets of 'derived rights' (that focus on the specification of admissible behavioural strategies), and recognize that values and preferences can have an important role in the allocation of basic or fundamental rights (e.g. Hammond 1996; Van Hees 1996; Pattanaik and Suzummura 1994, 1996; Suzummura 1999, 2000). For example, Hammond (1996: 83) notes that 'one could think of choosing a configuration of rights as being equivalent to choosing a game form that induces these rights', whilst Pattanaik and Suzumura (2000) embed the game-theoretic formulations of individual rights in a broader social choice model that involves the social choice of a 'rights-structure'. This broader model relates the conferment of individual rights to individual preferences (through a social welfare function) and to outcomes (by building in consequence-sensitive informational loops). Fleurbaey and Van Hees (2000) interpret the distinction between basic rights (defined in terms of guarantees of states of affairs) and derived rights (defined in terms of admissible strategies in a game form) in terms of the distinction between human rights that everyone should have, and the actual positive rights that are codified in particular legal systems. Their contributions to the development of the game-theoretic approach also include the incorporation of the ideas of rights-incompatibility and rights-realizations, and (with Fleurbaey and Gaertner 1996), of broad distinctions between different categories of rights (active/passive rights, negative/positive).[8]

Extended game-theoretic models and the concept of a 'rights-structure'

The 'extended' game-theoretic model developed by Pattanaik and Suzumura (1994, 1996) makes analytical space for the *conferment of a rights structure* by society. The starting point for this model is the elaboration of an extended social choice framework that goes beyond the traditional approach—and incorporates the idea of *process sensitivity*. The traditional informational basis for the purposes of social choice and welfare is the set of individual preference orderings over the set X of conventionally defined social alternatives. In contrast, Pattanaik and Suzumura introduce an expanded informational base comprising individual preference orderings over the Cartesian product of X and M, where X is the set of conventionally defined social alternatives except for the social decision-making mechanism (defined as 'a complex set of rules referring to individual rights and other matters'), and M stands for the set of social decision-making mechanisms through which actual social choices are made. If the extended preference ordering of individual i in this sense is denoted by Q_i, and

---

[8] Peleg's (1998) model is also relevant here. Based on the idea of an *effectivity function* (with individuals being characterized as 'effective' if they can guarantee the outcome of a decision process), this model can accommodate rights that can be readily interpreted in terms of restrictions on behavioural strategies (and that can be captured and formalized in terms of sets of available individual strategies in a game form), and 'higher level' rights that cannot be readily interpreted, captured, or formalized in this way (through the 'alpha function').

Box 4.7 EXTENDED GAME-THEORETIC FORMULATION OF INDIVIDUAL RIGHTS TO TAKE ACCOUNT OF THE IDEA OF A 'RIGHTS STRUCTURE' (EXPOSITION IN PATTANAIK AND SUZUMURA (1996))

Let:

N denote the set of individuals in the society. More specifically, let $N := \{1, \ldots, i, \ldots, n\}$, where $2 = n < 8$;

X be the set of social alternatives (by assumption, a social alternative is a complete description of the society except for the social decision-making mechanism);

A denote the set of all non-empty finite sub-sets of X. Each element A of A represents an issue, that is, a physically feasible sub-set of X for some specified underlying conditions.

For each issue $A \in A$, an A-based game-form G_A is defined by an $(n+2)$-tuple $(N, S_{1A}, \ldots, S_{nA}, g_A)$, where, for every $i \in N, S_{iA}$ denotes the set of permissible strategies of i and g_A is the outcome function that maps each strategy n-tuple $s^N = (s_1, \ldots, s_n) \in S_A^N := X_{i \in N} S_{iA}$ into A. A rights-structure G is a specification of an A-based game-form G_A for each $A \in A$, that is, $G = \{G_A \backslash A \in A\}$. G denotes the set of all conceivable rights-structures. Given an issue $A \in A$ and an A-based game form G_A, once each individual $i \in N$ chooses a permissible strategy $s_i \in S_{iA}$, an outcome $g_A(s^N) \in A$, where $s^N = (s_1, \ldots \ldots, s_n) \in S_A^N$, will be determined by g_A. However, to see which permissible strategies the respective individuals actually choose, individual preferences over the set of outcomes X must be specified. For any given set K, let R (K) be the set of all possible orderings over K. Each element of $R^n(K)$, the n-fold Cartesian product of $R(K)$ represents a profile of individual preference orderings over K. Then a game form G_A and a profile $R^N = (R_1, \ldots, R_n) \in R^n(X)$ of individual preference orderings jointly describe a game (G_A, R^N).

(x, m) and $(x'\, m')$ are two representatives of $X \times M$, then $(x, m)Q_i(x'm')$ means that, according to i's judgement, having x through m is at least as desirable as having x' through m'. Having expanded the informational basis for social choice framework in this way, Pattanaik and Suzumura assume that rules relating to the decision-making structure other than those referring to individual rights are fixed, and develop the idea of an extended social alternative—a combination of a conventional defined social alternative x and a rights structure G, with everything else held constant.

A significant feature of this approach is that the game (G_A, R^N) is embedded in a broader model of social choice, whereby the *rights structure G* is variable and is represented as being determined by 'society' through a social decision-making process. The game (G_A, R^N) is played as the second part of a two-stage process, whereby:

(1) The rights-structure G^* is conferred by society through a social decision-making procedure formulated as an extended social welfare function;

(2) Given the rights-structure G^*, the game $(G_A^*, R_{G^*}^N)$ is played.

The first stage of this process involves the determination of the rights-structure G^* 'by society' through a social decision-making procedure. Pattanaik and Suzumura introduce an 'extended social welfare function' that permits process sensitivity (taking note of the value of an outcome being achieved through different rights-structures) and is *sensitive to outcomes*. *Outcome-sensitivity* is achieved by the incorporation of an 'informational loop' that permits the respecification of the rights-structure G^* in the light of expected outcomes of the exercise of rights for any given rights-structure. If there is uncertainty, this will involve the formulation of an *expectation* or *prediction* about how the individuals will exercise their rights, given the conferment of a rights structure.[9] In the second stage of the process, the rights-structure G^* is taken as given, and the game $(G_A^*, R_{G^*}^N)$ is played. The final social outcome (x^*) that emerges from this process is contingent on how individuals choose to exercise these rights in practice, given their preferences. Pattanaik and Suzumura fully acknowledge that when it comes to the conferment of rights, and the social realization of an outcome in accordance with the conferred rights, this model assigns an important role to individual preferences. In the first part of the two-stage process, individual preferences are critical (*a*) in the social evaluation of generalized extended alternatives; (*b*) in predicting possible 'narrowly defined social outcomes' for each rights-structure; and (*c*) in identifying the 'feasible generalized extended alternatives'. In the second stage, given an issue A, once the rights-structure G^* is established by the society, $R_{G^*}^N$ determines the game $(G_A^*, R_{G^*}^N)$ to be played, individual prefer-

---

[9] In the Pattanaik–Suzumura model, a pair (x,G) of $x \in X$ and $G \in G$ represents an *extended social alternative*—a combination of a conventional defined social alternative x and the rights structure G, with everything else held constant. X_+ denotes $X \times G$, that is, $X_+ = \{(x, G) \ x \in X$ and $G \in G\}$. Each individual *i*'s evaluation of the elements of X_+ is given by a preference ordering $Q_i \in R(X_+)$, where ($i \in N$). An *extended social welfare function*, F, specifies exactly one ordering $Q \in R(X_+)$ for every $Q^N = \{Q_1, \ldots, Q_n\} \in R(X_+)$. The role of the *extended social welfare function* is to determine an *extended social welfare ordering* for each profile of individual preference orderings over *extended social alternatives*. An *extended social welfare ordering* $Q = F(Q^N) \in R(X_+)$ embodies the social evaluation of extended alternatives and corresponds to the profile $Q^N \in R^n(X_+)$. 'Society' predicts what will happen if the rights-structure G is granted. For a given issue $A \in A$, a rights-structure is $G \in G$, and given the rights-structure G, the profile of individual preference orderings over X is given by $R_G^N \in R^n(X)$. Pattanaik and Suzumura then introduce a five-stage procedure for predicting expected possible outcomes of the game, given a conferred rights-structure; and for determining an actually realized social outcome from the possible range of feasible outcomes, given actual individual preference profiles, and the exercise of individual rights in practice.

ences are critical in the *realization of a social outcome* (x^*) for a given rights structure G^*. Nevertheless, Pattanaik and Suzumura deny any 'intrinsic conceptual link' with individual preferences of the Sen-type and emphasize the distinction between (*a*) the formal contents of conferred rights; (*b*) the reasons for conferring rights; (*c*) the determination of social outcomes reflecting the conferred rights. Emphasizing the importance of the Nozickian position, they suggest that whereas there is a role for preferences in the establishment of a rights-structure in the extended game-form model, the formal content of individual rights is 'fully articulated' by the specification of the permissible sets of strategies for each individual.

By the very nature of rights, it is intuitively compelling to assume that the society must first determine the rights-structure . . . and then let a conventionally defined social alternative emerge as a result of the individual's free exercise of their respective rights granted by the established rights-structure. . . . The objective of social choice is not to choose the narrowly defined social outcome *per se*, but to choose the set of rules of the game that people play; the realisation of a social outcome through the chosen set of rules is left to the play of the game by the individual players. (Pattanaik and Suzumura 1996: 198–204)

Conclusion

This chapter has provided an analytical overview of Sen's work in economics from the perspective of fundamental freedoms and human rights. It has explored Sen's far-reaching critique of standard frameworks in theoretical and empirical economics that fail to take account of fundamental freedoms and human rights, and has assessed the ways in which he has pioneered the development of new paradigms and approaches that focus on human rights-centred concerns. It has been argued that Sen's contributions have resulted in an important body of statistical evidence on human rights issues and have expanded and deepened human rights discourse by opening up new lines of enquiry and by promoting cross-fertilization and integration across traditional disciplinary divides. The development of a 'scholarly bridge' between human rights and economics has been shown to be an innovative and important contribution that has methodological as well as substantive importance, and that provides a prototype and stimuli for future research.

5

Poverty and Human Rights: The International Legal Framework

This chapter analyses the emergence of a body of legally binding international standards in the field of poverty and human rights. Section 5.1 examines the basis of international legal obligation in the field of poverty and human rights. Section 5.2 discusses the nature and scope of international legal obligation in this field (with particular emphasis on the question of whether resource and feasibility constraints pose a 'theoretical obstacle' to the establishment of legally binding international obligations regulating the protection and promotion of economic and social rights). Section 5.3 examines the development of evaluative principles that facilitate judicial scrutiny of the 'reasonableness' of actions undertaken by states under conditions of resource and feasibility constraints. Section 5.4 analyses the emergence of a body of case law in the field of poverty and human rights. Section 5.5 considers the issue of collective obligation.

This chapter aims to establish the ways in which Sen's development of the 'capability perspective' in ethics and economics might be reinforced and supported through the embryonic and underdeveloped—but nevertheless widening and deepening—body of international standards in the field of global poverty and human rights. The 'capability approach' does not require or entail linkages with the actual system of international human rights law. Indeed, Sen's work in ethics has emphasized the important role of the idea of human rights outside the legal domain, and suggests that the justification and elucidation of this idea is not contingent on the degree of precision necessary for codification and judicial enforcement (Sen 2000a; Chapter 3, this volume). At the same time, his work in economics highlights the important role of different complementary institutions (economic, political, legal, etc.) in avoiding 'capability deprivation' and achieving 'capability expansion' (see Chapter 4, this volume). This chapter moves the discussion forward by considering the 'capability approach' and the international human rights framework as mutually reinforcing systems. It establishes the ways in which international treaties, authoritative international standard-setting, and jurisprudence reinforce and support the idea of the capability to achieve a standard of living adequate for survival and development—including adequate nutrition, safe water and sanitation, shelter and housing, access to basic health and social services, and education—as a basic human right that governments have individual and collective obligations to respect, protect, and promote. Eight key correspondences between the 'capability approach' and evolving standards in international human rights law and jurisprudence are identified and discussed. These are:

(1) The ways in which the international human rights system, supported by international law, provides authoritative recognition of a broad class of fundamental freedoms and human rights that takes account of global poverty.

(2) The ways in which the international human rights system, supported by international law, provides authoritative grounds for rejecting 'absolutism' and the view that 'resource constraints' represent a 'theoretical obstacle' to the establishment of international legal obligation in the field of global poverty and human rights.

(3) The ways in which the international human rights system, supported by international law, provides authoritative recognition of positive obligations of protection and promotion (as well as negative obligations of omission and restraint).

(4) The ways in which the international human rights system, supported by international law, provides authoritative recognition of general goals (as well as specific actions) as the object of human rights.

(5) The ways in which the international human rights system, supported by international law, provides an authoritative evaluative framework for assessing the 'reasonableness' of state actions in the field of global poverty and human rights.

(6) The ways in which the international human rights system, supported by international law, provides authoritative recognition of the importance of rights to policies and programmes (or 'meta-rights') when resource constraints are binding.

(7) The ways in which the international human rights system, supported by international law, recognizes collective international obligations of co-operation, assistance, and aid.

(8) The ways in which the international human rights system, supported by international law, provides authoritative recognition of the importance of outcomes and results to the evaluation of human rights.

5.1 The Basis of International Legal Obligation in the Field of Global Poverty and Human Rights

This section establishes the basis of international legal obligation in the field of global poverty and human rights, and sets out the ways in which key international treaties in the field of human rights reinforce and support the notion that the capability to achieve a standard of living adequate for survival and development—including adequate nutrition, safe water and sanitation, shelter and housing, access to basic health and social services, and education—as a basic human right that governments have individual and collective obligations to respect, protect, and promote. An overview of the embryonic—but nevertheless deepening and widening—framework of international standards in the field of global poverty and human rights is set out in Box 5.1. In order to be legally binding under international human rights law, an international standard must fall within the three sources of international law defined in the Article 38(1) of the Statute of the International Court of Justice (ICJ) (and therefore fall within the scope of an international treaty, international custom, or the 'general principles of international law').[1]

---

[1] Article 38(1) of the Statute of the International Court of Justice (ICJ) establishes three primary sources of international law. These are:

- **International conventions.** An *international convention* (or a *treaty*) is a *written* agreement expressing the consent of two or more states to be legally bound by certain rules. The consent of a state to become party to a treaty must be made explicit by a formal declaration such as ratification or accession, and states that have not made such a declaration are not directly legally bound by the rules expressed in a treaty. At the time of ratification or accession, states may enter reservations that exclude or alter the legal effect of certain treaty provisions.
- **International custom.** An *international custom* is an *unwritten* expression of a general practice that is accepted as law. The legal force of an international custom is *not* contingent on a formal declaration of consent by states and international custom is legally binding on *all* states with no possibility of derogation.
- **The general principles of law as recognized by civilized nations.** The third source of international law recognized in Article 38(1) of the ICJ Statute—*the general principles of law as recognized by civilized nations*—has also given rise to considerable legal debate. The classic approach of Western jurists has been to view general principles as an independent source of international law from which no derogation is possible. General principles, it has been maintained, are fundamental principles derived from the underlying municipal legal systems of 'civilized' nations. Alston and Simma (1996 [1992]: 23–6) argue that, under modern conditions,

---

Box 5.1 GLOBAL POVERTY AND HUMAN RIGHTS: THE EMERGING INTER-
NATIONAL FRAMEWORK

UN Charter Articles 55 and 56
Universal Declaration
Article 1(1), 25, 26 Universal Declaration on Human Rights
International treaty framework
Preamble, Article 6 International Covenant on Civil and Political Rights
The International Covenant on Economic, Social, and Cultural Rights (especially the
Preamble and Articles 11, 12, 13, 14)
Article 5 (e) of the International Convention on the Elimination of All Forms of Racial
Discrimination
Articles 11, 12, 13, 14 (1–2) of the Convention on the Elimination of All Forms of
Discrimination against Women
Articles 6, 24, 26, 27, 28, 29 of the Convention on the Rights of the Child
Authoritative international standard-setting
General Assembly Resolutions
Resolutions of the Commission on Human Rights
General Comments of the UN Treaty Monitoring Committees (especially: UN Com-
mittee Economic, Social, and Cultural Rights General Comments 2, 3, 4, 7, 11, 13,
14, 15; Human Rights Committee General Comment 6); Committee on the Rights
of the Child (especially General Comment 5).
Fact-finding activities of UN human rights machinery
Other authoritative interpretative guides: e.g. Limburg Principles, Maastricht Guide-
lines
Responsibilities of non-state actors: e.g. constituent instruments of UN specialized
agencies (e.g. WHO and FAO constitutions), World Bank Inspection Panel
UN Declaration on the Right to Development
Regional Agreements: e.g. African Charter on Human and Peoples Rights',
American Convention on Human Rights, European Convention on Human Rights,
European Union Charter of Fundamental Rights.
National constitutions and jurisprudence
Establishment of positive obligation in the field of civil and political rights
Invoking civil and political rights as a basis for the protection of economic and social
rights
Increasing constitutional protection of economic and social rights (e.g. South Africa,
India) and emerging body of case law in this field

---

there is no necessity to restrict the notion of general principles to those principles developed in
foro domestico. Given the existence of international organizations, these authors argue that
general principles can now be made objective through some sort of general acceptance or
recognition by states at the international level.

The ICJ statute is available electronically at http://www.icj-cij.org/icjwww/ibasicdocume. For further
analysis of the sources of international law, the nature and scope of international legal obligation,
and the principles of international state responsibility, see Harris (1998) and Higgins (1994).

Human rights-standards in the UN Charter

The legal competence of the UN in the field of human rights is prescribed in the UN Charter. The Charter is an international treaty. As such, it is legally binding on all states parties, and states parties are required to comply with its provisions in good faith.[2] The principles and purposes of the Charter include the reaffirmation of 'faith in fundamental human rights' (preamble), and the promotion and encouragement of 'respect for human rights and for fundamental freedoms for all without distinction as to race, sex, language, or religion' (Article 1, para. 3). State parties to the Charter undertake to be bound by two key international obligations in the field of human rights. These are the obligation to act in such a way as to promote 'universal respect for, and observance of, human rights and fundamental freedoms for all' on the basis of non-discrimination (Article 55); and the obligation 'to take joint and separate action' in cooperation with the UN to achieve this purpose (Article 56). Institutional responsibility for pursuing the human rights objectives of the UN is vested in a number of UN organs including the General Assembly (Article 13), the Economic and Social Council (Article 62), and the Trusteeship system (Article 76). Other Charter provisions may limit the potential power of the UN in the field of human rights. For example, the Charter recognizes the principle of 'sovereign equality' and neither authorizes the UN to 'intervene in matters which are essentially within the domestic jurisdiction of any State' nor requires state parties to 'submit such matters to settlement under the present Charter' (Article 2).

The Universal Declaration

The human rights content of the UN Charter was given clarity and scope in the Universal Declaration on Human Rights. This instrument is a resolution of the UNGA and was adopted in 1948.[3] The Preamble to the Universal Declaration emphasizes the importance of a common understanding of human rights and fundamental freedoms for the international legal obligations undertaken by states party to the UN Charter. Member

---

[2] Article 38(1) of the Statute of the ICJ establishes that international treaties express the written consent of two or more states to be legally bound by certain rules, and constitute one of the three primary sources of international law. Article 26 of the Vienna Convention on the Law of Treaties establishes that every treaty in force is binding upon the parties to it, and that treaty obligations must be performed in good faith. See comment in note 1 and Brownlie (1995: 388).

[3] Adopted and proclaimed by UNGA Resolution 217 A (III), December 10, 1948. UN Doc. A/811. The voting was forty-eight for, none against, with eight abstentions.

states have pledged to achieve, in cooperation with the UN, the promotion of universal respect for and observance of human rights and fundamental freedoms, and a common understanding of these rights and freedoms is of greatest importance for the full realization of this pledge. Article 1 and 2 elaborate the basic Charter principles of equality and non-discrimination. Article 1 states that '[a]ll human beings are born free and equal in dignity and rights'. Article 2 states that everyone is entitled to the rights and freedoms set forth in the Universal Declaration. No distinction should be made on the grounds of race, colour, sex, language, religion, political opinion, national or social origin, property, birth, or the political, jurisdictional, or international status of the country or territory to which a person belongs. Articles 3–21 of the Universal Declaration spell out the political and civil rights to which all individuals everywhere are entitled:

- Articles 3–5 prescribe rights to life, liberty, and security and prohibit slavery, servitude, the slave trade, torture and cruel, inhuman, or degrading treatment or punishment. Articles 6–11 prescribe rights to recognition before the law, to equality before the law, to equal protection of the law, to effective remedy, to a fair trial, and to the presumption of innocence. These articles also prohibit arbitrary arrest, detention, exile, and the introduction of retrospective offences. Article 12 prohibits arbitrary interference with privacy, family, home and correspondence, and arbitrary attacks on honour or reputation. Articles 13–16 prescribe rights to freedom of movement, to seek and enjoy asylum, to nationality, and to marry and found a family. Article 17 prescribes the right to property and prohibits arbitrary interference with property. Articles 18–20 prescribe rights to freedom of thought, conscience, religion, opinion, expression, peaceful assembly, and association, and Article 21 prescribes rights to political participation, to periodic and genuine elections, to universal and equal suffrage, and to free voting procedures.

- Articles 22–26 of the Universal Declaration spell out certain economic, social, and cultural rights. Article 22 prescribes the right to social security and the entitlement of everyone to the realization, in accordance with the organization and resources of each state, of the economic, social, and cultural rights indispensable for dignity and the free development of personality. Articles 23 and 24 prescribe the rights to work, to free choice of employment, to just and favourable conditions of work, to protection against unemployment, to equal pay for equal work, to just and favourable remuneration, to form and join trade unions, and to rest and leisure. Article 25 prescribes the right to a standard of living adequate for health and well-being, including food, clothing, housing, medical care, and necessary social services, and provides for special protection for motherhood and childhood. Article 26 prescribes the right to education and to free and compulsory education in the elementary stage and article 27 prescribes the right to participate in the cultural life of the community. Article 28 states that 'everyone is entitled to a social and international order in which the rights and freedoms set forth in this Declaration can be fully realised'.

The standard view is based on an interpretation of articles 10–14 of the UN Charter, which establish that UNGA resolutions in matters other than budgetary ones are mere *recommendations*—that is, declarations or statements of intentions or goals—and are *not* directly binding on states. According to this view, the Universal Declaration is an important declaration of intent by states, and possesses significant moral and political value, but does *not* establish legally binding international legal obligations.[4] However, the 'restrictivist' characterization of the Universal Declaration is increasingly being challenged. An advisory opinion of the ICJ concluded that although such resolutions are manifestly not binding, they are 'not without legal effect'[5] and human rights advocacy strategies aimed at establishing the legal significance of the Universal Declaration focus on the following arguments:

- **UNGA resolutions in the form of *Declarations* are adopted only in very rare cases relating to matters of major and lasting importance, where maximum compliance is expected.**[6] The Universal Declaration is a rare example of a UNGA resolution passed without opposition and formally recognized by a very large number of states, and this trend towards the universal or quasi-universal formal acceptance and recognition of the Universal Declaration has continued to date. The normative validity of many of the rights and duties prescribed in the Universal Declaration has been referred to by many multilateral and international treaties and bodies and is affirmed in the constitutions, laws, and judicial processes of a large number of

---

[4] See comment in note 2.

[5] Interpretation in Higgins (1994: 24–5) of the reasoning in Legal Consequences for States of the Continued Presence of South Africa in Namibia (South West Africa), ICJ Reports (1971) at 50.

[6] Official Records of the Economic and Social Council, Thirty-fourth Session, Supplement No.8, UN Doc. E/3616/Rev.1, para. 105.

states. Violations of human rights standards are frequently condemned as breaches of international law by multilateral and international bodies, governments, and state officials.

- **Some or all of the provisions of the Universal Declaration strengthen, or are constitutive of, customary international law and are therefore legally binding sources of international law under the ICJ statute.** This argument is reflected in the *Third Restatement* of *The Foreign Relations Law of the United States*, which stipulates in its characterization of customary international law that a state violates international law if, as a matter of state policy, it practices, encourages or condones (*a*) genocide; (*b*) slavery or slave trade; (*c*) the murder or causing the disappearance of individuals; (*d*) torture or other cruel, inhuman, or degrading treatment or punishment; (*e*) prolonged arbitrary detention; (*f*) systematic racial discrimination; or (*g*) a consistent pattern of gross violations of internationally recognized human rights.[7] This argument was also reflected in the judgement in the Filartiga case in the USA, where the Court of Appeal interpreted General Assembly Resolution 2635 (XXV) (October 24, 1970) on the Principles of International Law as declaring that the Charter precepts embodied in the Universal Declaration 'constitute basic principles of international law'. Having examined the sources from which customary international law is derived, the Court concluded that 'official torture is now prohibited by the law of nations. The prohibition is clear and unambiguous, and admits of no distinction between treatment of aliens and citizens'.[8]

---

[7] American Law Institute (1987).

[8] Filartiga Versus Pena-Irala, 630 F. 2d 876 (1980); (1980) 19 I.L.M. 966. US Circuit Court of Appeals, 2nd Circuit, cited in Alston and Simma (1996 [1992]). However, the question of whether or not some or all of the provisions of the Universal Declaration satisfy the threshold for international custom is subject to a far-reaching and complex jurisprudential debate. Evaluated on the basis of traditional criteria, international custom is established by 'the emergence of a general, uniform, consistent, and settled state practice' followed by 'the emergence of a sense of legal obligation embodied in *opinio juris*, the belief that a norm is accepted as law' (Alston and Simma (1996 [1992]: 9). This classic test implies that state practice, repetition, and *opinio juris* are all necessary requirements for the establishment of international custom and that international custom *cannot* be established on the basis of a UNGA resolution alone. Higgins supports this classic test while arguing that under modern conditions, the collective acts of states—'repeated by and acquiesced in by sufficient numbers of states with sufficient frequency'—can eventually attain legal status. Furthermore, she contends that UNGA resolutions—as *manifestations of state practice*—can provide evidence of developing trends in customary international law, depending on the importance of subject matter concerned, the extent of the majority in favour of the resolution, evidence of repeated practice, and evidence of *opinio juris* (Higgins 1994: 18–28). The following are some representative views in the literature:

- Some or all of the provisions of the Universal Declaration fall within the scope of 'general international law' and are therefore legally binding sources of international law under the ICJ Statute. Alston and Simma invoke general international law as a basis for international legal obligation in the field of human rights. They contend that *jus cogens* norms that are recognized and accepted by states

- Schachter (1991: 138) contends that evidence that some important human rights included in the Declaration have become customary law is rarely to be found in 'traditional patterns of State practice involving claims and counterclaims between two States' but in the international forums where human rights issues are 'discussed, debated, and sometimes resolved by general consensus'.

- Higgins upholds the view that evidence of the importance of the subject matter of the Universal Declaration and of the widespread recognition and acceptance of certain human rights standards *in principle* must be balanced against evidence of the violation of these standards by many states *in practice*. In balancing up this evidence, she notes that although international rules relating to the prohibition of genocide and torture are widely recognized and accepted by states *in principle*, whereas majority state practice complies with the international rules prohibiting genocide, the vast majority of states probably violate the international rules prohibiting torture. Yet Higgins rejects the view that state practice is a necessary condition for the continued survival of an international custom (so that, in a situation where an existing international custom is violated in practice by states on a widespread basis, the international custom is de-established). In her view, 'an existing norm does not die without the great majority of states engaging in both a contrary practice and withdrawing their *opinio juris*'. She concludes that the international rules prohibiting both genocide and torture can be classified as rules of customary international law (Higgins 1994: 20–2).

- In the Nicaragua Case, the ICJ de-emphasized the role of state practice in the establishment and survival of international custom. The Court considered the implications of the non-compliance of states with certain *jus cogens* or peremptory rules relating to the non-use of force. It deemed it sufficient that in deducing the existence of customary rules, the conduct of states should, in general, be consistent with such rules; and that where there is widespread evidence of the acceptance and recognition of an international rule *in principle*, state non-compliance in practice does not de-establish the rule. More specifically: '[I]nstances of State conduct inconsistent with a given rule should generally be treated as breaches of that rule, not as indications of the recognition of a new rule. If a State acts in a way prima facie incompatible with a recognized rule, but defends its conduct by appealing to exceptions or justifications contained within the rule itself, then whether or not the State's conduct is in fact justifiable on that basis, the significance of that attitude is to confirm rather than to weaken the rule.' See: Military and Paramilitary Activities in and against Nicaragua (Nicaragua versus United States of America), Merits, Judgment, ICJ Reports (1986) at 186.

- Alston and Simma are highly sceptical of the idea that international custom can provide sufficient grounds for holding all states accountable for violations of human rights, and have argued that the basis for grounding substantive human rights-obligations in international custom is very weak. They are particularly critical of the proposition that the declaration of human rights standards *in principle* can strengthen or establish international custom, even when these standards are widely violated in practice. Insisting that international custom is established *not* by the articulation of rules in principle, but by the generalization of state conduct in practice, they contend that although the characterization of non-compliance as a breach of a peremptory international rule is valid where state practice and *opinio juris* have had a chance to establish themselves solidly in an initial, formative state, it is not valid where an inconsistency between words and factual behaviour is evident from the beginning. For this reason, they are critical of the judgement in the Nicaragua Case, concurring with the view (attributed to the International Law Association) that 'norms that fail to pass a generality of practice test may not be constitutive of international custom' (Alston and Simma 1996 [1992]: 11–21).

in principle, but are widely violated *in practice*, should be characterized not as international custom but as *recognized general principle of international law*, and that some human rights principles may fall within the reach of Article 38(3) of the ICJ Statute. Support for this position can also be found in the judgement in the *Barcelona Traction Case*, where the ICJ ruled that certain international obligations in the field of human rights standards relating to genocide and the basic rights of the person, including protection from slavery and racial discrimination, are legally binding *erga omnes* and have 'entered into the body of general international law'.[9]

- **The Universal Declaration constitutes an *authoritative interpretation* of the international obligations of states under articles 55 and 56 of the UN Charter.** Another argument emphasizes that the characterization of the Universal Declaration constitutes an *authoritative interpretation* of the international obligations of states under articles 55 and 56 of the UN Charter and therefore is directly relevant to the interpretation of the legally binding international obligations of state parties to this international treaty. For example, articles 55 and 56 of the UN Charter establish an international legal obligation to examine UNGA recommendations in the field of human rights *carefully* and in *good faith*, and many legal experts argue that, at the very least, the practices of systematic obstruction and/or of total rejection of UNGA recommendations in the field of human rights may be contrary to this obligation. Alston and Simma build on this idea, suggesting that state parties to the UN Charter, having undertaken in good faith international legal obligations to respect 'human rights', may, for the purposes of interpreting their treaty obligations, be subsequently bound to accept the definition of 'human rights' that has evolved from the recommendations and practices of relevant UN organs (Alston and Simma 1996 [1992]: 21–7).[10]

The international treaty framework

The negotiation process aimed at codifying the human rights recognized in the Universal Declaration into legally binding international treaty form

---

[9] ICJ Rep 1970: 33.

[10] This view also seems to be supported by Judge Tanka in his dissenting option in the South West Africa Case (Second Phase, 1966, ICJ Reports 6 294/9), which highlights Article 38(1)c of the ICJ Statute as a basis for human rights concepts and points out that this provision contains natural law elements.

began in 1948. However, with the onset of the cold war, a long and protracted debate over the form and substance of international treaties in the field of human rights ensued.[11] The International Bill of Human Rights was eventually all adopted by the General Assembly at its twenty-first session in 1966 and immediately opened for signature, ratification, and accession.[12] The International Bill comprises the ICCPR, which codifies civil and political rights; Optional Protocols to the ICCPR relating to machinery for individual complaints and the abolition of the death penalty; and the ICES, CR. Other key international treaties in the field of human rights include ICRC, the CEA Forms of RD, and the CEDAW. These international treaties had been signed and ratified by the vast majority of states, with the number of state parties approaching quasi-universal and universal levels by 2004 (Box 5.1).[13]

International treaty obligations are binding under international law. The compliance of states with their legal obligations under international treaties in the field of human rights is monitored by the international machinery set out in Box 5.2. The UN system for the promotion and protection of human rights consists of two main types of institutional arrangements created under the UN Charter (including the Commission on Human Rights) and bodies created under the international human rights treaties, with the implementation of the core international human rights treaties being monitored by seven UN Committees. Four of these (HRC, CERD, CAT, and CEDAW) can receive petitions from individuals who claim that their rights under the treaties have been violated by countries.[14] The need to strengthen accountability under the ICESCR has received increased international attention in recent years and a Draft Optional Protocol that would give the Committee on Economic, Social, and Cultural Rights competence to consider individual complaints is currently under consideration.[15]

---

[11] This debate was largely ideological in character and turned on the issue of whether there should be one convention covering all human rights, or two conventions, one for political and civil rights, and one for economic, social, and cultural rights. For a general discussion, see UN (1995: 38–47); Alston and Steiner (1996: 256–75); Craven (1995: 16–22).

[12] In Resolution 2200 (XXI) of 16 December 1966.

[13] OHCHR Status of ratifications of the principle international human rights treaties as at 1 October 2004, together with details of the reservations of state parties, are available at: http://www.unhchr.ch/.

[14] See http://www.ohchr.org/english/bodies/treaty/index.htm for further details of the functioning and responsibilities of the monitoring Committees.

[15] E.g. see UN Doc E/CN.12/2004/44.

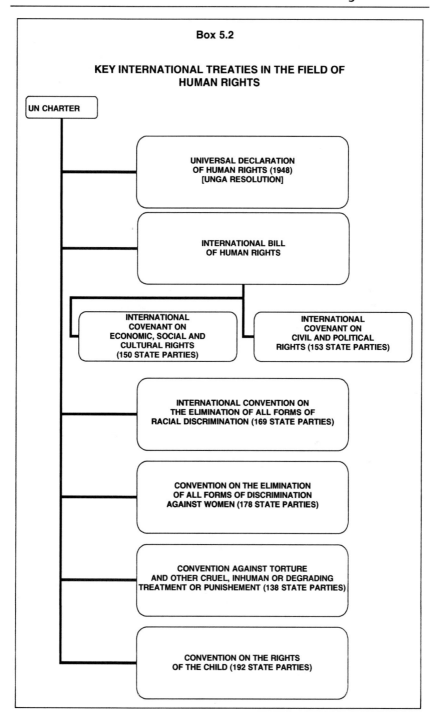

Box 5.2

KEY INTERNATIONAL TREATIES IN THE FIELD OF HUMAN RIGHTS

UN CHARTER

UNIVERSAL DECLARATION
OF HUMAN RIGHTS (1948)
[UNGA RESOLUTION]

INTERNATIONAL BILL
OF HUMAN RIGHTS

INTERNATIONAL
COVENANT ON
ECONOMIC, SOCIAL AND
CULTURAL RIGHTS
(150 STATE PARTIES)

INTERNATIONAL
COVENANT ON
CIVIL AND POLITICAL
RIGHTS (153 STATE PARTIES)

INTERNATIONAL CONVENTION ON
THE ELIMINATION OF ALL FORMS OF
RACIAL DISCRIMINATION (169 STATE PARTIES)

CONVENTION ON THE ELIMINATION
OF ALL FORMS OF DISCRIMINATION
AGAINST WOMEN (178 STATE PARTIES)

CONVENTION AGAINST TORTURE
AND OTHER CRUEL, INHUMAN OR DEGRADING
TREATMENT OR PUNISHEMENT (138 STATE PARTIES)

CONVENTION ON THE RIGHTS
OF THE CHILD (192 STATE PARTIES)

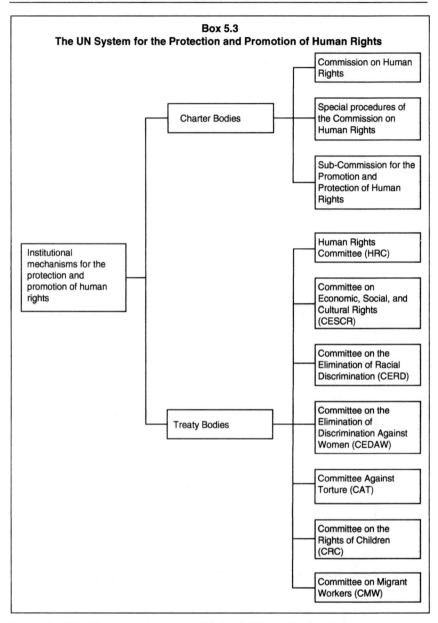

Box 5.3
The UN System for the Protection and Promotion of Human Rights

Institutional mechanisms for the protection and promotion of human rights

Charter Bodies
- Commission on Human Rights
- Special procedures of the Commission on Human Rights
- Sub-Commission for the Promotion and Protection of Human Rights

Treaty Bodies
- Human Rights Committee (HRC)
- Committee on Economic, Social, and Cultural Rights (CESCR)
- Committee on the Elimination of Racial Discrimination (CERD)
- Committee on the Elimination of Discrimination Against Women (CEDAW)
- Committee Against Torture (CAT)
- Committee on the Rights of Children (CRC)
- Committee on Migrant Workers (CMW)

Source: See http://www.ohchr.org/english/bodies/treaty/index.htm.

International treaty obligations dealing with global poverty and human rights

The major international human rights treaties create legally binding international obligations on state parties progressively to implement the human rights to life, to adequate food and nutrition, to safe water and sanitation, to adequate health care facilities, and to education, both individually and collectively through international assistance and cooperation. The key international treaty obligations relevant to the establishment of global poverty as a human rights issue include:

- Article 6 of the International Convention on ICCPR codifies the human right to life.
- Article 11 of the ICES, CR codifies the human right of everyone to an adequate standard of living including adequate food, clothing, and housing, an adequate standard of living, and the fundamental right of everyone to be free from hunger; Article 12 codifies the human right of everyone to the enjoyment of the highest attainable standard of physical and mental health; Articles 13 and 14 the human rights to education and to free and compulsory basic primary education; and Article 9 the right to social security. The Covenant also establishes legally binding obligations in relation to non-discrimination and equality in the field of economic, social, and cultural rights (Articles 2 and 3) and legally binding international obligations in relation to work and working conditions (Articles 6–8).
- Article 6 of the CRC legally codifies the rights of the child to life. Article 24 codifies the right of the child to the enjoyment of the highest attainable standard of health and to facilities for the treatment of illness and rehabilitation of health; Article 26 the right of the child to benefit from social security; Article 27 the right of every child to a standard of living adequate for physical, mental, spiritual, moral, and social development; Articles 28 and 29 the right to education.
- Articles 11, 12, 13, 14(1–2) of the ICEDAW codify legally binding state obligations relating to non-discrimination and equal access in the areas of employment, health care, credit, family benefits, and to take into account the particular problems faced by rural women.
- Article 5(e) of the ICER codifies state obligations to eliminate discrimination in relation to economic and social rights including work, housing, health, and education.

Articles 55 and 56 of the Charter of the UN, together with Articles 2 (1) and 23 of the ICESCR, and Article 5 of the CRC, establish international legal obligations in relation to international cooperation in the field of economic, social, and cultural rights. These articles underpin the characterization of the international obligation in the field of human rights in multiparty terms—where achievement of internationally recognized human rights cannot always be achieved by single obligation holders acting alone, and may require international cooperation, assistance, and aid.

Can international treaties have implications for non-state parties?

Like the question of the legal status of the Universal Declaration, the question of whether international treaties can have implications for non-state parties raises complex jurisprudential debates focussing on the issue of whether international treaty obligations can strengthen or be constitutive of international customary and general international law. Higgins contends that the repeated practice of a UN organ in interpreting an international treaty may establish a practice that, if the treaty deals with matters of general international law, can ultimately harden into custom (Higgins 1994: 24). Alston and Simma maintain that the repeated practices of UN human rights institutions have contributed to the establishment of a widely accepted *droit de regard*—entitling the UN to respond to gross violations of human rights in various ways without encroaching upon the *domaine reserve* of sovereign states. In this respect, intensive state practice in the field of human rights has been joined by *opinio juris*, and has led to firmly established customary international law (Alston and Simma 1996 [1992]: 19–20). These theoretical debates have important implications for the widening and deepening of international accountability in the field of global poverty and human rights. In addition to specific principles relating to certain basic human rights such as genocide, torture, and non-discrimination, multilateral treaties which have been signed by large numbers of states are most likely to be accepted as treaty rules which have become binding on non-parties (Higgins 1994: 25; Alston and Steiner 1996). For example, the CRC has 192 states parties. As the basis of international legal acceptance of this treaty deepened and widened to quasi-universal levels, UNICEF (2000) maintained that although the CRC was not formally binding in countries that had neither signed nor acceded, its provisions were nevertheless not without legal significance on the grounds that:

- The Convention has an effect on all countries as part of international customary law;
- The Convention represents an international consensus on child rights;
- The Convention was adopted unanimously by the UNGA after a long process, with a large number of countries having been actively involved;
- The importance of the Convention as a guide for work on behalf of children was underlined by the seventy-one Heads of State/Government plus observers at the World Summit for Children;
- The support of the standards contained in the Convention by a large number of countries through ratification, and the actual implementation of the standards by countries that already are states parties, will influence and guide much of the debate on child rights at the international level, with inevitable consequences for all countries;
- The UNICEF Executive Board decided in 1991 (decision 1991/9) that all programmes should reflect the principles of the Convention, meaning that UNICEF must use the Convention as a frame of reference for all programmes, whether a country has ratified or not.

Establishing the responsibilities of non-state actors

The question of the responsibilities of non-state actors including individuals, businesses, and transnational corporations also raised important debates. The standard position is that international law is a horizontal order binding states and that only the acts and omissions of the state and its representatives can constitute breaches of international law. Under this conception, states are nevertheless responsible for regulating the actions of non-state actors and providing a legal and institutional framework that aims to prevent violations of human rights by third parties. Furthermore, the responsibilities of states can be viewed as extending to responsibility for the organizations of which they are members, including their participation in international and regional organizations. In addition, human rights advocacy strategies are currently focusing international attention on the possibility of establishing more direct responsibilities of non-state actors under international human rights law. In relation to international organizations, it has been emphasized that UN agencies are creatures of the UN Charter and are directly bound by articles 55 and 56, by authoritative interpretations of these articles, as well as by the human rights content of their constituent instruments (as reflected, for example, in the WHO and FAO constitutions). In relation to businesses and transnational corporations, human rights-advocacy strategies aim to build on other areas where international law establishes more direct responsibilities for non-state actors (e.g. individuals can commit crimes under international criminal law/international humanitarian law binds armed opposition groups) to establish direct forms of accountability for the violations of human rights by transnational organizations and businesses (e.g. ICHR 2004: 2). The development of new norms in this area is reflected in the recent adoption of the UN Norms on the Responsibilities of Transnational Corporations and other Businesses.[16]

5.2 The Nature and Scope of International Legal Obligation in the Field of Global Poverty and Human Rights

The previous section analysed the basis of international legal obligation in the field of global poverty and human rights. An important aim was to establish the ways in which the international system for the protection and promotion of human rights reinforces and supports the 'capability approach' through the authoritative international recognition of a broad characterization of fundamental freedoms and human rights that takes account of global poverty. A second way in which the international legal system can be viewed as reinforcing and supporting the 'capability approach' is by casting doubt on the view that human rights can be adequately conceptualized as absolute, non-conflicting rights that are logically co-possible and feasible in all circumstances—and that resource constraints consequently constitute a 'theoretical obstacle' to the conceptualization of human rights. Key international treaties in the field of human rights provide for exceptional but justifiable limitations of and qualifications to internationally recognized human rights in pursuance of other goals (e.g. the public interest, public health, and national security), whilst international case law in the field of human rights establishes that the duties flowing from civil and political rights cannot always be regarded as mutually co-possible and irreducibly absolute constraints that avoid all issues of hierarchies, trade-offs, and balancing.[17] The case law discussed in

---

[16] UN Norms on the Responsibilities of Transnational Corporations and other Businesses, E/CN.4/Sub.2/2003/12/Rev.2, available at: http://daccessdds.un.org/doc/UNDOC/GEN/G03/160/08/PDF/G0316008.pdf?OpenElement.

[17] Formal typologies often characterize human rights in terms of their 'absolute', 'limited', and/or 'qualified' nature. For example, in relation to the human rights enshrined in the European Convention

Section 5.4 establishes the 'positive' implications of civil and political rights (including the far-reaching resource implications of contemporary interpretations of civil and political rights) and recent jurisprudence relating to the human right to life raises the possibility of *conflicting* positive obligations of a legal as well as a moral and social nature.[18] In the field of economic and social rights, Section 5.4 establishes that when resource constraints are binding, human rights may be interpreted in terms analogous to Sen's category of 'meta-right'—in terms of human rights to policy measures that facilitate the realization of human rights over time (rather than being of immediate realization). The next two sections discuss the legal foundations of this approach. This section examines how whereas in the past, allowances for resource and feasibility constraints were often cited as the grounds of 'theoretical obstacles' to the legal enforceability and justiciability of economic and social rights, the legal status of economic and social rights is much more widely accepted. Section 5.3 then sets out some the evaluative principles that have been developed at the international level for delimiting the nature and scope of international legal obligation in the field of economic and social rights. Particular emphasis is placed on the ways in which these evaluative principles facilitate the judicial scrutiny of the 'reasonableness' of state actions under conditions of resource and feasibility constraints.

Is there a theoretical distinction between the status of civil and political rights, and the status of economic, social, and cultural rights, in international human rights law?

In the past a hierarchical approach to internationally recognized human rights was often adopted—with many of the international treaty obligations

of Human Rights, some rights, e.g., the right to life, to freedom from torture, inhuman and degrading treatment, and from enforced labour, are often interpreted as being absolute; others as limited rights (with derogation possible under certain specified conditions but otherwise unqualified); and others as qualified rights (with qualifications permissible under regulated conditions with proper justification and process). See, for example, UK Department of Constitutional Affairs, *Study Guide 2nd Edition, Human Rights Act 1998, October 2002*, para 3.9, available at http://www.humanrights.gov.uk/ studyguide.

[18] For exambple, the Judgement in Case of Mary versus Jodie delivered by the UK Court of Appeal referred to a situation of conflicting positive duties—of a legal, social, and moral nature. The limitations on the performance of duties in this case related to feasibility constraints rather than resources, with the Court reasoning that a proposed operation to separate Siamese twins that would result in the death of one of the twins. The judgement established that both girls fell within the scope of the definition of personhood and both had human rights to life and bodily integrity that should be protected and promoted. However, it suggested that the case involved a situation of conflicting positive obligations—where the doctors treating Jodie and Mary having conflicting legal, social, and moral duties. See: (Draft) Judgement Lord Justices Ward, Brook and Walker on the Case of the Siamese Twins, Case No.B1/2000/2969 in the UK Supreme Court of Judicature Court of Appeal (Civil Division), especially paras. 30–3.

relevant to the eradication of global poverty being downgraded and neglected. This approach was often justified on the basis of a (claimed) distinction between the status of civil and political rights, and the status of economic, social, and cultural rights, in international human rights law. Civil and political rights were generally characterized as legally binding, but economic, social, and cultural rights were often characterized as being *without legal significance*—as mere programmatic policy goals. It was often suggested that this distinction was affirmed by the division of the human rights recognized in the Universal Declaration (1948) into two legally binding international instruments—the ICCPR (1966) and the ICESR (1966)—and the idea of a *legal hierarchy* between the two clusters of human rights was often reflected in debates about the nature and scope of international legal obligation during the cold war period. For example, in a classic article on human rights, Cranston argued that whereas civil and political rights are 'real' rights that can be readily secured in positive law, economic, social, and cultural rights are of a 'different logical category' (Cranston 1967). In addition, it is sometimes argued that when compared to Article 2 of the ICCPR, the textual formulation of the general legal obligations of states parties under Article 2 of the ICESCR is relatively vague and imprecise, and that the obligations of states parties to the ICESCR cannot, as a result, be adequately determined.

The nature and scope of the general legal obligations of states parties to the ICESCR and the ICCPR are prescribed in Article 2 of each respective Covenant. Under both treaties, Article 2 has a dynamic relationship with the other articles recognized in each of these treaties and, in order to

ICCPR	ICESCR
'[E]ach state party to the present Covenant undertakes to take the necessary steps . . . to adopt such legislative or other measures as may be necessary to give effect to the rights recognized in the present Covenant.'	'Each state party to the present Covenant undertakes to take steps, individually and through international assistance and cooperation, especially economic and technical, to the maximum of its available resources, with a view to achieving progressively the full realization of the rights recognized in the present Covenant by all appropriate means, including particularly the adoption of legislative measures.'

determine the nature and scope of the human rights and the legal obligations on states prescribed in each Covenant, each of the articles in each treaty must be read in conjunction with Article 2 of each respective treaty.

A number of distinctions can be drawn between the textual formulation of these articles. Sieghart (1983: 56–63) interprets the general legal obligations under Article 2 of the ICCPR as being of an immediate and absolute nature. That is, the general legal obligation incumbent on each state party to take the necessary steps to ensure and respect political and civil rights is an immediate obligation that is legally binding on a state party at the moment in time that the Covenant comes into force, and is an absolute obligation that is not limited by the fulfilment of certain conditions or contingencies (such as the resources available to a state). In contrast, he interprets the general legal obligations of states parties spelt out in Article 2 of the ICESCR as being of a qualified and limited nature. Article 2 of the ICESCR obliges states parties to 'take steps' to achieve the 'full realization' of the economic, social, and cultural rights recognized in that Covenant. However, the general legal obligation to achieve this objective is qualified by the provision that the full realization of economic, social, and cultural rights may be achieved 'progressively' over time, and is limited by the provision that steps towards this objective shall be taken 'to the maximum of available resources.' In addition, the textual formulation of these articles are often contrasted on the basis of the degree of determination on the one hand, and the degree of discretion on the other, in relation to the means by which the general legal obligations on states parties under each respective Covenant are to be achieved. Article 2 of the ICCPR stipulates that states parties must undertake 'the necessary steps' to ensure and respect political and civil rights. Arguably, this provision implies a high degree of determination, and a correspondingly low degree of discretion and choice, over the means by which this general legal obligation is to be performed. That is, certain actions to ensure and respect political rights are necessary and mandatory, and, in order to comply with the provisions of the ICCPR, a state party must perform or refrain from these specific actions or omissions. In contrast, the word 'necessary' is omitted from the general legal obligations on states parties spelled out in Article 2 of the ICESCR. This omission reduces the degree of determination, and correspondingly increases the degree of discretion, over the means by which the general legal obligation on states parties under the ICESCR is to be achieved. That is, there may be a range of options or choices over the actions which states parties may take in order to comply with the general legal obligation to take progressive steps, to the maximum of available resources, towards the full realization of economic, social, and cultural rights.

The significance of different theoretical perspectives on the nature and functions of international law

The proposition that economic, social, and cultural rights are of a lower legal status than those associated with particular theoretical perspectives on the *nature* and *functions* of international law. Legal positivism entails (*a*) that legally binding rules must, by definition, be strictly deduced from the text of authoritative legal documents; and (*b*) that the ability of an individual to enforce the performance (or non-performance) of an obligation is an essential characteristic of a legally binding right.[19] These positivist criteria are associated with the view that if the textual formulation of Article 2 of the ICESCR is vague and imprecise, then determinate legal obligations cannot be deduced from this article. For example, Vierdag has argued that the imprecise nature of the textual formulation of the ICESCR means that the obligations on state parties cannot be determined in a sufficiently concrete way for enforcement and justiciability. Assuming that the existence of specific legal remedies is essential to the characterization of rights,[20] he contends that economic, social, and cultural rights cannot be enforced and are not justiciable, and cannot be 'real' rights at all.

[E]xcept in circumstances of minimal or minor economic, social or cultural relevance [and subject to certain distinctions]...the rights granted by the ICESCR are of such a nature as to be legally negligible. (Vierdag 1978: 105)

In contrast, other legal paradigms challenge positivist views, questioning whether international law can be meaningfully characterized as a static body of text from which legally binding rules can be deduced. For example, Higgins proposes that international law is a '...continuing process of authoritative decisions' which requires that choices be made between alternative norms. Rather than disguising the fact that legal interpretation

---

[19] See, generally, Freeman (1994: 205–70).

[20] Vierdag notes that he 'will not examine the question whether, in legal theory, the doctrine does or does not prevail that there can be no "subjective right" of an individual unless there is also a remedy (procedural capacity, *jus standi*, action, capacity to claim, etc.) attached to it'. Nevertheless he reserves the term individual rights 'for those rights that are capable of being enforced by their bearers in courts or law, or in a comparable manner'. He also suggests that enforceability is an 'essential element' of the characterization of individual rights in the practice of international law and that '[i]n order to be a legal right, a right must be legally definable; only then can it be legally enforced, only then it can be said to be justiciable'. Vierdag cites Kelsen as an authority for this position: '[T]he essential element (of a right) is the legal power bestowed upon the [individual] by the legal order to bring about, by a law suit, the execution of a sanction as a reaction against the nonfulfilment of the obligation. ... Only if the legal order confers such a power are we faced by a "right" in [the] specific, technical sense of the word' (Vierdag 1978: 73, 93).

entails an element of value judgement, she suggests that ' . . . it is desirable that the policy factors are dealt with systematically and openly', and that, in making choices, consideration should be given to ' . . . the humanitarian, moral, and social purposes of the law' (Higgins 1994: 2–9). Normative and dynamic approaches of this type tend to emphasize the role of international standard-setting in clarifying and elaborating the international legal obligations of states. Approaches of this type are particularly influential in the field of human rights, because, when compared with other areas of international law, the textual formulation of *many* international instruments in the field of human rights is relatively vague and abstract. There is, for example, a tendency in the field of human rights to make reference to the object and purposes of international human rights law as spelled out in the preambles to international human rights treaties—to principles such as *human dignity* and *human equality*.[21] In addition, the role of international standard-setting in clarifying the nature and scope of international obligations in relation to civil and political rights is now accepted as standard.

The role of authoritative international standards in clarifying the nature and scope of the obligations of states in the field of economic, social, and cultural rights

For these reasons, many legal analysts argue that normative and dynamic approaches have critical roles to play in clarifying the nature and scope of the obligations of states parties under Article 2 of the ICESCR. For example, Eide acknowledges that, when contrasted with the degree of precision with which most civil and political rights have been elaborated, the formulation of economic, social, and cultural rights seems vague and imprecise, and suggests that this relative vagueness and imprecision has encouraged their neglect at the national and international levels. Nevertheless, rather than responding to imperfections in the ICESCR by suggesting that economic, social, and cultural rights are non-justiciable and are not 'real rights', he contends that appropriate response should be 'legal

---

[21] For example, Jasudowicz (1994: 26) has challenged the positivist thesis that the preamble to an international treaty expresses general principles and goals, but does not establish legally binding international rules, so characterizing the preamble of international treaties in the field of human rights as the *animus* and *ratio legis* of such treaties, and proposing that the preamble constitutes an 'integral' part of international human rights law that is 'essential' for the interpretation and application of human rights-standards.

creativity to make the obligations on states clear and enforceable'.[22] Similarly, Van Hoof recommends a strategy of deducing the legal obligations from rules, even if these are vaguely formulated, and enhancing the effectiveness of these rules through standard-setting (Van Hoof 1984: 105–8). As the sub-sections that follow will show, normative standard-setting by authoritative bodies in the field of economic, social, and cultural rights has accelerated in recent years. The jurisprudence of the UN Committee on Economic, Social, and Cultural Rights (CESCR), together with important interpretative statements issued by other authoritative bodies, have clarified the nature and scope of the international legal obligations of states in the field of economic, social, and cultural rights. These authoritative international standards have helped to create a common understanding of Article 2 of the ICESCR, and of the normative content of the human rights recognized in this instrument—including the normative content of the human rights to adequate food and clothing, to the highest attainable standard of health, and to education, including free and compulsory primary education. Given the emergence of this body of authoritative standards—together with changing international priorities since the end of the cold war—the hierarchical approach to human rights has now been widely rejected. The legal significance of economic, social, and cultural rights is now firmly established.

The principle of 'interdependence and indivisibility'

The rejection of 'hierarchical' approaches has been reflected in the development of important normative standards relating to the 'indivisible, interdependent, and interrelated' nature of international human rights over the past decade. These standards emphasize that human rights enumerated in the Universal Declaration for the physical survival and integrity of the person include both civil, political, economic, social, and cultural rights and that no categorical distinction is made between civil and political rights (Articles 3–21) and economic, social, and cultural rights (Articles 22–27). This absence of a categorical distinction can be interpreted as implying that the Universal Declaration does not establish a hierarchy of human rights, and that although political and civil rights on

---

[22] See 'Right to Adequate Food as a Human right', Report of the Special Rapporteur of the Sub-Commission on Prevention of Discrimination and Protection of Minorities, submitted in 1987 and reprinted in Human Rights Study Series No. 1 (1989), UN Publications, New York. Para. 40. For the minutes of the General Discussion on the Right to Food by CESCR, see UN Doc. E/C.12/1989/SR.20: 2–12.

the one hand, and economic, social, and cultural rights on the other, are codified in two separate international treaties, they are on an equal footing. The ICCPR and the ICESCR are both international treaties and the object and purposes of each treaty as set out in the preamble recognizes the important of all human rights—civil, political, economic, social, and cultural.

[I]n accordance with the Universal Declaration of Human Rights, the ideal of free human beings enjoying freedom from fear and want can only be achieved if conditions are created whereby everyone may enjoy his economic, social and cultural rights, as well as his civil and political rights. (Preamble, ICESCR; cf. Preamble, ICCPR).

The principle that the promotion and protection of the two categories of rights are go hand in hand, and the promotion and protection of one category of rights does not exempt or excuse states from the promotion and protection of the other, has been reflected in international standard-setting in recent years. This principle was reflected, for example, in UNGA resolution 32/130 and the UN World Conference on Human Rights convened in 1993, which recognized that:

All human rights are universal, indivisible and interdependent and interrelated. The international community must treat human rights globally in a fair and equal manner, on the same footing, and with the same emphasis.... [I]t is the duty of States, regardless of their political, economic and cultural systems, to promote and protect all human rights and fundamental freedoms. (Commitment 5)[23]

This principle is also reflected in the UN Declaration on the Right to Development, which states that the promotion of respect for and enjoyment of particular human rights and fundamental freedoms cannot justify the denial of other human rights and fundamental freedoms'.[24] It is also central to the jurisprudence and practice of authoritative UN human rights organs. For example, the CESCR has reasoned that the principles of interdependence could be expected to give rise to the equal treatment of all human rights, with the same level of urgent consideration being given to both categories of rights, and proportionality in the implementation machinery.[25]

---

[23] UN Doc. A/Conf.157/24 Part One, Ch. III.
[24] General Assembly resolution 41/128 of 4 December 1986.
[25] CESCR, 'Statement to the UN World Conference on Human Rights', UN Doc. E/1993/22, Annex III–IV.

5.3 Evaluative Principles for Assessing the 'Reasonableness' of State Actions in the Context of Resource and Feasibility Constraints

This section sets out some the evaluative principles that have been developed at the international level for delimiting the nature and scope of international legal obligation in the field of economic and social rights. Particular emphasis is placed on the ways in which these evaluative principles facilitate the judicial scrutiny of the 'reasonableness' of state actions under conditions of resource and feasibility constraints.

International standard-setting relating to the meaning of 'progressive realization'

Authoritative international interpretations of the nature and scope of the international obligations of states under Article 2 of the ICESCR are set out in the General Comments of the UN Committee on Economic, Social, and Cultural Rights[26] and other authoritative documents including the Limburg Principles[27] and Maastricht Guidelines.[28] The principal obligation is to take steps to achieve *progressively* the full realization of the rights recognized in the Covenant. In General Comment 3, the Committee suggests that the provision for 'progressive realization' under Article 2 of the ICESCR provides an acknowledgement that resources may be limited and that where resource constraints are binding, the full realization of these economic, social, and cultural rights may be achieved over time. Nevertheless, states parties are expected to be in compliance with convention obligations within a reasonable time after ratification or accession.

[26] See especially General Comment 1, 'Reporting by States parties', UN Doc. E/1989/22 (subsequently, 'General Comment 1'); General Comment 3, 'The nature of States parties obligations (Article 2: para. 1)', UN Doc. E/1991/23 (subsequently, 'General Comment 3'); General Comment 1, 'Plans of Action for Primary Education', General Comment 9, 'The Domestic Application of the Covenant', UN Doc. E/C.12/1998/24 (subsequently, 'General Comment 9'); UN Doc. E/C.12/1999/4 (subsequently, 'General Comment 11'); CESCR, General Comment 12, 'The Right to Adequate Food', UN Doc. E//C.12/1995/5 (subsequently, 'General Comment 12'); General Comment 13, 'The Right to Education', UN Doc. E/C.12/1999/10 (subsequently, 'General Comment 13'); General Comment 14, 'The Right to the Highest Attainable Standard of Health', UN Doc. E/C.12/2000/4 (subsequently, 'General Comment 14'); General Comment 15, 'The Right to Water', UN Doc. C/C.12/2002/11 (subsequently, 'General Comment 15'). Available electronically at http://www.ohchr.org/english/bodies/cescr/comments.htm.
[27] 'The Limburg Principles on the Implementation of the International Covenant on Economic, Social, and Cultural Rights', UN Doc. E/CN.4.1987/17, Annex: 122–35 (subsequently, 'The Limburg Principles').
[28] 'The Maastricht Guidelines on Violations of Economic, Social, and Cultural Rights', published in *Human Rights Quarterly* 20.3 (1998: 691–704) (subsequently, 'The Maastricht Guidelines').

General Comment 3 stipulates that 'progressive realization' is an immediate obligation and is not conditional on increased resources. The objective of the Covenant is the *full* realization of economic, social, and cultural rights, and Article 2 does not relieve states parties of the general legal obligation to move as expeditiously and effectively as possible towards that goal. The burden is on the state to demonstrate that it is making measurable progress toward the full realization of the rights in question. 'Progressive realization' should not, therefore, be interpreted as implying for states the right to defer indefinitely efforts to ensure the full realization of the rights, and states cannot use the 'progressive realization' provisions of the Covenant as a pretext for non-compliance.[29]

Immediate and unconditional obligations

The jurisprudence of the CESCR further establishes that whilst Article 2 provides for progressive realization and acknowledges the constraints due to the limits of available resources, it also imposes various unconditional obligations on states parties that are of immediate effect.[30] In particular, the general obligation 'to take steps' under Article 2 is not itself qualified or limited by other considerations. All states parties have an obligation to begin immediately to take steps towards the full realization of the rights contained in the Covenant[31] and there is no reason to defer the implementation of human rights whose realization is independent of resources. The importance of the right to non-discrimination has been highlighted in this context. The prohibition of discrimination in Article 2(2) of the Covenant stipulates that states parties are obliged to 'guarantee' that the rights recognized in the Covenant be exercised without discrimination, and Article 3 obliges states parties to ensure the equal rights of men and women to economic, social, and cultural rights. The jurisprudence of the Committee, the Limburg Principles, and the Maastricht Guidelines suggest that the 'undertaking to guarantee' that the rights recognized in the Covenant 'will be exercised without discrimination' is an unconditional obligation suitable for immediate implementation that should be implemented in full immediately.[32] Some of the other provisions in the Covenant—including Article 8 (the right to join a trade union)—are also capable

---

[29] CESCR, General Comment 3, 'The nature of States parties obligations (Article 2, para. 1)', Limburg Principles 1, 21, 22, 23, 24; and Maastricht Guideline 8.

[30] General Comment 3 paragraph 1; Limburg Principles 8, 22.

[31] General Comment 3 paragraph 2; Limburg Principle 1; and Maastricht Guideline 8.

[32] CESCR, General Comment 1, and Limburg Principle 22.

of immediate application by judicial and other organs. The Committee has also emphasized the importance of states parties giving effect to the ICESCR in the domestic legal order in this context.[33]

The development of general principles for evaluating the adequacy or reasonableness of the measures adopted by states under Article 2 of the ICESCR

A number of general principles have been developed that provide a basis for assessing the adequacy or reasonableness of the actions performed by states. The UN Committee on Economic, Social, and Cultural Rights emphasized that ICESCR is compatible with diverse political, economic, and legal systems and that states enjoy a 'margin of appreciation', allowing for different routes to the implementation of the Covenant in different cultural settings, and in countries with different levels of resources.[34] Under circumstances where resource constraints are binding, good faith effort must nevertheless be demonstrated towards the achievement of economic, social, and cultural rights. The steps undertaken by states towards the implementation of the ICESCR should for example be '...deliberate, concrete, and targeted as clearly as possible towards meeting the obligations recognized in the Covenant'.[35] This principle is set out in General Comment 3 and provides the framework for the analysis of the international obligations of states in relation, for example, to the human right to food (General Comment 12), the human right to health (General Comment 14), and the human right to water (General Comment 15). The Limburg Principles stipulate that '[i]n the use of the available resources due priority shall be given to the realization of rights recognized in the Covenant'[36] and that in determining whether or not adequate measures have been taken for the realization of the rights recognized in the Covenant, 'attention shall be paid to equitable and effective use of and access to the available resources'. The Maastricht Guidelines also emphasize the importance of the effective use of resources available, and reiterate that the burden is on the state to demonstrate that it is making measurable progress toward the full realization of the rights in question.[37] The

[33] UN Committee on Economic, Social, and Cultural Rights, General Comment 9.

[34] These principles are affirmed in the Limburg Principles and Maastricht Guidelines, which stipulate that, as in the case of civil and political rights, states enjoy a margin of discretion in selecting the means for implementing their respective obligations.

[35] UN Committee on Economic, Social, and Cultural Rights, General Comment 3, paras. 2–5.

[36] Limburg Principle 28.

[37] Limburg Principles 23 and 27; and Maastricht Guideline 8.

principle of no 'deliberate retrogression' has also emerged as an important element of international standards in this field and places a burden of justification on the state in relation to deliberately retrogressive measures in the field of economic and social rights (CESCR, General Comment 3).

The obligations to monitor and plan

Resource constraints do not relieve a state of its duty to monitor the non-fulfilment of economic, social, and cultural rights. General Comment 1 establishes that the obligation to monitor the extent of the realization and non-realization of economic, social, and cultural rights, with special attention being paid to disadvantaged, poor, and vulnerable groups, is an unconditional and immediate obligation, which is not limited by resource constraints. Likewise, the obligation to design and implement a plan for progressively realizing the full realization of the human rights set out in the ICESCR is also an immediate and unconditional obligation. States are in this context required to introduce and implement a detailed plan of action, including the identification of human rights indicators in relation to each of the human rights set out in the ICESCR, and a series of intermediate benchmark targets on the basis of which the progress over time can be evaluated (CESCR General Comment 1; CRC, General Comment 5).

Authoritative international recognition of the negative and positive dimensions of international legal obligation

International human rights law also provides authoritative recognition of the view that fundamental freedoms and human rights are associated with positive obligations of protection and promotion (as well as negative obligations of omission, non-intervention, and restraint). The Principles of State Responsibility elaborated by the International Law Commission (ILC) clearly establish that international obligations can be breached by both acts of *omission* and acts of *commission*. Whereas in the past there was a tendency to characterize civil and political rights in negative terms, and economic and social rights in positive terms, there is by now a significant body of authoritative standards that clearly establish that all human rights—civil, political, economic, social, and cultural—can give rise to both negative and positive obligations. The interpretative framework developed by the UN CESCR identifies three essential aspects of international obligation in relation to all human rights:

(1) At the primary level, states are required to *respect* human rights. This implies immunity from interference with the enjoyment of all human rights—civil, political, economic, social, and cultural—by the government and its representatives such as freedom from arbitrary arrest and torture, freedom from arbitrary forced evictions, and freedom to work and to satisfy one's basic needs. Thus the right to housing is violated if the state engages in arbitrary forced evictions.

(2) At the secondary level, states are required to *protect* human rights. This implies that states are under a positive obligation to ensure the protection of individuals from violations by third parties (including violations by private individuals, businesses, and transnational corporations). This can be achieved, for example, by the establishment of a legal and institutional framework that prevents actions that violate human rights and that ensures appropriate action when violations both are alleged and are shown to have occurred (e.g. by investigations, monitoring, remedies, and relief). Violations occur when the state fails to take adequate, reasonable measures and/or fails to exercise due diligence in these respects.

(3) At the tertiary level, states are required to *fulfil* the enjoyment of human rights. This implies that states are under a positive obligation to take measures effectively to secure the full realization of human rights. This can be achieved, for example, by taking legislative, budgetary, administrative, and other measures to promote the achievement of human rights by facilitating opportunities for the achievement of human rights (e.g. by the adoption of policies and programmes) and by directly providing for the fulfilment human rights (for people whose human rights would otherwise be denied).[38]

This interpretive framework has had a major influence on international thinking about the nature and scope of international legal obligation in the field of economic and social rights. It is also reflected, for example, in the Committee's General Comment 12 on the human right to adequate food, and General Comment 14 on the human right to the highest attain-

---

[38] See 'Right to Adequate Food as a Human right', Report of the Special Rapporteur of the Sub-Commission on Prevention of Discrimination and Protection of Minorities, submitted in 1987 and reprinted in Human Rights Study Series No. 1 (1989), UN Publications, New York. Para. 40; General Discussion on the Right to Food by CESCR see UN Doc. E/C.12/1989/SR.20: 2–12; 'The Right to Food in Theory and Practice', http://www.fao.org/docrep/; 'Report Updating the Study on the Right to Food prepared by Mr. A. Eide', UN Doc. E/CN.4/Sub.2/1998/ 9; and 'The Right to Adequate Food and to be Free From Hunger, Updated Report by Special Rapporteur Mr Eide', UN Doc. E/CN.4/Sub.2/1999/12: paras 51 and 52; General Comments 12, 13, 14, and 15 of the UN Committee on Economic, Social, and Cultural Rights; ICHR (2004: 1).

able standard of health and General Comment 15 on the human right to water. The Maastricht Guidelines also emphasize international obligations to *respect, protect,* and *fulfil* all human rights and stipulate that the failure to perform any one of these obligations constitutes a violation of such rights (Guideline 6). This interpretive framework also underpins the deepening and widening of international obligation in the field of economic and social rights at the regional and domestic levels. It is reflected, for example, in the South African Constitution, which establishes that '[t]he state must respect, protect, promote, and fulfil' human rights[39] and in the emerging body of international case law in the field of economic and social rights discussed below.

The 'Minimum Core Obligations' approach

The General Comments of the UN CESCR also establish that resource scarcity does not relieve states of *minimum* obligations in relation to certain human rights recognized in the ICESCR. Although the full realization of economic, social, and cultural rights may be achieved progressively over time, all states parties are under a minimum core obligation to ensure the satisfaction of, at the very least, minimum essential levels of each of the rights recognized in the Covenant. The Limburg Principles (25–28) and the Maastricht Guidelines (9–10) confirm that this is an immediate and unconditional obligation and is legally binding at the moment that the Covenant comes into force in a particular state. The 'minimum threshold approach' places a floor under each right, below which any state will be in violation of Article 2 (Alston and Quinn 1987). Minimum core obligations to ensure respect for minimum subsistence rights for all apply irrespective of the availability of resources in the country concerned or any other factors and difficulties, and irrespective of the level of economic development of the state party concerned,[40] and violations of the Covenant occur when a state fails to satisfy the minimum core obligation to ensure the satisfaction of, at the very least, minimum essential levels of each of the rights recognized in the Covenant. Thus:

[A]ny situation in which any significant number of individuals is deprived of essential foodstuffs, of essential primary health care, of basic shelter and housing, or of the most basic forms of education constitutes *prima facie* evidence that a State

---

[39] South African Bill of Rights, Section 7.2.
[40] General Comment 3; Limburg Principle 25; and Maastricht Guideline 8.

party is failing to discharge its obligations under the Covenant. (General Comment 3 and Maastricht Guidelines 9–10)

In order for a state party to be able to attribute its failure to meet at least its minimum core obligations to a lack of available resources, it must demonstrate that every effort has been made to use all resources that are at its disposition in an effort to satisfy, as a matter of priority, certain minimum obligations. The incapacity of a state to fulfil its minimum obligations from its own resources under the ICESCR might also be taken as a 'trigger' for international cooperation, assistance, and aid (see Section 5.5).

The relevance of the distinction between 'international obligations of conduct' and 'international obligations of result'

The analytical distinction between 'international obligations of conduct' (requiring the performance or non-performance of specific actions) and 'international obligations of result' (requiring the realization of a particular situation or result, without determining the specific means by which this situation or result is to be achieved) has been highlighted by various authoritative international bodies, recognized in constitutions, and applied in case law.[41] In elaborating and codifying principles of State Responsibility, the ILC (1978) reasoned that international obligations can be structured differently with respect to the ways and means the state is expected to ensure their fulfilment, and that these differences have significant implications for the conditions of a possible breach of an international obligation, and hence for the assessment of the compliance of a state with its international legal obligations.

- International obligations that call 'categorically' for the use of 'specific means', and that require a 'specific conduct' from a state—where the specific conduct in question may be an action or a course of action, or an act of omission—are classified by the ILC (1978) as *international obligations of conduct*. A breach by a state of an international obligation of conduct arises 'in virtue of the adoption of a course of conduct different from that specifically required' (Article 20).

- International obligations that require that a state '...ensures a particular situation or result' but leaves the state 'free to do so by what-

---

[41] The distinction was set out in Articles 20 and 21 (and the attached Commentary) of the Principles of State Responsibility elucidated by the International Law Commission in 1977. (See: *Yearbook of the International Law Commission* 1977. New York, United Nations Publications).

ever means it chooses' are classified by the ILC (1978) as *international obligations of result*. The *degree* of freedom of choice allowed to the state in determining the means by which the obligation of result is to be achieved may vary. In some cases, the state may have complete freedom to choose between the means available to it, while in other cases, an international obligation may express a preference and suggest that a particular means is most likely to produce the required result, without making recourse to that means compulsory. A breach of an international obligation of result exists 'if, by the conduct adopted in exercising its freedom of choice, the State has not in fact achieved the internationally required result' (Article 21).

The 'Articles of State Responsibility' adopted by the ILC in (2001) do not directly refer to the distinction between 'obligations of conduct' and 'obligations of result'.[42] This is explained on the grounds that although the distinction between 'obligations of conduct' and 'obligations of result' may assist in ascertaining when a breach of an international obligation has occurred, it has relevance for the *classification* of primary rules, rather than direct significance for the establishment of state responsibility for internationally wrongful acts.[43] In contrast to the analysis suggested above, the Commentary to the 2001 'Articles of State Responsibility' also emphasizes that the evaluation of compliance with international obligations of result cannot be inferred from the evaluation of the results achieved per se, but will often entail the evaluation of both (*a*) state conduct and (*b*) the results achieved. For example, in the Colozza Case, the European Court of Human Rights characterized Article 6(1) of the European Convention on Human Rights (the right to a fair and public trial) as an obligation of result and stated: 'States enjoy a wide discretion as regards the choice of means calculated to ensure that their legal systems are in compliance with the requirements of article 6(1). The Court's task is to determine whether the result . . . [required] has been achieved.' In determining whether a breach of this Article had occurred in this case, the Court took into account (*a*) the result required (the opportunity for a fair and public trial); (*b*) the result achieved in practice (the lack of that opportunity for a trial in the presence

---

[42] Articles of responsibility of states for internationally wrongful acts adopted in 2001 after the second reading: http://www.law.cam.ac.uk/rcil/ILCSR/Statresp.htm.

[43] See Second Report on State Responsibility by Mr Crawford, Special Rapporteur, UN Docs A/CN.4/498, paras. 52–80.

of the accused); (c) the adequacy of the measures adopted by the state party to make the right effective.[44]

The role of statistical indicators and benchmarks in evaluating compliance with 'obligations of result'

The UN CESCR has relied on the distinction between international obligations of conduct and international obligations of result in its jurisprudence, stipulating that situations or results—as well as specific actions and omissions—constitute relevant benchmarks in terms of which the compliance of states parties with their treaty obligations under Article 2 of the ICESCR can be assessed.[45] The UN CESCR has placed much emphasis on the effective realization of human rights in practice, and has highlighted the de facto as well as the *de jure* aspects of the realization of economic, social, and cultural rights. The Reporting Guidelines issued to states parties by the CESCR suggest that information relating to the law pertaining in a state should be supplemented with statistical information relating to the achievement of the human rights enumerated in the Covenant by individuals and groups in practice. The Committee has repeatedly criticized states parties that have focused on 'legalistic and theoretical aspects and [have] not placed sufficient emphasis on tangible facts reflecting the actual situation prevailing in the country',[46] and has highlighted the use of statistical indicators and benchmarks as evaluative tools for assessing the achievement of economic and social rights by individuals and groups.[47] This approach is further developed in the Maastricht Guidelines, which also emphasize that a situation or result, as opposed to an act or an act of omission, can constitute a relevant benchmark against which the compliance of states parties with their treaty obligations can be judged. Guideline 7 stipulates that whereas 'the obligation of conduct requires action reasonably calculated to realize the enjoyment of a particular right',

[44] See Colozza and Rubinat vs Italy, ECHR Series A, No. 89 (1985), and Commentary on Article 12 (para.11), *Yearbook of the International Law Commission 2001*, http://www.un.org/law/ilc/sessions/53/53sesss.htm.

[45] Also see Maastricht Guidelines 7, 8.

[46] For example, see the Committee's criticisms in its 'Concluding Observations' on Reports submitted by Panama and the Democratic People's Republic of Korea, in CESCR, 'Report on the Sixth Session', UN Doc. E/1992/23, paras. 134 and 157.

[47] 'The New International Economic Order and the Promotion of Human Rights: Realization of Economic, Social, and Cultural Rights', First and Second Progress Reports, Mr. D. Türk, UN Docs. E/CN.4 Sub.2/1990/19 and E/CN.4 Sub.2/1991/17. This conclusion was discussed by CESCR in 'General Discussion on Economic and Social Indicators and their Role in the Realization of Economic, Social, and Cultural Rights', UN Doc. E/1992/23, Chapter VII, 81.

the obligation of result 'requires States to achieve specific targets to satisfy a detailed substantive standard'. Applied to Article 12 of the ICESCR, the human right to health:

[T]he obligation of conduct could involve the adoption and implementation of a plan of action to reduce maternal mortality [while the] obligation of result requires States to achieve specific targets, such as the reduction of maternal mortality to levels agreed at the 1994 Cairo International Conference on Population and Development and the 1995 Beijing Fourth World Conference on Women.

Implications for the establishment of evidentiary thresholds in the field of economic and social rights

The concept of an 'international obligation of result', therefore, has far-reaching implications for discussions about evidentiary thresholds in the field of economic and social rights, highlighting the relevance of both the specified results and the results achieved in practice in the determination of compliance with international obligations under the ICESCR. However, as emphasized in the reasoning in the Commentary accompanying ILC (2001), violations of Article 2 of the ICESCR by national states cannot, for example, be inferred from the non-fulfilment of the human rights set out in the ICESCR, per se. The compliance of states under Article 2 of the ICESCR might, for example, be taken to require evaluation of (*a*) whether the human rights set out in the ICESCR have been realized; (*b*) the adequacy of state conduct (e.g. the application of a 'best efforts' or 'reasonableness' criterion). The reasonableness of state action should be evaluated in terms of the results specified in the Covenant (i.e. the full realization of the economic, social, and cultural rights) taking account of reasonableness of state conduct (evaluated in terms of the general principles set above, intermediate benchmark targets, and the 'minimum threshold approach'). However, even evaluation of state compliance with even its core obligations under the 'minimum threshold approach' will in the final analysis take account of the evaluation of state conduct as well as the results achieved. For example, whilst resource scarcity does not relieve states of certain minimum obligations under Article 2 of the ICESCR, any assessment as to whether a state has discharged its minimum core obligation must nevertheless take account of resource constraints applying within the state party concerned.[48] Thus the failure of population groups within a particular jurisdiction to achieve adequate nutrition provides

[48] Maastricht Guideline 8.

prima facie rather than direct evidence of human rights violations by the national state.

5.4 The Emergence of a Body of Case Law in the Field of Global Poverty and Human Rights

This section analyses the ways in which an emerging body of case law and jurisprudence reinforces and supports the idea of the capability to achieve a standard of living adequate for survival and development—including adequate nutrition, safe water and sanitation, shelter and housing, access to basic health and social services, and education—as a basic human right that governments have individual and collective obligations to respect, protect, and promote. The analysis begins with a review of authoritative interpretations of civil and political rights that support the principle that human rights give rise to positive obligations (of protection and promotion) as well as to negative obligations (of omission and restraint). The ways in which the positive implications of civil and political rights (especially the human right to life) can be invoked as a basis for the protection of economic and social rights are then discussed. Finally, emerging case law in the field of economic and social rights is examined. Particular emphasis is placed on the ways in which authoritative jurisprudence emphasizes the notion of rights to policies and programmes (or 'meta-rights') when resource and feasibility constraints are binding.

The positive implications of civil and political rights

The European Court of Human Rights has established an important body of precedents establishing the positive implications of human rights. Under Article 1 of the Convention, states parties are obliged to 'secure to everyone within their jurisdiction the rights and freedoms' defined in the Convention. In the case of Airey versus Ireland, the Court reasoned that the objective of the Convention is to guarantee rights that are 'practical and effective' and that the fulfilment of a duty under the Convention, including the fulfilment of the duty to secure an effective right of access to court, can on occasion necessitate 'some positive action on the part of the State'.[49] Furthermore, whilst the object of Article 8 of the Convention is to protect the individual against arbitrary interference by public authorities, this article does not merely compel the state to abstain from such inter-

---

[49] Airey v Ireland (6289/73) [1979] ECHR 3 (9 October 1979). Available at http://www.worldlii.org/eu/cases/ECHR/1979/3.html.

ferences, but can involve 'positive obligations inherent in an effective respect for private or family life'.[50] This principle was affirmed in the cases of Marckx versus Belgium[51] and X and Y versus the Netherlands,[52] while in the case of Plattform 'Ärzte für das Leben' versus Austria, the Court recognized that 'genuine effective freedom of peaceful assembly' could not be reduced to a mere negative duty of non-interference on the part of the state. Article 11 sometimes requires positive measures to be taken—even in the sphere of relations between individuals.[53]

The 'obligation to protect' and the test of 'due diligence'

The principle that the *adequate protection* of human rights can entail positive obligations on the part of states is clearly established in case law. For example, Article 22(2) of the Vienna Convention on Diplomatic Relations provides that '[t]he receiving State is under a special duty to take all appropriate steps to protect the premises of the mission against any intrusion or damage and to prevent any disturbance of the peace of the mission for impairment of its dignity'; although the obligation of protection stipulated by this article might be interpreted as a negative obligation of result, where a breach takes place only if a particular result (intrusion, damage, etc.) cannot be seen to have been ensured, and does not involve a warranty or guarantee against intrusion. However, in the *Case concerning United States Diplomatic and Consular Staff in Tehran*, the International Court of Justice referred to these provisions as imposing on a state 'the most categorical obligations ... to take appropriate steps to ensure' protection, holding that:

[T]he Iranian Government failed altogether to take any 'appropriate steps' ... [this failure] to take such steps was due to more than mere negligence or lack of appropriate means. ... This inaction ... by itself constituted clear and serious violation of Iran's obligation.[54]

In the field of human rights, the principle that the obligation to protect can have positive as well as negative dimensions has also been invoked as a basis for establishing state responsibility for violations by third parties. For example, in the Rodriguez Case, the Inter-American Court of Human Rights analysed the conditions under which violations by third parties can be 'imputed' to a state. The Court reasoned that the precept contained in Article 1 of the American Convention on Human Rights, whereby states

[50] UN Doc. ECIIR A32 (1979) at 24–32.   [51] UN Doc. ECHR A31 (1979) at 31.
[52] UN Doc. ECHR A 91 (1985) at 23.   [53] UN Doc. ECHR A 139 (1988) at 32.
[54] UN Doc. ICJ Reports (1980) at 61–7.

parties 'undertake to respect the rights and freedoms recognized [in the Convention] and to ensure to all persons subject to their jurisdiction the free and full exercise of those rights and freedoms, without any discrimination...' constitutes the generic basis of the protection of the rights recognized by the Convention. Under this article, states parties are obligated to prevent, investigate, and punish alleged human rights-violations. Furthermore, the obligation *to prevent* requires states parties to take reasonable steps to prevent human rights-violations by using means of a legal, political, administrative, and cultural nature that promote the protection of human rights, and to ensure that any violations are considered and treated as illegal acts. Failure to comply with this duty can lead to the international responsibility of a state. Hence:

An illegal act which violates human rights and which is initially not directly imputable to a State (for example, because it is the act of a private person or because the person responsible has not been identified) can lead to international responsibility of the State, not because of the act itself, but because of the lack of due diligence to prevent the violation or to respond to it as required by the Convention.[55]

The 'due diligence' test established in this case has become an important element of international efforts to widen and deepen international accountability in the field of human rights. It has become an important influence on case law focusing on the protective function of the state in the field of human rights—both in terms of actions that the state should itself perform and in terms of the broader obligations in relation to the regulation of the behaviour of non-state actors. For example, some human rights advocacy organizations contend that the 'due diligence' test imposes a requirement on states parties to take reasonable and adequate measures to prevent or respond to violations by private actors (e.g. ICHR 2004: 1)

Positive interpretations of the human right to life

The jurisprudence of the Human Rights Committee also establishes that positive as well as negative obligations flow from civil and political rights. This principle is clearly stated in the Committee's General Comment on Article 6 (the right to life). This suggests that the right to life imposes on

---

[55] Inter-American Court of Human Rights (Ser.C) No. 4 (1988): 163–72.

states not only a duty to refrain from interfering with life, but also a 'positive duty' to 'take steps to safeguard life':

[T]he right to life has been too often narrowly interpreted. The expression 'inherent right to life' cannot properly be understood in a restrictive manner, and the protection of this right requires that States adopt positive measures. In this connection, the Committee considers that it would be desirable for States parties to undertake all possible measures to reduce infant mortality and to increase life expectancy, especially measures to eliminate malnutrition and epidemics.[56]

The idea that the human right to life can give rise to positive obligations is also reflected in an expanding body of domestic case law. For example, the jurisprudence of the Supreme Court in India has interpreted the right to life under Article 21 of the Indian Constitution so as to impose positive obligations on the state in relation to the basic needs of its inhabitants, invoking the human right to life as a basis for the protection and promotion of economic and social rights and linking this to directive principles of state policy under the Indian Constitution (especially Article 39(a) providing that the state shall direct policy towards securing the right to an adequate means of livelihood, and Article 41 providing that the state shall, within the limits of its economic capacity and development, make effective provision for securing the right to work in cases of unemployment and of undeserved want). For example, in the *Paschim Banga Khet Mazdoor Samity and others v State of West Bengal and another*, the Supreme Court reasoned that Article 21 imposes an obligation on the state to safeguard the right to life of very person and that '[f]ailure on the part of a Government hospital to provide timely medical treatment to a person in need of such treatment results in violation of his right to life guaranteed under Article 21.7'.[57] Other cases have established similar important precedents. In the Case of Olga Tellis versus Bombay Municipality Corporation, the Indian Supreme Court found that the right to livelihood should be treated as an integral component of the right to life guaranteed by Article 21, supported by constitutional directive principles concerning adequate means of livelihood and work:

The sweep of Article 21 is wide and far-reaching. It does not mean merely that life cannot be extinguished or taken away.... An equally important facet of that right is the right to livelihood because, no person can live without the means of living, that

---

[56] CCPR, General Comment 6, The Right to life (Article 6), Sixteenth Session, 30/7/82.
[57] AIR 1996 SC 2426–29. Available at: http://www.escr-net.org/EngGeneral/CaseLawSearch Result.asp. Quotation at para. 9.

is, the means of livelihood....That, which alone makes it possible to live...must be deemed an integral component of the right to life.

In the case at hand (where the State of Maharashtra and the Municipal Council moved to evict pavement and slum dwellers from Bombay City), the Court held that the authorities' action amounted to a deprivation of the citizen's right to livelihood as they required housing for their livelihoods in order to secure their right to life. The Court further reasoned that deprivation of the right to livelihood could occur if there was a just and fair procedure undertaken according to law and that this condition was satisfied by the Supreme Court proceedings. Finally, whilst finding that there was no right to an alternative site, the Court found that the government should ensure alternative sites to those with 1976 census cards and to those resident for twenty years; that high priority should be given to the resettlement of other residents; and that the evictions should be delayed until after the monsoon.[58]

Deriving the 'human right to food' from the 'human right to life'

More recent cases in India have addressed the positive obligations of the government to prevent malnutrition and starvation deaths during periods of drought and famine. In the *Case of People's Union for Civil Liberties*, the Indian Supreme Court addressed the occurrence of starvation deaths despite the availability of surplus food reserved for famine situations. The People's Union alleged that in various locations, established policies and arrangements for preventing starvation deaths were inadequately implemented—with incomplete coverage of the population at risk, inefficient delivery mechanisms, and inadequate provision for meeting minimum needs. This included uneven implementation of the 'Famine Codes' introduced to protect people from death through starvation under officially recognized famine conditions; the failure of the public food distribution system, restricted to families below the poverty line, to meet minimum nutritional standards; and 'Food-For-Work' programmes with 'labour ceilings' and inadequate cash and food provision. The People's Union argued that various economic and social rights including shelter, an adequate standard of living, and medical care are derivable from the right to life under the Indian Constitution. The situation at hand was alleged to represent a violation of the right to food, derived from the right to life

---

[58] Olga Tellis and Ors. versus Bombay Municipal Corporation and Ors. Etc., July 10, 1985, available via: http://www.escr-net.org. Quotation on p. 23.

under Article 21, and supported by directive principles. The Supreme Court of India found systematic failure by the government to implement and finance the various policies and arrangements in operation and ordered that Famine Codes be implemented for three months, and that 'Food-for-Work' schemes be strengthened through increased grain allocations and finances. The Court further ordered that the access of families below the poverty line to grain at the set price at ration shops be improved and that individuals without means of support (including older persons, widows, and disabled adults) be granted ration cards for free grain. Finally, state governments were ordered to implement the 'mid-day meal scheme' in schools on a progressive basis.[59]

Application of the 'Minimum Core' and the concept of 'meta-rights' as interpretative principles

Articles 26–29 of the Bill of Rights attached to the South African Constitution (1996) entrench a cluster of socio-economic rights essential for an adequate standard of living—including housing, access to health care, sufficient food and water, social security, and education.[60] The justiciability of these rights has been put beyond question by jurisprudence of the South African Constitutional Court, which has upheld claims for the violation of socio-economic rights in two landmark judgements—the first regarding the human right to housing, and the second regarding the human right to health.[61] These cases (discussed below) establish that resource constraints do not relieve the government of the positive obligations to fulfil socio-economic rights established in Articles 26–29 of the constitution by taking measures to eliminate or reduce the large areas of severe deprivation that afflict South Africa. However, the government is not required to go beyond available resources or to realize the rights immediately. Rather, the extent of the positive obligation on the state is delimited by three key elements: the obligation (*a*) to take reasonable legislative and other measures; (*b*) within available resources; (*c*) to achieve the progressive realization of the rights.

---

[59] Supreme Court of India, 2001, unreported, 2 May 2003; order of the Supreme Court as summarized in COHRE (2003: 24).

[60] The Constitution of the Republic of South Africa [Act 108 of 1996, www.concourt.gov.za.].

[61] See: Government of the Republic of South Africa, the Premier of the Province of the Western Cape, Cape Metropolitan Council, Oostenberg Municipality vs Grootboom and others, decided on 4 October 2000, Case CCT 1100 Constitutional Court of South Africa (subsequently 'Grootboom'); Minister of Health and others vs Treatment Action Campaign and others, decided on 5 July 2002, Case CCT 8 / 02. Available at: www.concourt.gov.za.

In developing its jurisprudence on this issue, the South African Court has recognized the importance of the concept of the 'Minimum Core' as a guiding principle for evaluating state compliance in the field of economic and social rights. The Court has reasoned, however, that this concept may be of relevance to the evaluation of the *reasonableness* of the actions taken by the South African state in relation to its constitutional obligations under Articles 26–29; the binding nature of resource constraints precluded the possibility of an application in terms of an immediate positive entitlement to goods and services.

[E]vidence in particular case may show that there is a minimum core of a particular service that should be taken into account in determining whether measures adopted by the state are reasonable.... [However] the socio-economic rights of the Constitution should not be construed as entitling everyone to demand that the minimum core be provided to them.... It is impossible to give everyone access even to a 'core' service immediately. All that is possible, and all that can be expected of the state, is that it act reasonably to provide access to...socio-economic rights...on a progressive basis.[62]

The Court has further reasoned that there are two counterbalancing elements to Articles 26–29: a first element recognizing the general right, and a second element establishing and delimiting the scope of the positive obligation imposed on the state. In weighing up these elements, the Court has reasoned that the state is not obliged to go beyond available resources or to realize the rights immediately. Rather, the state must act *reasonably* to ensure the progressive realization of these rights over time. This can involve (*d*) the adoption of a comprehensive policy or programme that is (*d*.1) is capable of facilitating the realization of the right in question and (*d*.2) makes appropriate provision for short, medium, and term needs. The Court has developed two central principles for evaluating the adequacy of the programmes and policies adopted by the South African government.

(1) First, the programmes and policies adopted must be capable of facilitating the realization of the right. Measures cannot leave out of account the degree and extent of the denial of the right they endeavour to realize, and a programme that excludes a significant segment of society cannot be said to be reasonable.

(2) Second, the programmes and policies adopted must make appropriate provision for short, medium, and term needs. Policies that do not take

---

[62] TAC 26–39; quotation TAC at paras. 34 and 35.

adequate account of immediate desperate and crisis needs cannot be said to be reasonable.[63]

In the cases referred to above, the policies and programmes adopted by the government failed to comply with these principles, and the government was held to be in violation of the positive obligations established in the constitution.

Interpretation of the human right to adequate housing

The Grootboom case concerned the alleged violation of the right to housing due to the forced the evictions of Mrs Grootboom and hundreds of people from the private land they were informally occupying, in extremely adverse conditions and without access to minimal basic services and sanitation, and the failure of the state to make adequate provision for the temporary relief for those in crisis situations and in desperate need. In considering this case, the South African Constitutional Court reasoned that, although the government had introduced a comprehensive programme aimed at meeting medium- and long-term housing development needs, there was a failure to make reasonable provision within available resources for the immediate needs of people who had no access to land and no roof over their heads and were living in intolerable conditions. 'Those whose needs are the most urgent' should not be ignored 'by the measures aimed at achieving realization of the right', and in order to be reasonable, a housing development programme should plan, budget, and monitor the fulfilment of immediate needs and the management of crisis. The policy adopted and in force in the Cape Metro fell short of the obligations imposed on the state by Section 26(2) of the South African Bill of Rights, in that it failed to provide for any form of relief to those desperately in need of access to shelter or housing. The Court ordered the state to provide a comprehensive, coordinated programme designed to meet its Section 26 obligations by realizing the right of access to adequate housing on a progressive basis within available resources. It stipulated that the programme should include reasonable measures to provide relief for people who have no access to land, no room over their heads and who are living in intolerable conditions or crisis situations.[64]

---

[63] Grootboom paras. 43 and 44; TAC para. 68.
[64] Grootboom paras. 41–4 / 52 / 65–9 / 95.

Box 5.4 JURISPRUDENCE OF SOUTH AFRICAN CONSTITUTIONAL COURT
(GOOTBROOM CASE)

'[H]undreds of thousands of people [are] living in deplorable conditions throughout the country. The Constitution obliges the state to act positively to ameliorate these conditions. The obligation is to provide access to housing, health-care, sufficient food and water, and social security to those unable to support themselves and their dependents.... Those in need have a corresponding right to demand that this be done'.

'[It] is an extremely difficult task for the state to meet these obligations in the conditions that prevail in our country. This is recognised by the Constitution which expressly provides that the state is not obliged to go beyond available resources or to realise these right immediately. ... [D]espite all these qualifications, these are rights, and the Constitution obliges the State to give effect to them. This is an obligation that Courts can and in appropriate circumstances, must enforce'.

Source: Grootboom Case paras. 93–5

Interpretation of the human right to adequate health care

The second case (the Treatment Action Campaign case) referred to above concerned the alleged violation of the right to health due to restricted access to essential medicines necessary to prevent mother-to-baby transmission of HIV in public hospitals and clinics. The Court recognized that the government had devised a programme and identified a drug (nepravine) for dealing with mother-to-baby HIV transmission. However, geographical restrictions on access to the drug in public sector hospitals meant that nepravine could not be prescribed where medically indicated in large areas of South Africa. The Court found that a programme that excludes a significant segment of society is not capable of facilitating the realization of the human right to health over time. The failure by the government to provide a comprehensive programme to prevent mother-to-child transmission of HIV was unreasonable and unconstitutional. The state was ordered to introduce a reasonable programme to ensure access to treatment to prevent mother-to-child transmission of HIV at public hospitals and clinics.[65]

Application of the concept of 'obligation of result'

The approach to evidentiary thresholds set out in Section 5.3 is also supported by the jurisprudence of the South African Constitutional

---

[65] TAC, especially 26–39, 67–95, 135.

Court, which has reasoned that '[t]he state is obliged to act to achieve the intended result' under Articles 26–29 of the Bill of Rights and that legislative measures 'will invariably have to be supported by appropriate, well-directed policies and programmes'. However, the 'reasonableness' threshold adopted by the Court suggests that, where resource constraints are binding, a violation *cannot* be inferred from the non-fulfilment of Articles 26–29 of the Bill of Rights per se. Rather, the state must act *reasonably* to ensure the progressive realization of these human rights over time, and this can involve the adoption of a comprehensive policy or programme that is capable of facilitating the realization of the rights on a progressive basis and that makes appropriate provision for short, medium, and term needs. Programmes or policies that exclude a significant segment of society, or that do not take adequate account of immediate crisis needs, cannot be said to be reasonable, and constitute a violation of the positive obligations established in Articles 26–29 of the constitution.[66]

Basic services, essential medicines and vaccines, and 'neglected diseases'

The growing body of case law in the field of economic and social rights also includes a number of other important cases relating to basic services, essential medicines and vaccines, and 'neglected diseases'. In another landmark decision relating to positive obligations in the field of economic and social rights, the African Commission on Human and People's Rights reasoned that the human right to health under Article 16 of the African Charter on Human and People's Rights established a positive obligation on Zaire in relation to the provision of basic services and medicines:

Article 16 of the African Charter states that every individual shall have the right to enjoy the best attainable state of physical and mental health, and that States Parties should take the necessary measures to protect the health of their people. The failure of the Government to provide basic services such as safe drinking water and electricity and the shortage of medicine ... constitutes a violation of Article 16.[67]

[66] See para. references in notes 38–41 above.
[67] Free Legal Assistance Group, Lawyers' Committee for Human Rights, Union Interafricaine des Droits de l'Homme, Les Témoins de Jehovah vs. Zaire, African Comm. Hum. & Peoples' Rights, Comm. No. 25/89, 47/90, 56/91, 100/93 (1995). Available at: http://www1.umn.edu/humanrts/africa/comcases/25-89_47-90_56-91_100-93.html.

In Argentina, in the Viceconte case, the courts ruled that the measures undertaken by the government to make available a vaccine against hemorrhagic fever were inadequate. The reasoning here referred to the fundamental right to life under the Argentine Constitution, as well as to the right to health under Article XI of the American Declaration of the Rights and Duties of Man, the right to essential medicine under Article 25 of the Universal Declaration, and the right to health under Article 12 of the ICESCR. Taking into account both the gravity of the disease and the large numbers of people affected (with 3.5 million people living in areas at risk from the disease), the court found that the government measures taken to protect the people at risk were inadequate. It ordered that the state manufacture a vaccine to protect from hemorrhagic fever and comply with its formal plans within a reasonable time schedule.[68]

The importance of special measures to protect children living in poverty

In the Case of the Guatemalan Street Children, the Inter-American Court of Human Rights considered the alleged violation of various articles of the American Convention on Human Rights including Article 4 (the Right to Life) resulting from the murder of five street children by National Police Force agents and of Article 19 (the Rights of the Child) because of the failure of the state to take special measures to protect children. Initial considerations of the case had emphasized the *jus cogens* nature of the right to life and the fact that it is the essential basis for the exercise of the other rights recognized in the American Convention. It had been suggested that compliance with Article 4 presumes not only that no person shall be deprived of his life arbitrarily (negative obligation), but also that the states should take all necessary measures to protect and preserve the right to life (positive obligation). In the case at hand, when the events took place, the 'street children' involved were the object of different types of persecution, including threats, harassment, torture, and murder. The Court reasoned that states parties are required under Article 4 to take measures not only to prevent and punish deprivation of life by criminal acts, but also to prevent arbitrary killing by their own security forces, and that Article 4 had indeed been violated. There were many complaints to which the state should have responded with effective investigations, prosecutions, and punishment; however, the state agents who were respon-

---

[68] Viceconte, Mariela Cecilia versus Argentinian Ministry of Health and Social Welfare, Poder Judicial de la Nación, Causa no 31.777/96, June 2, 1998, available via: http://www.escr-net.org.

Box 5.5 THE INTER-AMERICAN COURT OF HUMAN RIGHTS

'The right to life is a fundamental human right, and the exercise of this right is essential for the exercise of all other human rights. If it is not respected, all rights lack meaning. Owing to the fundamental nature of the right to life, restrictive approaches to it are inadmissible. In essence, the fundamental right to life includes, not only the right of every human being not to be deprived of his life arbitrarily, but also the right that he will not be prevented from having access to the conditions that guarantee a dignified existence. States have the obligation to guarantee the creation of the conditions required in order that violations of this basic right do not occur and, in particular, the duty to prevent its agents from violating it'

Source: The 'Street Children' case, para. 144.

---

sible were rarely investigated or convicted, giving rise to de facto impunity that allowed and encouraged the continuation of violations against the 'street children' and increased their vulnerability. The Court further reasoned that Guatemala had violated Article 19 (Rights of the Child). The Convention on the Rights of the Child together with Article 19 provide comprehensive international *corpus juris* regarding the importance of special measures of protection and assistance for the children, but such measures had not been taken.[69]

Protection from third party violations

The principle of state responsibility for third party violations of economic, social, and cultural rights is reflected in Guideline 18 of the Maastricht Guidelines, which stipulates that the obligation to protect includes the state's responsibility to ensure that private entities or individuals, including transnational corporations over which they exercise jurisdiction, do not deprive individuals of their economic, social, and cultural rights. States are responsible for violations of economic, social, and cultural rights that result from their failure to exercise due diligence in controlling the behaviour of such non-state actors. The application of these principles was taken forward in the Case of the Ogoni People, in which the African Commission on Human and People's Rights considered allegations that a former (military) government of Nigeria was guilty of violations of various rights under the African Charter due both to its direct involvement in oil production and by its failure to prevention violations by oil corporations

---

[69] Inter-American Court Of Human Rights, Villagran Morales et al. Case (The 'Street Children' case), Judgment Of November 19, 1999, especially articles 137–46, 195, available at: http://www.worldlii.org/int/cases/IACHR/1999/17.html.

in Ogoniland. The alleged violations related to the destruction, contamination, and despoilation of land, housing, villages, and crops and to other forms of violence and intimidation. The African Commission on Human and People's Rights applied the tripartite analysis of the nature and scope of state obligations in the field of human rights set out above and reasoned that the state had obligations to respect, protect, and promote the human rights of the Ogoni people. Building on the judgement in the Rodriguez Case, it reasoned that when a state allows private persons or groups to act freely and with impunity to the detriment of human rights, it would be in violation of the obligation to protect the human rights of its citizens. In particular, the obligation to protect 'entails on the State to take measures to protect beneficiaries of the protected rights against political, economic, and social interferences', and requires an effective framework of laws and regulations for protecting individuals against third party violations. In the case at hand, the Commission ruled that violations of several articles of the African Charter had occurred—both as a result of the direct actions of the government and security forces and as a result of the failure of the government to monitor the health and environmental impact of oil production and to prevent violations by non-state actors through an appropriate regulatory framework—including violations of the right to health (Article 16) and to a clean environment (Article 24). In addition, the government's treatment of the Ogonis—both through the direct action of state representatives, and as a consequence of its failure to take adequate measure to ensure protection from third party violations—was found to violate the obligations to respect, protect, and fulfil an 'implied' right to food.

'The government's treatment of the Ogonis has violated all three minimum duties of the right to food. The government has destroyed food sources through its security forces and State Oil Company; has allowed private oil companies to destroy food sources; and, through terror, has created significant obstacles to Ogoni communities trying to feed themselves'.[70]

---

[70] http://www1.umn.edu/humanrts/africa/comcases/155-96b.html. The Commission found Nigeria to be in violation of Article 2, 4, 14, 16, 18, 21, and 24 of the African Charter on Human and People's Rights. Quotations at paras. 47 and 69. The significance of this case was discussed in Chinkin (2003).

5.5 International Recognition of Collective Obligations in the Field of Global Poverty and Human Rights

A final way in which the international system for the protection and promotion of human rights, supported by international human rights law, can be viewed as reinforcing and supporting the 'capability approach' is by providing authoritative recognition of collective obligations of co-operation, assistance, and aid in the field of global poverty and human rights. Articles 55 and 56 of the Charter of the United Nations, together with Articles 2(1) and 23 of the ICESCR, establish international legal obligations in relation to international cooperation and assistance. The importance of collective obligations are reaffirmed in General Comment 3 of the UN CESCR on the nature and scope of international legal obligation under Article 2 of the ICESCR focuses international attention on the obligation of all states parties to take steps, 'individually and through international assistance and cooperation, especially economic and technical', towards the full realization of the rights recognized in the Covenant. Collective obligations are also set out to the interpretative framework set out in other General Comments. For example, General Comment 14 on the nature and scope of international legal obligation under Article 12 of the ICESCR, the human right to adequate health, emphasizes, *inter alia*, individual and joint obligations of governments relating to the control of disease, and the physical and economic accessibility and affordability of essential medicines. The provision of essential drugs (as defined by WHO) is recognized as a 'Minimal Core Obligation' for national governments, while other governments are recognized as having individual and joint obligations to promote access to essential health facilities, goods, and services in other countries; to ensure that the right to health is given due attention in international agreements; and to ensure that their actions as members of international organizations take due account of the right to health. The General Comment also stipulates that the UN specialized agencies, the World Bank, regional development banks, the IMF, and the WTO should cooperate effectively with states parties in these respects. Collective obligations are also central to the interpreting of the nature and scope of international legal obligation under the CRC. The framework of international cooperation is established in Article 4 of the Convention and in its interpretive statements; the UN Committee on the Rights of the Child has stipulated in its General Comments that when states ratify the CRC 'they take upon themselves obligations not only to implement it within their jurisdiction, but also to contribute, through international cooperation, to global implementation'. States are required to take actions to ensure the achievement of the rights 'to the maximum of available resources' and where necessary within the framework of international cooperation. The CRC has further emphasized that 'international cooperation' entails international development and financial cooperation, including international cooperation to support states in fulfilling their obligations under the Convention, and to ensure that international organizations including the World Bank, the IMF, and the WTO give primary consideration to the full implementation of the Convention.[71]

The Declaration on the Right to Development

Increased emphasis on the need for international cooperation to eliminate obstacles to the achievement of internationally recognized human rights is also central to the *Declaration on the Right to Development* adopted by the UNGA in 1986. Articles 3 and 4 of the Declaration of the Right to Development (RTD) stipulate that states have a duty to cooperate with each other in ensuring development and eliminating obstacles to development and recognize the obligation of states 'to take steps, individually and collectively, to formulate international development policies with a view to facilitating the full realization' of the RTD. The analysis of the nature and scope of these obligations by the UN Independent Expert on the RTD suggests that, although the primary duty-holders in the field of development and human rights are national states, the achievement of all human rights in developing countries cannot be ensured by national governments alone; other members of the international community (including other states and international organizations) also have duties to cooperate to achieve this objective. In taking this analysis forward, the Independent Expert characterizes international obligations in the field of development and human rights law in terms of (*a*) the 'primary obligations' of national states to adopt appropriately formulated development programmes that secure the progressive realization of internationally recognized human rights; (*b*) the 'contingent obligations' of other actors (including other states and international organizations) to support this process by eliminating 'obstacles' and cooperating in trade, debt, finance, technology transfer, and development assistance. Sengupta reasons that in situations of 'complex multilateral interdependence' the performance of human rights-based duties can be complemented by the actions performed by other

---

[71] CRC/GC/2003/5, paras. 1–12, 60–4.

agents (complementary actions) or negative linked (where the actions performed by one agent can be neutralized or 'blocked' not only by exogenous events, but also by the actions of another agent), and that strategic interactions of this type have particular resonance in the context of the protection and promotion of internationally recognized human rights under conditions of globalization (Sengupta 2004*b*). Proposals for 'Development Compacts' (in Sengupta 1999: 65–80; 2000: 68–9; 2001: 44–6; 2002*a*: 880–9; 2002*b*: 42–74; 2002*c*; 2004*a*) reflect the need for an enhanced international mechanism that coordinates the actions of the various obligation holders in the field of development and human rights (national states, other states, international organizations, etc.) and ensures effective bilateral and multilateral cooperation in multiparty situations where the internationally recognized human rights cannot be guaranteed by single agents acting alone (and where cooperation may be required to achieve the complete realization of a human right). Whereas the United Nations Human Rights Treaty bodies monitor the rights contained in the respective human rights instruments on a country-by-country basis, 'Development Compacts' would provide an institutional mechanism that reflects the characterization of international human rights law in terms of a complex system of interdependent and indivisible duties that takes account of (*a*) the primary duties of national states and (*b*) the contingent duties of other actors (including other states and international organizations).

The analysis of 'structural obstacles'

Although the jurisprudence of the Committee has not directly addressed the question of the financial and material preconditions for the full achievement of economic, social, and cultural rights, the Committee has required states parties to report on all obstacles to the achievement of these rights,[72] and the identification of specific obstacles that can impede their full achievement has been an important element of the Committee's analytical and fact-finding framework. In its consideration of Country Reports, the Committee has highlighted the importance of specific obstacles—including as resource constraints, significant foreign debt, economic transition, and structural adjustment can restrict progress in

[72] CESCR, 'Revised general guidelines regarding the form and contents of report to be submitted by states parties under Articles 16 and 17 of the International Covenant on Economic, Social, and Cultural Rights' ('Reporting Guidelines'), UN Doc. E/C.12/1991/1.

achieving the full realization of economic, social, and cultural rights. For example, the Committee has also taken note of difficulties—'notably the foreign debt problem'[73]—in Ecuador; of structural factors such as '... considerable foreign indebtedness' in Mexico;[74] and of '...economic factors...such as external debt servicing...' in Senegal.[75] It has also expressed 'serious concern' for the 'negative consequences' of structural adjustment measures and the privatization of state property for the enjoyment of economic, social, and cultural rights in Nicaragua,[76] and has noted the 'particular obstacles faced by the transition economies in Eastern Europe in realizing economic, social, and cultural rights'.[77] Authoritative international fact-finding on the identification of obstacles to the achievement of economic, social, and cultural rights has also been undertaken by UN Independent Experts in relation to extreme poverty,[78] national and international income inequality,[79] and country level external debt.[80]

---

[73] UN Doc. E/1991/23 paras. 130–58.   [74] UN Doc. E/C.12/1993/16 at 5.

[75] UN Doc. E/C.12/1993/18 at 5.   [76] UN Doc. E/C.12/1993/14 at 6.

[77] 'Declaration on the Right to Development', Adopted by UN GA Resolution 41/128 of 4 December 1986.

[78] For example, 'Human Rights and Extreme Poverty', UN Docs. A/RES/51/97, A/RES/53/146; 'Human Rights and Extreme Poverty', UN Docs. E/CN.4/RES/1994/12, 1995/16, 1996/10, 1997/11, 1998/25, 1999/26, 2000/12; 'Human Rights and Extreme Poverty', UN Docs. E/CN.4/SUB.2/RES/ 1994/41, 1995/28, 1996/23; 'Second interim report on human rights and extreme poverty prepared by the Special Rapporteur, Mr. Leandro Despouy', UN Doc. E/CN.4/Sub.2/1995/15; 'Report(s) of the Special Rapporteur on human rights and extreme poverty', UN Doc. E/CN.4/Sub.2/1995/14, E/CN.4/ Sub.2/1996/13; 'Report of the seminar on extreme poverty and the denial of human rights', UN Doc. E/CN.4/1995/101

[79] For example, 'Human Rights and Income Distribution', UN Docs. E/CN.4/RES/1994/40, E/CN.4/ RES/1995/30, and E/CN.4/RES/1996/26; 'Report of the Special Rapporteur on the Relationship Between the Enjoyment of Human Rights, In Particular Economic, Social, and Cultural Rights, and Income Distribution', UN Doc. E/CN.4/Sub.2/1996/14; 'Final report prepared by the Special Rapporteur on the Relationship Between the Enjoyment of Human rights, in Particular Economic, Social, and Cultural Rights, and Income Distribution', UN Doc. E/CN.4/Sub.2/1997/9; 'Human rights and income distribution', UN Doc. E/CN.4/Sub.2/RES/1996/26.

[80] For example, 'Effects on the full enjoyment of human rights of the economic adjustment policies arising from foreign debt, in particular, on the implementation of the Declaration on the Right to Development', UN Doc. E/CN.4/RES/1997/10; 'Question of the realization in all countries of the economic, social, and cultural rights', UN Doc. E/CN.4/RES/1997/17; 'Effects on the full enjoyment of human rights of the economic adjustment policies arising from foreign debt and, in particular, on the implementation of the Declaration on the Right to Development', UN Doc. E/ CN.4/RES/1996/12; 'Effects on the full enjoyment of human rights of the economic adjustment policies arising from foreign debt and, in particular, of the implementation of the Declaration on the Right to Development', UN Doc. E/CN.4/RES/1995/13; 'Effects on the full enjoyment of human rights of structural adjustment programmes', UN Doc. E/CN.4/Sub.2/RES/1995/32; 'The realization of economic, social, and cultural rights', UN Doc. E/CN.4/Sub.2/RES/1996/25.

The human rights impact of international economic and financial arrangements

The human rights impact of international economic and financial arrangements including trade arrangements and rules, agricultural subsidies, international arrangements, and the global development architecture have come under increased scrutiny in recent years. The OHCHR together with human rights campaigning organizations have helped to focus international attention on the impact of agricultural subsidies on the human right to achieve an adequate standard of living in countries in West and Central Africa, including the impact of cotton subsidies in the European Union, China, and America on cotton producing countries such as Benin, Mali, and Burkina Faso (e.g. EGI 2004). Another example relates to campaigns around the impact of intellectual property rights on the accessibility of essential medicines. For example, in interpreting the individual and joint obligations in relation to the progressive realization of the human right to health and the availability of essential medicines, Robinson suggests that 'access to medication in the context of pandemics such as HIV/AIDS, malaria, tuberculosis' is fundamental to the progressive realization of the human right to health, and that accessibility—geographically, economically, and on the basis of non-discrimination—implies that essential medicines should be available in adequate numbers in countries where there is a need. However, the achievement of this objective is limited both by the nature of international trading rules embodied in WTO agreements (including the rules relating to intellectual property rights embodied in 'TRIPS') and by the failure of research and development to address the needs of those living in poverty (for example, by making new drugs available for the treatment of 'neglected diseases'). Emerging advocacy strategies in this area are emphasizing, in addition to the human right to health recognized in Article 14 of the ICESCR and accepted by 153 countries, the right to share in the benefits of scientific progress and its applications (including the right to share in the benefits of medical research and its applications) under Article 15 (Robinson 2004: 3–4). Recent legal and policy developments in these areas include modifications in WTO rules relating to the export of generic drugs; out-of-court settlements in South Africa between private companies and the Treatment Action Campaign in cases relating to the production and import of cheap generic versions of patented antiretroviral drugs; and new international policy proposals aimed at increasing access to essential vaccines.

The World Bank Inspection Panel

The World Bank Inspection Panel provides a strengthened mechanism for ensuring Bank accountability in relation to its compliance with Bank operational guidelines rather than directly focusing on human rights monitoring. Nevertheless, a number of the cases that come before the Inspection Panel raise important issues relating to social and human rights impact of Bank programs. For example, in 1999, the Inspection Panel found that budget cuts to a social protection program in Argentina would have harmed the intended beneficiaries—the absolute poor—and that Bank supervision and monitoring of social protection measures accompanying structural adjustment agreements (including programs in the areas of food and nutrition, disease control, emergency employment, education, and support for vulnerable groups) had been inadequate. The case concerned the Pro-Huerta Program which had been officially listed as a social protection programme in the structural adjustment agreement between Argentina and the Bank, and which provided nutritional support to people classified as having basic needs unsatisfied by assisting them to produce food for their own consumption. The Inspection Panel ruled that although Loan Agreements did not stipulate how budgetary allocations for social programmes should be specifically allocated between the various social programmes officially listed in structural adjustment agreements; the Bank's supervision and monitoring of compliance activities appeared to have been limited to reviewing the amounts allocated in the federal budget to social programmes, with no attempt to contact the executing agency or programme beneficiaries to ascertain whether proposed budgetary allocations were sufficient to sustain programmes through the fiscal year. There had therefore been a failure to recognize the implications of proposed budgetary allocations to the Pro-Huerta Program, which the Inspection Panel found would have reduced the number of beneficiaries and eventually forced the termination of the Program's activities.[81]

Establishing the responsibilities of the international development organizations in the field of human rights

The Maastricht Guidelines place particular emphasis on establishing the human rights responsibilities of the international development organizations. Maastricht Guideline 19 establishes that the obligations of states to protect economic, social, and cultural rights extend also to their partici-

---

[81] World Bank Inspection Panel 1999 (especially paras. 3, 5, 7, 8, 23, 26), analysed in COHRE (2004: 171–5).

pation in international organizations, where they act collectively. According to this Guideline, it is particularly important for states to use their influence to 'ensure that violations do not result from the programmes and policies of the organizations of which they are members' and '(i)t is crucial for the elimination of violations of economic, social and cultural rights for international organizations, including international financial institutions, to correct their policies and practices so that they do not result in deprivation of economic, social and cultural rights'. Member states of such organizations, individually or through the governing bodies, as well as the secretariat and NGOs, are required under Maastricht Guideline 19 to 'encourage and generalize the trend of several such organizations to revise their policies and programmes to take into account issues of economic, social and cultural rights'

The international human rights framework and 'poverty reduction strategy papers'

The OHCHR (2002, 2004) emphasizes the importance of integrating international human rights standards into the Poverty Reduction Strategy Papers (PRPS), accompanying agreements between national states and international development organizations including the World Bank and the IMF. The international human rights framework provides the appropriate legal framework in which PRSP should be drawn up and establishes the relevance of the principles of accountability, participation, and non-discrimination to the development and implementation of PRPS. In addition, OHCHR (ibid.) suggests that the application of the 'Minimum Core Obligations' concept of the minimum core establishes two key principles in relation to PRSP. First, the 'Minimum Core Obligations' approach establishes core obligations of states relating to minimum and essential levels of various rights including food, health protection, education, and housing, and for states to ensure that all individuals within their jurisdiction are free from starvation. OHCHR (2004: 26) suggests that if a poverty reduction strategy does not reflect these core obligations, it is legally inconsistent with the binding obligations of states under international human rights law. Second, when grouped together, the 'Minimum Core Obligations' establish an 'international minimum threshold'. OHCHR (2004: 27) suggests that it is incumbent on states and international organizations in a position to help to provide international assistance and cooperation to enable developing states to fulfil their core obligations and reach the minimum international threshold.

Conclusion

This chapter analysed the emergence of a body of legally binding international standards in the field of global poverty and human rights. It aimed to establish the ways in which Sen's development of the 'capability perspective' in ethics and economics might be reinforced and supported through the embryonic and underdeveloped—but nevertheless widening and deepening—body of international standards in the field of global poverty and human rights. Although the 'capability approach' does not require or entail linkages with the actual system of international human rights law, eight key correspondences between the 'capability approach' and authoritative international standards in the field of global poverty and human rights have been identified. In Chapter 7, the ways in which these complementary and reinforcing elements provide the basis of cross-disciplinary 'Working Models' of international accountability and responsibility in the field of global poverty and human rights will be discussed. Before this, however, Chapter 6 turns to the analysis of the idea of 'freedom from poverty as a basic human right' using systems of formal logic.

6

Freedom From Poverty as a Basic Human Right: Formal Analysis Using Deontic Logic

This chapter is concerned with the formal analysis of the idea of freedom from poverty as a basic human right. It explores how formal analysis can crystallize broader conceptual debates about poverty and human rights (absolute versus non-absolute human rights, negative versus positive correlative obligations, conditions of violation versus conditions of fulfilment, etc.) and take these debates to a more rigorous level. The chapter contributes to a broader project aiming at the development of an integrated interdisciplinary framework linking the ongoing research programme on the formal representation of freedoms and rights in welfare economics and social choice with a broader range of rights-types (including ideas about fundamental human rights incorporated into international human rights law, jurisprudence, and moral philosophy) and with logical frameworks concerned with the formal analysis of these ideas.

The discussion in this chapter is aimed at (*a*) identification of an appropriate analytical framework for capturing and formalizing the idea of human rights; (*b*) expansion of this framework to take account of the idea of freedom from poverty as a basic human right. Section 6.1 establishes the rationale of a research programme aimed at the development of the formal representation of human rights. Section 6.2 considers work by Kanger (1971, 1972, 1985; and with Kanger, H. 1966) to develop a logical system aimed at the formal representation of all 'rights-types' that are possible, and to establish all of the human rights in the Universal Declaration as 'valid' rules of rights within the bounds of this system (Kanger, II. 1984 and Kanger 1985). Building on the classic distinctions between basic or fundamental rights-types set out in Hofeld (1925 [1919]), this important work has recently been revived in the literature (especially in Van Hees (1995, 1996)) and provides an appropriate starting point for the analysis of the formal representation of human rights. Section 6.3 discusses various attempts to refine and expand the Kanger System. In Section 6.4, it is argued that the proposals for the formal representation of human rights in H. Kanger (1984) fail to capture and formalize widely accepted ethical and legal language expressions of the idea of human rights. Various proposals for moving forward are discussed. These improve on past approaches by building on Sen's concepts of 'capability-rights' and 'meta-rights' and by capturing and formalizing some of the internationally recognized standards discussed in Chapter 5 (which establish a common element of 'claim' as well as a common element of 'immunity' in the field of global poverty and human rights).

6.1 The Need for a Research Programme on the Formal Representation of Human Rights

Formal thinking about human rights (and the obligations on governments and other actors that flow from these rights) is in relative infancy. As the discussion in Chapter 4 showed, in extending the formal representation of freedoms and rights in welfare economics and social choice, an important challenge is to move away from the former emphasis on individual liberty, and to incorporate a broader range of the types of rights and obligations that arise in moral and legal discourse. Past approaches have been limited in this respect and important 'rights-types'—including the idea of human rights—have been neglected.

In their formal models, social choice theorists have so far only embodied a very limited conception of rights. Human rights and the rights of the citizen, as usually understood, and especially the degree to which those rights are respected, should be included within the description of a social state—as should other conceptions of rights which have been discussed by philosophers and jurists, though they have been largely ignored by economists and social choice theorists. (Hammond 1998: 115)

The need for a research programme aimed at the incorporation of the formal language of deontic logic—the formal logic of obligations and permissions—into the mathematical structures of welfare economics and social choice has been highlighted in this context. For example, Brunel and Salles (1998) highlight the need to develop a more systematic approach to the incorporation of a full range of the types of rights and duties that arise in moral and legal discourse—including the possibility of the development of a complete typology of rights-types—and raise the need for a research programme on deontic logic in this context:

[A] lot of work remains to be done on the definition of rights and social states. ... [W]e need to base our future technical work on the most recent findings of logicians. (Brunel and Salles 1998: 109)

The 'Kanger System' provides a useful starting point for taking forward this work. Building on Hohfeld's (1925 [1919]) Fundamental Legal Conceptions, this System (comprising the results in Kanger (1971, 1972, 1985; and in Kanger and Kanger, H. 1966) aims to capture and formalize all possible rights-types and the interrelationships between them using a combination of action logic and deontic logic. As well as Kanger's pioneering contributions, the basic framework has been interpreted, criticized, and further developed by Lindahl (1977, 1994); Makinson (1986); Van Hees (1995, 1996); and applied to the characterization of the human rights in the Universal Declaration by Kanger, H. (1984). Van Hees (1995, 1996) has moved the research programme forward by forging links between the Kanger-Framework and the models of individual rights being developed in welfare economics and social choice. Whereas in the past formal treatments have failed to provide 'a systematic account and categorization of different types of right', Van Hees develops proposals for incorporating Kanger's 'rights-types' into game-theoretic models and for 'translating' these 'rights-types' into their game-theoretic equivalents—thus providing a basis for precise game-theoretic characterizations of different rights-types.

6.2 Formal Representation of Human Rights using the Kanger System

The starting point for the development of the Kanger System is the distinction between a *right*, on the one hand, and a *type of right* (a rights-type) on the other. Whereas a *right*, can be characterized as a two-place relation between an agent (x) and an agent (y), Kanger and Kanger characterize a *type of right* as a three-place relation between an agent (x), another agent (y), and a state of affairs involving x and y [$S(x,y)$]. The agents x and y could be individuals, states, governments, and so on, whilst the characterization of states of affairs is not restricted to actions (as in other approaches) and can be any type of condition. The *type* of relation could involve, for example, a relation between two individuals such that x receives from y what x has lent to y, or a relation between an individual and a state, involving the state of affairs that the individual is not tortured by the state (Lindahl 1977). Kanger and Kanger then build up a list of possible rights-types based on the classic distinctions set out in Hohfeld (1925 [1919]): 5).[1] Hohfeld's scheme (summarized in Box 6.1 below) is based on the identification of four categories of basic rights-types (claim, liberty, power, and immunity) and the analysis of legal relationships involving these basic rights-types in terms of the position of each of two parties (agent x and agent y) and two logical operators (correlation and negation).[2] The Kanger System captures and formalizes eight 'simple' rights-types comprising the four basic rights-types identified in Hohfeld (1925) (claims, liberties, powers, and immunities) and their negations or opposites (counterclaim, counterliberty, counterpower, and counterimmunity). The eight simple rights-types are explicated using the action operator Do and the deontoic operator $Shall$ using formal semantics and rules of logical validity developed in Kanger (1971, 1972, 1985) and Kanger and Kanger, H. (1966) and analysed in detail in Lindahl (1977, 1994) and Van Hees (1995). Summaries of the deontic operators involved and of the explication of the eight 'simple' rights-types are given in Boxes 6.2 and 6.3.

The list of possible rights-types

Kanger and Kanger finally exploit the rules of logical consequence and consistency to build up a complete specification of all of the complex

---

[1] Although the origins of formal thinking about rights and duties are generally traced back to Bentham and Austin, Hohfeld's (1925 [1919]) pioneering scheme for analysing and classifying different forms of jural relationships is widely invoked as providing the foundations of modern analytical jurisprudence. Having completed an extensive survey of judicial precedents, Hohfeld proposed that the widespread use of a single category (that of *legal right*) to classify a wide range of jural situations resulted in ambiguity and confusion in legal theory and practice, and that the term *legal right* is in practice used to signify not *one* but *eight* analytically distinct jural categories (*rights, duties, privileges, no-rights, powers, disabilities, immunities, and liabilities*). This abstraction from legal practice provides the foundations of the logical analysis of rights-types. For analyses, criticisms, and applications of the basic Hohfeld framework, see Freeman (1994: 392–87); Jones (1994); Hart (1982) and Lindahl (1977); Van Hees (1995,1996).

[2] Hohfeld's analysis suggests a further distinction between jural relations *in personam* (or 'paucital' relations) and jural relations *in rem* (or 'multital' relations) (Hohfeld 1925: 67; Jones 1994: 17). Focusing on the reciprocal categories of claim-rights and duties, a claim-right *in personam* is a unique claim-right residing in a specific agent (X) and entails a reciprocal duty that resides in a determinate agent (Y). In contrast, a claim-right *in rem* is a claim-right that resides in an agent (X) but which entails a reciprocal duty that resides in a large or indefinite class of people. For example, if X has purchased a property (P) from Y, then X has a paucital right, or a right *in personam*, to P, and Y has a reciprocal duty to transfer the ownership of P to X. In contrast, if agent X owns a property (P), then X has a multital right, or a right *in rem*, to P, and a reciprocal duty resides in an indefinite class of people (the class of people 'not P') not to enter the P.

Box 6.1	HOHFELD'S BASIC 'RIGHTS-TYPES' AND THEIR LOGICAL INTERRELATIONSHIPS			
Rights-type (relationship involving *x* and *y*, expressed from the position of *x*)	**Right/claim**	**Privilege/liberty/ freedom**	**Power/ empowerment**	**Immunity/ exemption**
Intuition	claim of *x* against *y* with respect to *z*	*x* is not subject to a claim by *y* with respect to *z*	*x* is empowered to alter the relationship between *x* and *y* with respect to *z*	exemption of *x* from the power of *y* with respect to *x*
Example	*x* has a claim that *y* pays *x* £100	*x* is not under a duty not to walk along the path adjacent to *y*'s land	*x* is empowered to sell a house to *y*	*x* is exempt from the power of *y* to intervene in *x*'s private life
Correlative rights-type (expressed from the position of *y*)I	**Duty**	**No right/no claim**	**Liability**	**Disability/ disempower- ment**
Intuition	*y* has a duty in relation to *x* with respect to *z*	*y* does not have a claim against *x* with respect to *z*	*y* is subject to the power of *x* with respect to *z*	*y* has a disability in relation to *x* with respect to *z*
Example	*y* has a duty to pay *x* £100	*y* does not have a claim that *x* refrains from walking along the path adjacent to *y*'s land	*y* is subject to the power of *x* with respect to the sale of a house by *x* to *y*	*y* is disempowered from intervening in *x*'s private life
Opposite rights-type	**No right**	**Duty**	**Disability**	**Liability**

combinations of rights-types that are logically possible. Given the explication of the eight simple rights-types in the Kanger System and certain logical postulates, Kanger and Kanger establish logical interrelationships between different rights-types including opposites, synonyms, and correlatives (Box 6.4) and interrelationships of logical consequence (Box 6.5). Kanger and Kanger then exploit these logical interrelationships in building up the list of the complex combinations of the eight simple rights types that are in logical terms possible. Some rights-propositions are demonstrated to be valid or invalid and others to be the logical consequence of others. For example, if *x* has versus *y* a right of type *claim* in relation to the

---

Box 6.2   THE DEONTIC OPERATORS

$x,y,z, \ldots$	Agents (e.g. individuals/states/governments)
$S(x,y)$	State of affairs involving x and y
$\sim$	Negation
$\rightarrow$	Logical consequence

Deontic operator 'Shall': permissions/obligations
Operates over $S(x,y)$
Shall operator: 'It shall be the case that'
May operator: 'It may be the case that'

[Where Shall and May are interdefinable in accordance with the scheme: May=not-Shall-not; hence: 'it may be the case that' implies 'not: it shall be the case that not']

Action operator 'Do': doing/seeing to it
Operates over an ordered pair [agent x or agent y and $S(x,y)$]
Do-operator: 'Sees to it'

Examples
Shall Do $[x, S(x,y)]$:   'it shall be the case that x sees to it that $S(x,y)$'
May Do $[y, S(x,y)]$:   'it may be the case that y sees to it that $S(x,y)$'
Shall $\sim$Do $[x, S(x,y)]$:   'it shall be the case that x does not see to it that $S(x,y)$'
Shall $\sim$Do $[x, \sim S(x,y)]$: 'it shall be the case that x does not see to it that not $S(x,y)$'

Source: Kanger and Kanger (1966); Lindahl (1977)

---

state of affairs $S(x,y)$, then, as a logical consequence of this relationship, x also has an immunity in relation to the state of affairs $S(x,y)$. Kanger and Kanger's (1966) proof establishes that the 256 logically possible complex combinations of rights-types reduces to exactly twenty-six possible complete rights-types (where completeness implies that in logical terms any additional specification in terms of the eight simple types of rights is either inconsistent or unnecessary). These twenty-six are listed in Box 6.6.[3]

Formal representation of human rights

Kanger (1985) and H. Kanger (1984) establish that all the human rights in the Universal Declaration can be captured and formalized as logically valid rules of right using the Kanger System. The Kanger System is intended to provide for the logical representation of all possible rights-types

---

[3] The proof begins by listing the conjunctions of the eight simple rights-types and proceeds by specifying the rights-types obtained by the negation of one or more element of this list. This generates 256 (twenty-eight) lists in total. Given the logical rules of the system (consequence, consistency, etc.) many of the 256 can be demonstrated either to be contradictory or to have elements that are unnecessary. Kanger and Kanger demonstrate that once these have been eliminated there remain twenty-six contradiction-free 'reduced' lists (or 'atomic' rights-types). Following a proposal by Makinson (1986: 404–5), each of the twenty-six can be conceptualized as a 'maxiconjunction'—that is, as a maximal consistent conjunction of the (finitely many) expressions covered by the Kanger system.

Box 6.3 THE EIGHT 'SIMPLE' RIGHTS-TYPES

Type of rights-relation	The four simple rights-types				Countertypes or opposites of the four simple types of rights (obtained by *negating* the state of affairs (or S-condition))			
	T1 Claim $[x,y,S(x,y)]$	**T2 Freedom** $[x,y,S(x,y)]$	**T3 Power** $[x,y,S(x,y)]$	**T4 Immunity** $[x,y,S(x,y)]$	**T5 Counterclaim** $[x,y,S(x,y)]$	**T6 Counterfreedom** $[x,y,S(x,y)]$	**T7 Counterpower** $[x,y,S(x,y)]$	**T7 Counter-immunity** $[x,y,S(x,y)]$
Expression of rights-relation	Agent x is said to have a claim in relation to agent y with respect to the state of affairs $S(x,y)$ iff:	Agent x is said to have a freedom in relation to agent y with respect to $S(x,y)$ iff:	Agent x is said to have a power in relation to agent y with respect to $S(x,y)$ iff:	Agent x is said to have an immunity in relation to agent y with respect to $S(x,y)$ iff:	Agent x is said to have a counterclaim in relation to agent y with respect to not $S(x,y)$ iff:	Agent x is said to have a counterfreedom in relation to agent y with respect to not $S(x,y)$ iff:	Agent x is said to have a counterpower in relation to agent y with respect to not $S(x,y)$ iff:	Agent x is said to have a counterimmunity in relation to agent y with respect to not $S(x,y)$ iff:
Explication of rights-relation	It shall be the case that/y sees to it that/$S(x,y)$.	It shall not be the case that/x sees to it that/not $S(x,y)$.	It shall not be the case that/x does not see to it that $S(x,y)$. Alternatively: It may be the case that/x sees to it that/$S(x,y)$	It shall be the case that/y does not see to it that/not $S(x,y)$.	It shall be the case that/y sees to it that/not $S(x,y)$.	It shall not be the case that/x sees to it that/$S(x,y)$.	It shall not be the case that/x does not see to it that/not $S(x,y)$.	It shall be the case that/y does not see to it that/$S(x,y)$.
Formula of rights-relation	Shall Do $[y, S(x,y)]$	$\sim$ Shall Do $[x, \sim S (x,y)]$	$\sim$ Shall $\sim$ Do $[x,S(x,y)]$ Alternatively: May Do $[x,S(x,y)]$	Shall $\sim$ Do $[y, \sim S (x,y)]$	Shall Do $[y, \sim S(x,y)]$	$\sim$ Shall Do $[x, \sim S(x,y)]$	$\sim$ Shall $\sim$ Do $[x, \sim S(x,y)]$ Alternatively: May Do $[x, \sim S(x,y)]$	Shall $\sim$ Do $[y, S(x,y)]$
Interpretation	y has an obligation to see to it that $S(x,y)$	x does not have an obligation to see to it that not $S(x,y)$	x does not have an obligation to refrain from seeing to it that $S(x,y)$ Alternatively: x may see to it that $[S(x,y)]$	y has an obligation to refrain from seeing to it that not $S(x,y)$	y has an obligation to see to it that $S(x,y)$	x does not have an obligation to see to it that not $S(x,y)$	x does not have an obligation to refrain from seeing to it that not $S(x,y)$ Alternatively: x may see to it that not $S(x,y)$	y has an obligation to refrain from seeing to it that $S(x,y)$

Source: Based on explications in Kanger and Kanger (1966); Lindahl (1977, 1994)

Box 6.4 INTERRELATIONSHIPS BETWEEN 'RIGHTS-TYPES': (A) OPPOSITES, SYNONYMS, AND CORRELATIVES

Opposite rights-types (counter-rights)

Rights-type [x,y,S(x,y)]
Counter-right [x,y,~S(x,y)]

	Claim / Counterclaim	Freedom / Counterfreedom	Power / Counterpower	Immunity / Counterimmunity

Synonym-pairs (rights-types with the same meaning)

	Claim Counterclaim	Freedom Counterfreedom	Power Counterpower	Immunity Counterimmunity
Rights-relation	x has versus y a claim that not S(x,y)	x has versus y a freedom that not S(x,y)	x has versus y a power that not S(x,y)	x has versus y an immunity that not S(x,y)
Synonym-pair	x has versus y a counterclaim that S(x,y)	x has versus y a counterfreedom that S(x,y)	x has versus y a counterpower that S(x,y)	x has versus y a counterimmunity that S(x,y)

Correlative rights-types (defined in relation to the position of agent x and the position of agent y)

Type of rights-relation expressed from the position of x	Claim [x,y,S(x,y)]	Freedom [x,y,S(x,y)]	Power [x,y,S(x,y)]	Immunity [x,y,S(x,y)]	Counter claim [x,y,S(x,y)]	Counter freedom [x,y,S(x,y)]	Counter power [x,y,S(x,y)]	Counter immunity [x,y,S(x,y)]
Formula of rights-relation, expressed from the position of x [x,y,S(x,y)]	Shall Do [y, S(x,y)]	~ Shall Do [x, ~ S(x,y)]	~ Shall ~ Do [x, S(x,y)]	Shall ~ Do [y, ~ S(x,y)]	Shall Do [y, ~ S(x,y)]	~ Shall Do [x,S(x,y)]	~ Shall ~ Do [x, ~ S(x,y)] Alternatively: May Do [x, ~ S(x,y)]	Shall ~ Do [y,S(x,y)]
Formula of permutation of rights-relation expressed from the position of y [y,x,S(x,y)]	Shall Do [x, S(x,y)]	~ Shall Do [y, ~ S(x,y)]	~ Shall ~ Do [y, S(x,y)]	Shall ~ Do [x, ~ S(x,y)]	Shall Do [x, ~ S(x,y)]	~ Shall Do [y,S(x,y)]	~ Shall ~ Do [y, S(x,y)] Alternatively: May Do [x, ~ S(x,y)]	Shall ~ Do [x,S(x,y)]
Correlative type of rights-relation expressed from the position of y	Not counter freedom [y,x,S(x,y)]	Not counter claim [y,x,S(x,y)]	Not counter immunity [y,x,S(x,y)]	Not counter power [y,x,S(x,y)]	Not freedom [y,x,S(x,y)]	Not claim [y,x,S(x,y)]	Not immunity [y,x,S(x,y)]	Not power [y,x,S(x,y)]

Source: Based on explications in Kanger and Kanger (1966); Lindahl (1977, 1994)

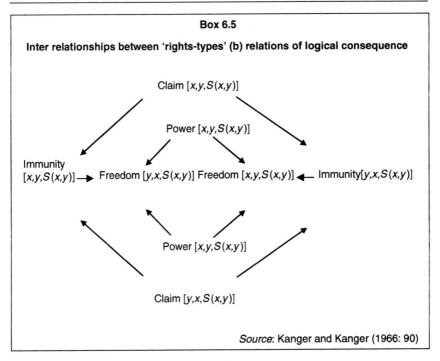

Box 6.5

Inter relationships between 'rights-types' (b) relations of logical consequence

Claim [x,y,S(x,y)]

Power [x,y,S(x,y)]

Immunity [x,y,S(x,y)] → Freedom [y,x,S(x,y)]   Freedom [x,y,S(x,y)] ← Immunity[y,x,S(x,y)]

Power [x,y,S(x,y)]

Claim [y,x,S(x,y)]

Source: Kanger and Kanger (1966: 90)

and therefore, a basis for establishing the validity or non-validity of rights–based claims. Given these arguments, Kanger illustrates the logical validity of human rights by capturing and formalizing Article 13.2 of the UN Declaration of Human Rights (1985: 72–3) as a valid rule of right. This Article states that '[e]veryone has the right to leave any country, including his own, and to return to his country'. Although this right expresses more than one right-relation, Kanger focused on the right of an individual to leave his or her country, which—according to Kanger's interpretation—implies that everyone has, in relation to the authorities of his or her country, both a *power* and an *immunity* to leave the country. Kanger derives the following rule from this right: 'Rule (A): For each individual x and state y, such that x is a normal non-criminal adult citizen of y residing in y, x has to y a rights-relation of the type power and immunity with respect to S (x, y), and also with respect to non-$S(x, y)$, where $S(x,y)$ is the state of affairs that x leaves the territory of y'. Given this interpretation of Article 13.2, Kanger reasons that the atomic rights relating to this right are sufficiently specified by the following conjunctions of formulas:

$$\sim Shall \sim Do[x,S(xy)]$$

$$Shall \sim Do[y, \sim S(x,y)]$$

203

Box 6.6 THE TWENTY-SIX 'ATOMIC' RIGHTS-TYPES

1. Power, not immunity, counterpower, not counterimmunity
2. Not power, immunity, not counterpower, counterimmunity
3. Claim, not counterfreedom
4. Not claim, power, immunity, counterfreedom, not counterpower, not counterimmunity.
5. Power, immunity, counterpower, counterimmunity
6. Claim, power, counterfreedom
7. Claim, not power
8. Power, immunity, counterfreedom, not counterpower, counterimmunity
9. Power, immunity, counterpower, not counterimmunity
10. Power, not immunity, not counterpower, counterimmunity
11. Not freedom, counterclaim
12. Freedom, not power, not immunity, not counterclaim, counterpower, counterimmunity
13. Freedom, counterclaim, counterpower
14. Counterclaim, not counterpower
15. Freedom, not power, immunity, counterpower, counterimmunity
16. Power, not immunity, counterpower, counterimmunity
17. Not power, immunity, counterpower, not counterimmunity
18. Not power, not immunity, not counterpower, not counterimmunity
19. Not claim, not counterfreedom, not counterimmunity
20. Not counterfreedom, counterimmunity
21. Not claim, not power, immunity, not counterpower, not counterimmunity
22. Power, not immunity, not counterpower, not counterimmunity
23. Not freedom, not immunity, not counterclaim
24. Not freedom, immunity
25. Not power, not immunity, not counterclaim, not counterpower, counterimmunity
26. Not power, not immunity, counterpower, not counterimmunity

Source: Kanger and Kanger (1966: 93)

$$\sim \text{Shall} \sim \text{Do}[x, \sim S(x,y)]$$

$$\text{Shall} \sim \text{Do}[y,S(x,y)]$$

This approach is systematically applied to the classification of the entire range of human rights recognized in the Universal Declaration by H. Kanger (1984). Her basic methodology entails the (*a*) interpretation of the nature and scope of the human right in question; and (*b*) capturing and formalizing human rights in terms of the categories 'claim', 'liberty', 'power', 'immunity', and in terms of complex combinations of these categories. The proposed classifications are summarized in Table 6.1 and imply that the human rights in the Universal Declaration fall within the reach of five key rights-types (Types 3, 6, 4, 5, and 9). H. Kanger then

Table 6.1 Summary of classifications of human rights in H. Kanger (1984)

Rights-type	Component elements	Illustrations of H. Kanger's (1984) characterizations	Example of explication (*x*: all individuals subject to any restrictions recognized in the Universal Declaration; *y*: all states that have adopted the Universal Declaration)
Type 6 'Claim rights'	• Claim power • Counterfreedom	• Article 9a,1.2.3: Freedom from arbitrary arrest, detention, or exile • Article 10a,1.2.3: Fair, public trial, by independent, impartial tribunal • Article 11.1a,1/2: Presumed innocent until proved guilty	$S(x,y)$: *x* has a fair and public trial • *y* has an obligation to see to it that $S(x,y)$ • *x* does not have an obligation to refrain from seeing to it that $S(x,y)$ • *x* does not have an obligation to see to it that $S(x,y)$
Type 4 'Integrity rights'	• Not claim • Power • Immunity • Counterfreedom • Not counterpower • Not counterimmunity	• Article 4a: Freedom from slavery and servitude • Article 5a,b: Freedom form torture and cruel or unusual punishment	$S(x,y)$: *x* is not held in slavery or servitude • Not: *y* has an obligation to see to it that $S(x,y)$ • *x* does not have an obligation to refrain from seeing to it that $S(x,y)$ • *y* has an obligation to refrain from seeing to it that not $S(x,y)$ • *x* does not have an obligation to see to it that $S(x,y)$ Not: *x* does not have an obligation to refrain from seeing to it that not $S(x,y)$ • Not: *y* has an obligation to refrain from seeing to it that $S(x,y)$
Type 5 'Freedom/ Integrity Rights'	• Power • Immunity • Counterpower • Counterimmunity	• Article 13.1a,b: Freedom of movement, residence • Article 13.2a,b: Exit, entry from country of residence • Article 18a,b: Freedom of thought, conscience, and religion • Article 19a: Freedom of opinion and expression • Article 20a,b: Freedom of assembly and association	$S(x,y)$: *x* leaves the country • *x* does not have an obligation to refrain from seeing to it that $S(x,y)$ • *y* has an obligation to refrain from seeing to it that not $S(x,y)$ • *x* does not have an obligation to refrain from seeing to it that not $S(x,y)$ • *y* has an obligation to refrain from seeing to it that $S(x,y)$

Table 6.1 Continued

Rights-type	Component elements	Illustrations of H. Kanger's (1984) characterizations	Example of explication (*x*: all individuals subject to any restrictions recognized in the Universal Declaration; *y*: all states that have adopted the Universal Declaration)
Type 9 'Service rights'	• Power • Immunity • Counterpower • Not counterimmunity	• Article 25.1a,b: Standard of living adequate for health and well-being	$S(x,y)$: x has an adequate standard of living • x does not have an obligation to refrain from seeing to it that $S(x,y)$ • y has an obligation to refrain from seeing to it that not $S(x,y)$ • x does not have an obligation to refrain from seeing to it that not $S(x,y)$ • Not: y has an obligation to refrain from seeing to it that $S(x,y)$
Type 3 'Claim rights'	• Claim • Not counterfreedom	• Article 26a,1: Education	$S(x,y)$: x is given free elementary education • y has an obligation to see to it that $S(x,y)$ • Not: x does not have an obligation to see to it that $S(x,y)$

distinguishes between four main groups of human rights ('claim rights', 'integrity rights', 'freedom rights', 'service rights'). She maintains that these categorizations 'are compatible with the traditional grouping into civil and political rights versus economic, social, and cultural ones', but are subtler in that they provide for the elucidation of 'the differences and similarities within the two main groups'.[4]

6.3 Proposals for Refining and Extending the Kanger System

Various limitations of the Kanger System identified in the literature are analysed in Lindahl (1977; 1994: 896–902); Makinson (1986); and

---

[4] Note that some of H. Kanger's (1984) characterizations of states of affairs are simplified in Table 6.1 and the subsequent analysis for brevity. Her categorizations, however, are as stated.

Herrestad and Krogh (1993, 1995). The first relates to an apparent lack of 'directionality' and 'relationality' in Kanger's scheme. As Lindahl (1994: 896–902) notes, classic theories of rights such as that elaborated by Mill suggest that when a right is not fulfilled a 'wrong has been done' and an identifiable bearer of a right 'has been wronged'. However, this inference is arguably problematic in Kanger's framework (the 'being wronged' concept can be understood as implying that (a) x has a claim-right versus y to the effect that $S(x,y)$ only if it is true that (b) if $S(x,y)$ is not the case, then x is wronged) because there are interpretations of x, y, and $S(x,y)$ such that (a) holds (i.e. Shall Do [y, $S(x,y)$]) whilst (b) is counterintuitive. Herrestead and Krogh (1995) give the following example. If a policeman y has an obligation to arrest a criminal x, it might be wrongly inferred from Kanger's equivalences that the criminal x has a claim that x is arrested by the policeman y (and is wronged if he or she is not in fact arrested). They conclude that Kanger's scheme fails to provide an adequate basis for distinguishing cases of this type. The Kanger System fails to capture and formalize what it means to be the counterparty of an obligation (in particular, that is, wronged in the case of non-fulfilment) and makes the identification of the counterparties of obligations problematic.[5] A second limitation relates to an alleged failure of the Kanger System to capture and formalize a common element in relationships signified by the term 'rights' (benefits, interests, choices, etc.). Makinson (1986) and Herrestead and Krogh (1993, 1995) emphasize here the failure of Kanger to capture and formalize a common element of 'legal power' (signalling the power to initiate legal proceedings), whilst Lindahl (1994: 896–902) emphasizes certain limitations relating to the claim-holders will (with Kanager's explications failing to capture and formalize a right-holder's, ability to refuse offers by obligation-holders).[6] Finally, a third limitation of Kanger's scheme identified in Lindahl (1994: 896–902) relates to the explication of rights of recipience without counterparties. As Lindahl notes,

---

[5] Herrestead and Krogh (1995: 211) note that it is not immediately apparent that the reference to the counterparty is missing in the Kanger model since Kanger specifies $S(x,y)$ in the scope of the action operator, but that Kanger (1985) notes that $S(x,y)$ could be any kind of state of affairs including those in which the parties x and y are redundant. Although Kanger defends his representation by stating that in ordinary cases x and y figure in a non-redundant way, and in many cases x and y can be described as being in a 'right-relation', that is, as the bearer and counterparty of a directed obligation. However, they are critical that 'Kanger does not make any suggestion concerning how to make representation in which these particular non-redundant cases may be distinguished from the redundant ones'. Lindahl (1977,1994) adopts the notation 'S' rather than $S(x,y)$.

[6] Lindahl suggests that the 'claim-holders' will' problem can be resolved by an appropriate respecification of states of affairs. This is the approach adopted below (see 'Capturing and formalizing x's right to refuse offers of assistance by y').

propositions relating to 'rights to receive' that do not imply statements about duties—such as the proposition 'children have a right to be nurtured' with no specification of counterpart duties—are not tractable in terms of Kanger's scheme.

The refined Kanger–Lindahl framework

Lindahl (1994) proposes a refined framework based on the notion of *being wronged by* (or *having a legitimate complaint*). A summary of the refined 'Kanger–Lindahl framework' is given in Box 6.7. Rights are explicated in terms of the two-place predicate $W(x,y)$, read as 'x is wronged by y'. Lindahl suggests that it is possible to reconstruct the complete lists of the four types of active rights and four types of passive rights on the basis of the two-place predicate W, reconstructing a theory of atomic rights by the method of 'maxi-conjunctions' (although the number of atomic types would be greater than in Kanger's scheme). In Lindahl's view, many of the difficulties associated with Kanger's scheme do not arise in this new system. In particular, the notion of 'x being wronged by y' captures and formalizes what it means to be bearer of a right, provides a clearer specification of the relationship between a bearer of an obligation and a beneficiary, and clarifies the identification of counterparties under the refined Kanger–Lindahl scheme.

The formal representation of rights without counterparties

Lindahl (1994: 906–8) further suggests that the predicate W can be used flexibly to explicate sentences that cannot be well interpreted even in terms of the reconstructed notions of rights against a counterparty. In particular, it is possible to explicate rights without a counterparty (i.e. statements of the kind 'x has a right to . . . ', without mentioning any counterparty) using W. For example, consider the proposition that all children have the right to receive nutrition. Suppose that x is a child and that $F(x)$ expresses that x receives nutrition. The sentence 'x has a right to nutrition' is compatible with:

$$\sim (\exists y)N[\sim Do(y,F(x)) \rightarrow W(x,y)],$$

That is, there need not be any particular agent by whom the child is wronged if that agent does not see to it that the child receives nutrition. Lindahl also suggests the following 'improved' interpretation:

$$N[\sim (\exists y)(Do(y,F(x))) \rightarrow (\exists y)(W(x,y))].$$

That is, if no one sees to it that x receives nutrition, then there is someone by whom x is wronged.

Box 6.7 OVERVIEW OF THE REFINED 'KANGER–LINDAHL' FRAMEWORK (LINDAHL (1994))	
Notation:	S - condition
Language:	The starting point of Lindahl's proposal is an interpretation of the deontic operator (O) in terms of Kanger's expression shall. According to this interpretation: Shall $S \longleftrightarrow N(\sim S \rightarrow B)$, where N stands for 'necessary', and B is a prepositional constant that can be understood in deontic terms, as 'a bad thing occurs'.
Rules of inference and axioms:	Lindahl introduces the following theorems: If A is a theorem, then Shall (A) is a theorem. Shall$(A \rightarrow C)$ and Shall$(A) \rightarrow$ Shall(C) Shall$(A) \rightarrow \sim$Shall$(\sim A)$.
Logic of rights-proper:	Lindahl introduces an axiom that expresses the idea that: if x is wronged by y, then a bad thing arises. That is: $W(x,y) \rightarrow B$.
Definition of rights-proper:	If A is a condition, $R(x,y,A)$ is read: 'x has a right-proper versus y to the effect that A' and is interpreted as follows: $R(x,y,A) \longleftrightarrow N[\sim A \rightarrow W(x,y)]$.
Deontic logic:	If, for fixed x,y, $R(x,y,.)$ is interpreted as an operator with x,y as parameters, then the logic of $R(x,y,.)$ is: If A is a theorem, then $R(x,y,A)$ is a theorem; $R(x,y,A) \& R(x,y,A \rightarrow C) \rightarrow R(x,y,C)$; $R(x,y,A) \rightarrow \sim R(x,y, \sim A)$ In addition, where x,y are not kept fixed: $R(x,y,A) \rightarrow \sim R(z,w, \sim A)$.
Example:	Claim (x,y,S) or $R[x,y,Do(y,S)]$ is explicated by: $N[\sim Do(y,S) \rightarrow W(x,y)]$

In addition, Lindahl suggests that, in cases of this type, it may be advantageous to introduce a one-place predicate W to a notion R(x,.), that is, a right-proper where there is no counterparty, according to the formula:

$$R(x,y,A) \longleftrightarrow N(\sim A \rightarrow W(x)).$$

The suggested interpretation is that A has been wronged, without specifying that y has done something wrong. In elaborating this idea, Lindahl suggests that it is possible to have rights in the absence of duties. For example, statements such as 'all children have the right to be nurtured' are not statements of *duty*. There are no identifiable counterbearers and it cannot be inferred from these statements alone any statement placing an obligation on any specific individuals to nurture children. Lindahl's one-place predicate formulation makes it possible to say that it is *wrong* if children are not nurtured, without specifying that specific counterparties failed to comply with an obligation.

'Directionality', 'the counterparty problem', and indexing

There have been a number of suggestions in the literature for solving the 'counterparty problem' through the introduction of indexed deontic operators (of the form $_xO_y$, read: 'x has a directed obligation towards y'). Following Makinson (1986), Herrestead and Krogh (1995) and Krogh (1995, 1996) proposed that directionality be re-established through the introduction of (*a*) *'bearer relativized ought-to-do statements'* of the form $_xOA$ (index before the deontic operator, read: 'it is obligatory for *x* that *x* sees to it that *A*'); (*b*) *'counter-party relatived ought-to-be'* statements of the form O_yA (index after the deontic operator, read: 'it ought to be the case for *y* that *A*'; (*c*) *'directed obligations'* of the form $_xO_y(_xEA)$ (read: '*x* has a directed obligation towards *y* that *x* sees to it that *A*') (where *A* expresses a state of affairs and $_xE$ is an 'intentional action operator'). 'Directed obligations' are defined in terms of the conjunction of an 'ought-to-do statement' and an 'ought-to-be statement' (where the first conjunct specifies the bearer and the object of the obligation, and the second conjunct specifies the counterparty of the directed obligation (i.e. the party who benefits from the fulfilment of the obligation). For example, the directed obligation '*x* is obliged towards *y* that *x* sees to it that *A*, if and only if, it is obligatory for *x* that *x* sees to it that *A*, and for *y* it ought to be that *x* brings about that *A*' is represented by:

$$_xO_y(_xEA) =_{def} xO(_xEA) \wedge O_y(_xEA)$$

The definition of a 'directed obligation' provides the basis of an explication of claim-rights (claim $(x,y,A) =_x O_y(_xEA)$. 'Bearer-free' rights of the type 'children have a right to be nurtured' are represented as 'counterparty relativized ought-to-be statements' of the form $_xO_y$ (with no bearer-relativized ought-to-do statement until further development of the law or some other principle for specifying the bearers of duties is provided).[7]

---

[7] The relational aspect of a 'directed obligation' is conserved by specifying deontic operators in terms of explicit action sentences. For this reason, Herrestead and Krogh distinguish between $xOy(xEA)$ (where sees to it that *A* through his or her personal actions) and xOA (where *x* has responsibility for seeing to it that *A* but not necessarily through his or her own personal actions). For related discussions of agency responsibility, 'acting as a representative', and delegation, see Royakkers (2000).

Van Hees' game-theoretic extensions

Van Hees (1995, 1996) has moved the research agenda on the formal modelling of individual rights forward by developing game-theoretic 'translations' of Kanger's rights-types. The underlying objective here is to introduce more refined rights-types into the game-theoretic modelling of the type reviewed in Section 4.7. Van Hees's 'Deontic Logic of Action' (DLA) is summarized in Box 6.8 and links action statements (describing actions performed by one or more agents at points of time leading to specific states of affairs) to the alethic and deontic modalities. The underlying logical language is applied in a game-theoretic context (to distinguish feasible strategies from admissible strategies) and to embed Kanger's typology of rights-types in a 'game-theoretic' setting. In order to embed Kanger's distinctions between rights-types in terms of a game-form, individual rights are defined (*a*) on the basis of the deontic operator Shall and the action operator Do; (*b*) with respect to formulas of DLA describing states of affairs existing between two individuals. An individual *x* is viewed as having permission to see that something is the case ('*x* may see to it that') if and only if he or she has an admissible strategy which leads to the state of affairs regardless of what the others do (with any play of the game form in which the individual opts for that strategy leading to an outcome in which the state of affairs is realized). The individual is viewed as having an obligation to realize a state of affairs ('*x* shall see to it that') if every admissible strategy of the individual leads to the state of affairs. Actions and inactions can be specified as being permissible ('*x* may see to it that') or obligated ('individual *x* shall see to it that'). The resulting statements and their negations are then used to distinguish between the eight simple types of right in Kanger's scheme. The game-theoretical translation of the first four simple rights-types is listed in Van Hees (1996: 85) as:

(1) claim if and only if each play of the game leads to an outcome in which *q* is true

(2) power if and only if *i* has an admissible strategy that always leads to *q*—that is, any play of the game-form in which the individual adopts that strategy which leads to an outcome in which *q* is true

(3) immunity if and only if *j* has no admissible strategy which always leads to an outcome in which *q* is not true

(4) freedom if and only if it is not true that any play of the game-form leads to an outcome in which *q* is not true

As with Kanger's original explications, Van Hees's 'game-theoretic' translations can be used to formulate logical relationships between simple types of

---

Box 6.8 VAN HEES'S 'DEONTIC LOGIC OF ACTION'

- **Action statements (doing statements embodying seeing to it that a state of affairs is realized / bringing about a state of affairs) of the form:**
  $Do_x(t_j,q)$: 'x performs an action at t_j such that whatever else may happen q is the case', where t_j is a point in time, and q is a well defined formula specifying a relation between two individuals x and y and a state of affairs q existing between them*.
- **Alethic modalities ('can' and 'must' statements embodying practical possibility/necessity) of the form:**
  Can $Do_x(t_j,q)$: x has the opportunity and ability to do q at time t_j (and has the opportunity and ability to not q at time t_j)
  Must $do_x(t_j,q)$: x has the opportunity and ability to do q at time t_j but does not have the opportunity and ability to not q
- **Deontic modalities (should/may statements embodying obligation/ permission to see to it that a state of affairs is realized) of the form:**
  Shall $Do_x(t_j,q)$: at t_j individual x shall (is obligated to) take an action that leads to q (although x can take an action that does not necessarily lead to q)
  May $Do_x(t_j,q)$ read: at t_j individual x may (has permission to) take an action that leads to q (and can take an action that does not necessarily lead to q)

*'Do' is taken to represent Van Hees's 'strong action operator' (an individual sees to it that something q is the case if any only if (a) the individual actions necessitates q; (b) the individual could have chosen a course of action that would not have necessitated q. In contrast, 'do' is taken to represent Van Hees's 'weak action operator' (that does not entail a true choice situation).

Source: Van Hees (1995: 25–44)

---

rights. Van Hees (1996: 86) gives the following examples. If x has a claim versus another y with respect to a state of affairs q, with each play of a game leading to an outcome in which q is true, then x does not have a counter-immunity or a counterpower versus that other person with respect to q. If all plays lead to q then it is trivially true that the other individual has at least one strategy that always leads to q (not counterimmunity), and x cannot have a strategy that always leads to not q (not counterpower). In addition, x can only have a claim versus another individual if x also has a freedom versus that person: if any play of the game-form leads to q then there is at least one play leading to q. Van Hees (1995: 107–25, 177–80) sets out the logical inter-relationships between the 'translated' rights-types and provides a recon-structed list of atomic rights-types for both individuals and collective agents.

The formal representation of the 'capacitive' element of 'acting'[8]

The extended logical framework for analysing 'rights-realizations' set out in Kanger (1985) introduces a *capacitive* condition for acting or doing that

[8] See Lindahl (1994: 890) for references to the expanded logical apparatus used by Kanger in developing the idea of the realization of rights.

relates to Sen's 'capability framework' in important ways. In considering the question of what it means to benefit from a human right, Kanger (ibid.) introduced an analytical distinction between the idea of *compliance with a rule of rights* and that of the *realization of a right*. For example, in relation to Article 13.2 of the UN Declaration on Human Rights, suppose that y is the state of India and x is a poor peasant in central India, such that x and y satisfy the C-condition of the rule. In this case, the rule of right implies:

$$\text{Shall} \sim \text{Do}[y, \sim S(x,y)]$$

$$\text{Shall} \sim \text{Do}[y,S(x,y)]$$

If y complies with the rule in relation to the peasant then:

$$\sim \text{Do}[y, \sim S(x,y)]$$

$$\sim \text{Do}[y,S(x,y)]$$

However, Kanger suggests that the rule of right cannot be said to be *realized* for x, if x *lacks the means* for leaving India. His argument is formalized in Box 6.9. In case of rule A, if y is a state and x is a normal non-criminal adult citizen of y residing in y, the rule is realized for x in relation to y if and only if:

$$\sim \text{Do}[y, \sim S(x,y)] \text{ and } \sim \text{Do}[y,S(x,y)]$$

$$\text{Cando}[x,S(x,y)]$$

$$\text{Cando}[x, \sim S(x,y)]$$

In Kanger's view, this idea of the *realization of a human right* underlies Article 28 of the Universal Declaration of Human Rights—the right of everyone to a social and international order in which the rights and freedoms recognized in the Universal Declaration can be fully realized. Kanger interprets this article as both a valid rule of rights and as a *direction* that can be formulated as a normative statement: 'It ought to be the case that the rules listed in the Declaration be realized for everyone' (ibid. 76–7).

In the Van Hees (2004) model, the capacitive element suggested by the capability approach is built into the underlying logic of action with action statements linked to the alethic modality and with Can $\text{Do}_x(t_j,q)$ interpreted as: x has the opportunity and ability to do q at time t_j (and has the opportunity and ability to not q at time t_j). Further development of this approach that makes explicit that what it is feasible for an individual to do (i.e. 'practical possibility'/'opportunity and ability') depends on the

---

Box 6.9   *REALIZATION* OF A RULE OF RIGHTS

Notation	Cando [$x, S(x,y)$]: There are measures M such that it is possible in practice that x sees to it that $S(x,y)$ by means of M.
Realization of a rule of rights	If rule R implies that x has both a power and immunity but not a claim in relation to y with respect to $S(x,y)$, then to be realized for x in relation to y it is not sufficient that R is complied with by y. There must also be some measure by means of which it is possible for x to see to it that $S(x,y)$.
Conditions for realization of a rule of rights	If $C(x,y)$, a rule of rights R is said to be realized for x in relation to y if:

(1) y complies with R in relation to x;
(2) Cando [$x, S(x,y)$], if $C(x,y)$ and R imply that $\sim$Shall $\sim$Do [$x, S(x,y)$], Shall $\sim$Do [$y, \sim S(x,y)$] and $\sim$Shall Do [$y, S(x,y)$];
(3) Cando [$x, \sim S(x,y)$], if $C(x,y)$ and R imply that $\sim$Shall $\sim$Do [$x, \sim S(x,y)$], Shall $\sim$Do [$y, S(x,y)$], if $C(x,y)$ and $\sim$ Shall Do [$y, \sim S(x,y)$].

The rule R is realized for x, if R is realized for x in relation to each y such that $S(x,y)$.

Source: Kanger (1985)

---

personal transformation of characteristics into functionings (and on which functionings are present) could provide an important logical representation of the 'capability approach'. The idea of a 'capability-right' could then be captured and formalized by mixing alethic with deontic operators (e.g. ShallDo$_y$CanDo$_x$q).

6.4 Updating the Formal Analysis of Key International Standards in the Field of Human Rights Using the Kanger System

The series of papers by Kanger and H. Kanger moved the human rights agenda forward in an important way. Their work challenged contemporary theories that ruled out the admissibility of certain human rights including the entire range of economic and social rights as universal human rights (including the influential work by Cranston (1967))[9] by establishing the validity of the human rights recognized in the Universal

---

[9] Cranston (1967) linked the admissibility of universal human rights to the feasibility of counterpart duties being performed by all individuals without exception. Cf. Sections 2.1, 2.4, 3.2, 3.3, and 3.4.

Declaration as 'rules of right' under the 'Kanger System'. Nevertheless, their underlying intuition relating to the interpretation of human rights in general—and economic and social rights in particular—has become outdated. The categorizations proposed in H. Kanger (1984) were intended to be 'compatible with the traditional grouping into civil and political rights versus economic, social, and cultural ones', but to be subtler in that they provided for the elucidation of 'the differences and similarities within the two main groups'. However, these categorizations fail to reflect widely accepted expressions of the idea of human rights in international human rights law, which suggest that all human rights incorporate common elements of claim (reflected in positive obligations to take actions to protect, promote, and fulfil human rights) as well as common elements of immunity (reflected in negative obligations of non-intervention, omission, and restraint). As a result, H. Kanger's categorizations of key civil and political rights—and of virtually the entire cluster of economic and social rights—fail to capture and formalize the common element of 'claim' established in international human rights law.

Authoritative international establishment of the 'claim element' of human rights

International human rights law also provides authoritative recognition of the view that fundamental freedoms and human rights are associated with positive obligations of assistance and aid (as well as negative obligations of non-intervention and restraint). As discussed in Chapter 5 (especially Section 5.4), the positive implications of human rights are well established in case law on civil and political rights, with the European Court of Human Rights reasoning that the objective of the European Convention on Human Rights guarantees rights that are 'practical and effective' and gives rise to obligations that necessitate 'positive action by the state'. Thus 'genuine effective freedom of peaceful assembly' cannot be reduced to a mere negative duty of non-interference on the part of the state; the right to life imposes on states not only a duty to refrain from interfering with life, but also a 'positive duty' to 'take steps to safeguard life'; whilst the prohibition on unusual and degrading treatment can under certain contingencies give rise to positive duties to provide food and shelter.[10] These approaches have been further developed by the UN CESCRs, which has set out an analytical framework that identifies three types of obligations on

---

[10] Full references are given on pages 174–8.

states in the field of human rights. These are: obligations to respect human rights (requiring states to refrain from violating human rights); obligations to protect human rights (requiring states to take measures to prevent violations of human rights by third parties); and obligations to fulfil human rights (requiring states to take measures towards the full realization of human rights, and giving rise in turn to obligations to facilitate opportunities for the enjoyment of human rights and to provide for the fulfilment of human rights that would otherwise be denied). This approach is also reflected in the South African Constitution, which establishes that '[t]he state must respect, protect, promote, and fulfil' human rights.[11]

Failure of the classifications in H. Kanger (1984) to capture and formalize the 'claim element' of certain civil and political rights

The failure of H. Kanger to incorporate a common element of claim as well as a common element of immunity in the formal representation of human rights has far-reaching implications for H. Kanger's proposals for the formal representation of important civil and political rights recognized in the Universal Declaration. H. Kanger's proposals for the formal representation of key civil and political rights fail, for example, to capture and formalize an element of positive state responsibility for the protection of individuals from violations of human rights by third parties. This limitation is particular pronounced in relation to the group of human rights classified by H. Kanger as 'integrity rights'. This includes Article 4a of the Universal Declaration (the human right of everyone to freedom from slavery and servitude) and Article 5a,b (freedom from torture and cruel and unusual punishment). Given the characterization of the relevant state of affairs 'x is not held in servitude or slavery', Kanger rejects the characterization of Article 4a of the Universal Declaration as a Type 6 right on the grounds that the state cannot be reasonably held to be under an obligation to prevent x from being forced into servitude by a third party. An important implication of this approach is that states are modelled as not being under a positive obligation to take positive steps to ensure, for example, that third parties such as private companies are prevented from using bonded labour. This approach fails to capture the positive obligations that states have to protect individuals from violations of human rights by third parties established in authoritative international jurisprudence (discussed below).

---

[11] Full references on pages 167–9.

Similarly, the element of claim is entirely absent from the group of human rights characterized by H. Kanger as 'freedom' or 'independence' rights, including Article 13.1 (freedom of movement and residence), Article 18 (freedom of thought, conscience, and religion), and Article 19 (freedom of opinion and expression). Thus the formal representation of Article 13.1 implies that states are not under a positive obligation to take actions to ensure that x has freedom of movement. Again, given the characterization of the relevant state of affairs 'x has freedom of movement between places a and b', H. Kanger rejects the characterization of Article 13.1 as a Type 6 right on the grounds that the state cannot be reasonably held to be under an obligation to ensure that x moves between a and b. However, this approach fails to capture and formalize the authoritative interpretations of international human rights law set out in authoritative international jurisprudence, which establish that states can be required to take positive actions to promote and fulfil human rights— and that human rights such as freedom of movement and freedom of peaceful assembly cannot be reduced to a mere negative duty of non-interference on the part of the state.

Strengthening the formal representation of the element of 'claim' in the field of civil and political rights

In moving forward, the introduction of broader specifications of the state of affairs can overcome H. Kanger's objections and enable the formal representation of key civil and political rights to be strengthened from the point of view of x's claim in a meaningful and coherent way. The objective here is to specify the relevant state of affairs in a way that delimits the nature and scope of the positive obligation of the state in respect of the state of affairs. This avoids the problem highlighted by H. Kanger—that is, the problem of specifying the rule of right in a way that gives the state full and open-ended responsibility for the complete achievement of the relevant state of affairs. For example, the state of affairs $S(x,y)$ might be specified as: 'reasonable actions are taken to ensure that x is not held in slavery or servitude'. Under this specification, Article 4a could be characterized as a Type 6 right, entailing x's claim and a corresponding obligation on y to take positive actions (see Box 6.10). Similarly, a broader formulation of the relevant state of affairs would provide a basis for the characterization of Article 13.1 (freedom of movement) as a Type 6 right—entailing x's claim and a corresponding obligation on y to take reasonable positive actions to protect, promote, and fulfil the human right to freedom from movement (see Box 6.11).

Box 6.10 ARTICLE 4A: FREEDOM FROM SLAVERY AND SERVITUDE

H. Kanger's classification

$S(x,y)$:	x is not held in slavery or servitude
Scope:	All individuals x resident in y subject to any restrictions recognized in the Universal Declaration, all states y that have adopted the Universal Declaration on Human Rights

Type 4: not claim, power, immunity, counterfreedom, not counterpower, not counterimmunity

Element:	**Not claim**
Explication:	Not: It shall be that case that/y sees to it that/$S(x,y)$
Formalization:	$\sim$ Shall Do [y, $S(x,y)$]
Interpretation:	Not: y has an obligation to see to it that $S(x,y)$
	y does not have an obligation to see to it that $S(x,y)$
Element:	**Power**
Explication:	It shall not be the case that/x does not see to it that/$S(x,y)$
Formalization:	$\sim$ Shall $\sim$ Do [$x, S(x,y)$] [May Do $(x, S(x,y))$]
Interpretation:	x does not have an obligation to refrain from seeing to it that $S(x,y)$, x may see to it that $S(x,y)$
Element:	**Immunity**
Explication:	It shall be the case that/y does not see to it that/ not $S(x,y)$
Formalization:	Shall $\sim$ Do [y, $\sim S(x,y)$]
Interpretation:	y has an obligation to refrain from seeing to it that not $S(x,y)$
Element:	**Counterfreedom**
Explication:	It shall not be the case that/x sees to it that/$S(x,y)$
Formalization:	$\sim$ Shall Do [x, $S(x,y)$]
Interpretation:	x does not have an obligation to see to it that $S(x,y)$
Element:	**Not counterpower**
Explication:	Not: It shall not be the case that/x does not see to it that/not $S(x,y)$
Formalization:	Not: $\sim$ Shall $\sim$ Do [x, $\sim S(x,y)$]
	Alternatively, Not: May Do [x, $\sim S(x,y)$]
Interpretation:	Not: x may see to it that not $S(x,y)$
Element:	**Not counterimmunity**
Explication:	Not: It shall be the case that/y does not see to it that/$S(x,y)$
Formalization:	Not: Shall $\sim$ Do [y, $S(x,y)$]
Interpretation:	Not: y has an obligation to refrain from seeing to it that $S(x,y)$

Alternative Classification

$S(x,y)$	reasonable measures are taken to ensure that x is not held in slavery or servitude
Scope:	All individuals x resident in y and satisfying relevant conditions, and all states y

Box 6.10 Continued

Type 6 right Claim, Power, Counterfreedom

Element:	**Claim**
Explication:	It shall be the case that/y sees to it that/$S(x,y)$
Formalization:	shall do [y, $S(x,y)$]
Interpretation	y has an obligation to see to it that $S(x,y)$
Element:	**Power**
Explication:	It shall not be the case that/x does not see to it that/$S(x,y)$
Formalization:	$\sim$ Shall $\sim$ Do [$x, S(x,y)$] [May Do $(x, S(x,y))$]
Interpretation:	x does not have an obligation to refrain from seeing to it that $S(x,y)$ x may see to it that $S(x,y)$
Element:	**Counterfreedom**
Explication:	It shall not be the case that/x sees to it that/$S(x,y)$
Formalization:	$\sim$ Shall Do [$x, S(x,y)$]
Interpretation:	x does not have an obligation to see to it that $S(x,y)$

Failure of the classifications in H. Kanger (1984) to capture and formalize the 'claim element' of economic and social rights

The failure of H. Kanger to incorporate a common element of claim as well as a common element of immunity in the formal representation of human rights also imposes limitations on H. Kanger's proposals for the formal representation of the idea of freedom from poverty as a basic human right. H. Kanger (1984) characterizes the cluster of economic and social rights enumerated in the Universal Declaration as Type 9 rights (see Box 6.12). This characterization implies the absence of a claim element in relation to this class of human rights, and fails to capture and formalize any degree of positive responsibility for the progressive realization of internationally recognized human rights in this field. For example, H. Kanger describes the state of affairs entailed by Article 25.1 of the Universal Declaration on Human Rights as 'x has an adequate standard of living'. Given this description, she classifies this as a Type 9 right, such that x has versus y, power, immunity, counterpower, and not counterimmunity. The power, immunity, and counterimmunity elements of this rights-type imply that y may see to it that x has an adequate of living, and may not prevent x from seeing to it that y has an adequate standard of living, but is not under an obligation to see to it that this is the case. The element of counterpower implies that x may refuse offers of assistance by y (contrasting with the element of not counterpower in H. Kanger's classification of the human right to freedom from slavery, whereby x may not enslave herself).

Box 6.11   ARTICLE 13.1*A*. FREEDOM OF MOVEMENT

H. Kanger's Classification
S(x,y): *x* has freedom of movement
Scope: All individuals *x* resident in *y* subject to any restrictions recognized in the Universal Declaration, all states *y* that have adopted the Universal Declaration on Human Rights

Type 5: Power, Immunity, Counterpower, Counterimmunity

Element:	**Power**
Explication:	It shall not be the case that/*x* does not see to it that/*S(x,y)*
Formalization:	$\sim$ Shall $\sim$ Do [*x*, *S(x,y)*] May Do [*x*, *S(x,y)*]
Interpretation:	*x* does not have an obligation to refrain from seeing to it that *S(x,y)*
	x may see to it that *S(x,y)*
Element:	**Immunity**
Explication:	It shall be the case that/*y* does not see to it that/ not *S(x,y)*
Formalization	Shall $\sim$ Do [*y*, $\sim$*S(x,y)*]
Interpretation:	*y* has an obligation to refrain from seeing to it that not *S(x,y)*
Element:	**Counterpower**
Explication:	It shall not be the case that/*x* does not see to it that/not *S(x,y)*
Formalization:	$\sim$ Shall $\sim$ Do [*x*, $\sim$ *S(x,y)*] May Do (*x*, $\sim$ *S(x,y*]
Interpretation:	*x* does not have an obligation to refrain from seeing to it that not *S(x,y)*
	x may see to it that not *S(x,y)*
Element:	**Counterimmunity**
Explication:	It shall be the case that/*y* does not see to it that/ *S(x,y)*
Formalization:	Shall $\sim$ Do [*y*, *S(x,y)*]
Interpretation:	*y* has an obligation to refrain from seeing to it that *S(x,y)*

Alternative Classification
S(x,y): all reasonable measures are undertaken to ensure that *x* has freedom of movement

Type 6: Claim, Power, Counterfreedom

Element:	**Claim**
Explication:	it shall be the case that/*y* sees to it that/*S(x,y)*
Formalization	shall do [*y*, *S(x,y)*]
Explanation:	*y* has an obligation to see to it that *S(x,y)*
Element:	**Power**
Explication:	It shall not be the case that/*x* does not see to it that/*S(x,y)*
Formalization:	$\sim$ Shall $\sim$ Do [*x*, *S(x,y)*] May Do [*x*, *S(x,y)*]

Box 6.11 Continued

Interpretation:	*x* does not have an obligation to refrain from seeing to it that *S(x,y)*
	x may see to it that *S(x,y)*
Element:	**Counterfreedom**
Explication:	It shall not be the case that/*x* sees to it that/*S(x,y)*
Formalization:	~ Shall Do [*x, S(x,y)*]
Interpretation:	*x* does not have an obligation to see to it that *S(x,y)*

Box 6.12   H. KANGER'S CLASSIFICATION OF ARTICLE 25.1*A.B.* (THE HUMAN RIGHT TO AN ADEQUATE STANDARD OF LIVING)

State of affairs *S(x,y)*:	*x* has an adequate standard of living
Scope:	All individuals *x* resident in *y* subject to any restrictions recognized in the Universal Declaration, all states *y* that have adopted the Universal Declaration on Human Rights
Type 9:	**_x_ has versus _y_, power, immunity, counterpower, not counterimmunity**
Element:	**Power**
Explication:	It shall not be the case that/*x* does not see to it that/*S(x,y)*
Formalization:	~ Shall ~ Do [*x,S(x,y)*] May Do [*x, S(x,y)*]
Interpretation:	*x* does not have an obligation to refrain from seeing to it that *S(x,y)*
	x may see to it that *S(x,y)*
Element:	**Immunity**
Explication:	It shall be the case that/*y* does not see to it that/not *S(x,y)*
Formalization:	Shall ~ Do [*y, ~S (x,y)*]
Interpretation:	*y* has an obligation to refrain from seeing to it that not *S(x,y)*
Element:	**Counterpower**
Explication:	It shall not be the case that/*x* does not see to it that/not *S(x,y)*
Formalization:	~ Shall ~ Do [*x, ~ S(x,y)*] May Do [*x, S(x,y)*]
Interpretation:	*x* does not have an obligation to refrain from seeing to it that not *S(x,y)*
	x may see to it that not *S(x,y)*
Element:	**Not counterimmunity**
Explication:	Not: It shall be the case that/*y* does not see to it that/*S(x,y)*
Formula:	Not: Shall ~ Do [*y, S (x,y)*]
Interpretation:	Not: *y* has an obligation to refrain from seeing to it that *S(x,y)*

Jurisprudential analysis of authoritative international standards in the field of poverty and human rights

In defending this characterization of Article 25.1 as a Type 9 right (with no element of claim) rather than a Type 6 right (incorporating an element of claim), H. Kanger (1984: 143) maintains that the state cannot be reasonably held to be under an obligation to see to it that everyone within its borders achieves an adequate standard of living, and that the characterization of the human right to an adequate standard of living as a Type 6 right (including the entailed element of claim) would be too strong. This interpretation fails to comply with contemporary international standards in the field of poverty and human rights discussed in Chapter 5, which support the recharacterization of Article 25.1 as a claim-right, with the appropriate qualifications to, and limitations on, the scope of the positive obligation on states being built into the description of the state of affairs (e.g. by building in the concepts of reasonable measures, maximum of available resources, and progressive realization into the description of the state of affairs). Authoritative international jurisprudence establishes that individuals have claims on states in relation to the human right to an adequate standard of living—albeit claims that are *qualified* and *limited*. For example, the positive obligation to *take steps* to the *maximum of available resources* is codified in legally binding international treaties including the ICESCR. The nature and scope of the positive obligations of state parties arising from is delimited in Article 2. The principal obligation is to achieve the progressive realization of the human rights set out in the ICESCR. States parties are obliged to take steps, 'individually and through international assistance and cooperation' towards this objective, by adopting 'all appropriate means'—including policies and programmes as well as legal measures. This provision for progressive realization provides an acknowledgement that resources may be limited and that the full realization of the human rights recognized in the Covenant may necessarily be achieved progressively over time. However, the obligation 'to take steps' is itself an immediate obligation and resource constraints do not relieve states parties of the general obligation to move as expeditiously and effectively as possible towards the full realization of the human rights set out in the Covenant. Furthermore, the 'Minimum Core Contents Approach' developed by the Committee stipulates that all states parties are under a minimum core obligation to ensure the satisfaction of, at the very least, minimum essential levels of each of the rights recognized in the Covenant. This has been interpreted as implying that violations can occur if a state fails to fulfil this minimum core obligation and that 'a State party in which any significant number of individuals is deprived of essential foodstuffs, of essential primary health care, of basic shelter and housing, or of the most basic forms of education is, prima facie, failing to discharge its obligations under the Covenant'.[12]

As discussed in Chapter 5, the South African Constitution (1996) also provides support for the recharacterization of Article 25.1 as a claim-right, with the appropriate qualifications to, and limitations on, the scope of the positive obligation on states being built into the description of the state of affairs. The Bill of Rights attached to the constitution entrenches a cluster of socio-economic rights essential for an adequate standard of living—including housing, access to health care, sufficient food and water, social security, and education. The justiciability of these rights has been put beyond question by jurisprudence of the South African Constitutional Court, which has upheld claims for the violation of socio-economic rights in two landmark judgements—the first regarding the human right to housing, and the second regarding the human right to health. These cases established that resource constraints do not relieve the government of the positive obligations to fulfil socio-economic rights established in Articles 26–29 of the constitution by taking measures to eliminate or reduce the large areas of severe deprivation that afflict South Africa. However, the Court has also sought to delimit the nature and scope of the duties that flow from this positive obligation. It has reasoned that there are two counterbalancing elements to Articles 26–29: a first element recognizing the general right, and a second element establishing and delimiting the scope of the positive obligation imposed on the state. In weighing up these elements, the Court has reasoned that the state is not obliged to go beyond available resources or to realize the rights immediately. Rather, the state must act reasonably to ensure the progressive realization of these rights over time.[13]

Formal representation of 'capability-rights' and 'meta-rights'

Sen's treatment of the general class of 'capability rights' and the general class of 'meta-rights' takes forward the analysis of authoritative international standards in the field of poverty and human rights in important ways. The focus on individual substantive freedoms (in the form of the

[12] Full references on pages 157–9, 164–7, and 169–70.
[13] Full references on pages 179–81.

capabilities and functionings that people can and do achieve)[14] provides a basis for the elucidation of a broad class of fundamental freedoms and human rights that takes account of poverty, hunger, and starvation. Sen's central idea of 'capability-freedom' is associated with derivate classes of 'capability-rights' (that have as their object the protection and promotion of valuable states of being and doing) and of obligations associated with 'capability-rights'. These include positive obligations to defend and support capability-rights (as well as negative obligations of omission and restraint) and obligations to promote goals (as well as obligations to perform or not to perform specific actions). Sen's treatment of the idea of 'goal-rights' breaks down the emphasis in some theories on a strict one-to-one binary correspondence between rights-fulfilments (and violations) and the performance (and non-performance) of specific duties or action. The general class of rights that focus on outcomes rather than on permissions and obligations to act (or not to act) is referred to as the class of 'contingent rights to "states of affairs" ' (Sen 1982a: 38; 1982d: 347; 1985c; 2000a; 2002: 645).

Sen's concept of 'meta-rights' also encapsulates a critical element in the establishment and development of international legal obligation in the field of poverty and human rights. Whereas the Nozickian model makes the feasibility of 'complete realization' a condition of the admissibility of rights-based claims, Sen has argued that feasibility cannot be a condition of coherence, and that fundamental freedoms and human rights-based claims can be meaningful in the context of cost and feasibility constraints. Sen (1982d; 2000a) has reasoned that where there are resource constraints, the positive obligations associated with 'capability-freedoms' and 'capability-rights' may not relate directly to valuable states of being and doing (x)—that may be currently unachievable—but to policies and programmes $p(x)$ that promote the achievement of (x) as an immediate or cumulative outcome. The violation of obligations of this type involves the *absence* and *inadequacy* of policies and programmes $p(x)$—rather than the *non-fulfilment of (x)* per se. This approach is reflected in the jurisprudence of the South African Constitutional Court, which has reasoned that the responsibilities of the South African Court under Articles 26–29 of the South African Constitution can be discharged through the adoption of policies and programmes that aim at the achievement of human rights over time rather

---

[14] The term 'functioning' refers to aspects of the states of being and doing that a person achieves., ranging from elementary personal states (such as achieving adequate nutrition) to complex personal states and activities (such as participation and appearing without shame). The term 'capability' refers to the alternative combinations of functionings that are within a person's reach. See, for example, Sen (1993a: 31).

than their immediate and/or complete fulfilment.[15] This can involve (*a*) the adoption of a comprehensive policy or programme that is (*a*.1) capable of facilitating the realization of the right in question and that (*a*.2) makes appropriate provision for short, medium, and term needs. Programmes or policies that exclude a significant segment of society, or that do not take adequate account of immediate crisis needs, cannot be said to be reasonable. In the cases referred to above, the policies and programmes adopted by the government failed to comply with these principles and the government was held to be in violation of the positive obligations established in the constitution.

Strengthening the formal representation of authoritative international standards in the field of poverty and human rights using the Kanger System

The formal representation of the idea of freedom from poverty as a basic human right can be captured and formalized as a claim-right using the 'Kanger System', through the incorporation of broad specifications of states of affairs that exploit key elements of emerging legal and ethical frameworks in the field of poverty and human rights. The proposals that follow build on:

- Incorporation of authoritative international standards in the field of poverty and human rights that delimit the nature and scope of the positive obligations on states into the description of states of affairs (especially progressive realization and adequacy or reasonableness).
- Incorporation of Sen's concepts of 'capability-rights' and 'meta-rights' into the description of states of affairs.

The proposed approach resolves two specific objections to the characterization of the human right to an adequate standard of living as a claim-right raised by H. Kanger. These relate to (*a*) *x*'s right to refuse offers of assistance made by *y*; (*b*) the failure to delimit the scope of the positive obligation on the state (and thus the failure to avoid non-feasible and conflicting duties).

Capturing and formalizing x's right to refuse offers of assistance by y

An important objection to the characterization of social and economic rights as claim-rights raised by H. Kanger (1984: 143) relates to *x*'s right to waive offers of assistance by *y*. Under the Type 9 characterization, *x* does

[15] See pages 179–81.

not have an obligation to refrain from seeing to it that *x* does not have an adequate standard of living. In contrast, *x*'s *claim* entails *x*'s *not counter-power*—depriving the individual of the right to *refuse* an offer by *y* to see to it that *x* has an adequate standard of living. However, this problem is a generic one. For example, the right of a rights-holder to refuse an offer of adequate nutrition (e.g. a hunger striker for reasons of principle) is in fact analogous to a situation where a person refuses an element of a free trial (e.g. representation by a barrister). Yet the right to a free trial is nevertheless characterized by H. Kanger as a Type 6 right. Indeed, agency issues of this type may be best dealt with in the Kanger framework not by weakening the characterization of the rights in question from the point of view of the rights-holder's claim, but rather by broadening the informational focus of the states of affairs entailed by particular rights. For example, the states of affairs entailed by *x*'s right can be related to a broad description of *x*'s access to opportunities *before x*'s choices are exercised (rather than to the situation that pertains *after x*'s choices). If this approach is adopted, then the classification of rights would be analytically independent of whether *x* chooses to take-up, or not to take-up, offers of assistance by *y*.

Formal representation of 'capability-rights'

Taking forward this approach, a possible informational focus would be whether or not *x* has the *capability* to achieve valuable states of affairs (e.g. an adequate standard of living). Thus the human right to an adequate standard of living could be elucidated as a 'capability-right' using the 'Kanger System'. H. Kanger's specification of the relevant state of affairs [$S(x,y)$: *x* has an adequate standard of living] could be superseded by the following formulation:

- **Incorporation of the concept of capability**
  $S(x,y)$1: '*x* has the capability to achieve an adequate standard of living adequate standard of living (including adequate nutrition, clothing, and shelter)'.[16]

Delimiting the nature and scope of the positive obligation on the state

Other objections raised by H. Kanger to the characterization of Article 25.1 as a claim-right relate to the failure to delimit the scope of the positive

---

[16] The approach developed is intended to introduce the notion of secure realization of states of affairs into the characterization of rights-based claims, without relying on the extended logical apparatus for rights-realizations introduced in Kanger (1985).

obligation on the state (and hence the failure to avoid the problem of non-feasible and conflicting duties). According to the formulation above, only the state has a positive obligation to see to it that steps are taken to ensure that x has the capability to achieve an adequate standard of living. Furthermore, the responsibility of the state is unqualified and open-ended and does not take account of the qualifications to and limitations on the positive obligations on the state under conditions of limited resources and other cost and feasibility constraints set out in international human rights law and authoritative international jurisprudence. However, these limitations can be resolved through the further incorporation of the ethical and jurisprudential concepts discussed above—including the assumption of the primary responsibility of the individual, the concept of meta-rights (or rights to policies and programmes), and the concepts of progressive realization, adequacy/reasonableness, and resource and feasibility constraints—into the characterization of states of affairs. In this way, H. Kanger's specification of the relevant state of affairs [$S(x,y)$: x has an adequate standard of living] could be superseded by the following formulations:

- **Incorporation of the assumption of individual responsibility:** $S(x,y)2$: 'For all x unable to secure the capability to achieve an adequate standard of living (including adequate nutrition, clothing, and shelter) by their own efforts, this capability will be secured.'

- **Incorporation of the concept of meta-rights:** $S(x,y)3$: 'For all x unable to secure the capability to achieve an adequate standard of living (including adequate nutrition, clothing, and shelter) by their own efforts, actions and programmes of actions aimed at the realization of this capability will be undertaken.'

- **Incorporation of the concepts of reasonableness/adequacy:** $S(x,y)4$: 'For all x unable to secure the capability to achieve an adequate standard of living (including adequate nutrition, clothing, and shelter) by their own efforts, all reasonable actions and programmes of actions aimed at the secure realization of this capability will be undertaken.'

- **Incorporation of the concepts of resource and feasibility constraints:** $S(x,y)5$: 'For all x unable to secure the capability to achieve an adequate standard of living (including adequate nutrition, clothing, and shelter) by their own efforts, actions and programmes of actions aimed at the secure realization of this capability will be undertaken subject to feasibility and resource constraints.'

Proposals for moving forward

This broad approach to specification of the relevant states of affairs in the field of poverty and human rights suggested above provides a basis for the formal representation of the human right to an adequate standard of living as a 'claim-right'. Under the classification of Article 25.1 of the Universal Declaration as a Type 6 in Box 6.13 below, the element of claim implies that if x cannot ensure the capability to achieve an adequate standard of living through his or her own efforts, then the state is under a positive obligation to take positive actions to ensure the secure realization of this capability. As a logical implication of x's claim, x also has an immunity with respect to this state of affairs, prohibiting y from taking actions that undermine the secure realization of the capability to achieve an adequate standard of living by x. The element of counterfreedom implies that responsibility for ensuring the secure realization of x's capability to achieve an adequate standard of living under these circumstances does not fall to x, whilst the element of power implies that x does not have an obligation to refrain from taking actions to achieve this objective. Similar approaches are proposed in relation to the formal representation of the human right to an adequate standard of living (including adequate food, clothing, and shelter) under Article 11 of the ICESCR (read in conjunction with the general obligations of states individually and in respect to international assistance and cooperation set out in Article 2) and the human rights to food and water under Articles 27 of the South African Bill of Rights in Box 6.14.[17]

Capturing and formalizing y's obligations relating to international assistance and cooperation

In addition, there is the question of *international assistance* and *cooperation* to consider. Kanger and H. Kanger introduce the ideas of international assistance and cooperation in relation to Articles 28 and 29 of the Universal Declaration (in discussions about rights-realizations). However, obligations of international assistance and cooperation are included in the

---

[17] The responsibility of the state for undertaking policies and programmes may point to the alternative classification of certain civil and political rights as well as economic and social rights as Type 7 rights (claim, no power) within the Kanger System. Since only the state can be meaningfully conceived as being authorized to 'steps' such as legal measures and other policies and programmes, it is possible to argue that the interpretation of the element of Type 6 rights giving rise to x's 'power' is problematic. Similar issues may arise in relation to the characterization of civil and political rights as Type 6 rights (e.g. x's power to ensure that x has a fair and independent trial is not easily grasped).

Box 6.13 PROPOSED RECLASSIFICATION OF AUTHORITATIVE INTERNATIONAL STANDARDS IN THE FIELD OF POVERTY AND HUMAN RIGHTS AS CLAIM-RIGHTS

Example 1 *Article 25.1 of the Universal Declaration of Human Rights*

- State of affairs $S(x,y)$:'For those x unable to achieve the capability of x to achieve adequate health and well-being (including adequate food, clothing, housing, and medical care), actions will be undertaken to ensure the secure realization of this capability'
- Scope: All individuals x resident in y subject to any restrictions recognized in the Universal Declaration, all states y that have adopted the Universal Declaration of Human Rights

Type 6:	x **has versus y claim, power, counterfreedom**
Element:	**Claim**
Explication:	it shall be the case that/y sees to it that/$S(x,y)$
Formula:	shall do $[y, S(x,y)]$
Interpretation:	y has an obligation to see to it that $S(x,y)$
Element:	**Power**
Explication:	It shall not be the case that/x does not see to it that/$S(x,y)$
Formalization:	$\sim$ Shall $\sim$ Do $[x, S(x,y)]$ May Do $[x, S(x,y)]$
Interpretation:	x does not have an obligation to refrain from seeing to it that $S(x,y)$ x may see to it that $S(x,y)$
Element:	**Counterfreedom**
Explication:	It shall not be the case that/x sees to it that/$S(x,y)$
Formalization:	$\sim$ Shall Do $[x, S(x,y)]$
Interpretation:	x does not have an obligation to see to it that $S(x,y)$

specification of the general obligations of states in Article 2 of the ICESCR and are therefore directly relevant to the characterization of the nature and scope of state responsibility under other Articles of the Covenant, including Article 11 (see Section 5.5). For each state taken separately, x's claim against y that steps be taken through international assistance and cooperation can be captured and formalized in the Kanger framework using the following formulations.

- State of affairs $S(x,y)$:'steps are taken through international assistance and cooperation to ensure that x has the capability to achieve an adequate standard of living'
- Scope: all individuals x resident in y (*a*) satisfying relevant conditions and (*b*) unable to secure the capability to achieve an adequate standard of living through own efforts; all states y that are party to the ICESCR
- Type of right no. 6: x has versus y claim, power, counterfreedom.

Box 6.14   PROPOSED RECLASSIFICATION OF AUTHORITATIVE INTERNATIONAL
STANDARDS IN THE FIELD OF POVERTY AND HUMAN RIGHTS

**Example 2   *Article 11a of the International Covenant on Economic, Social, and
Cultural Rights, read in conjunction with Article 2***

- State of affairs $S(x,y)$:'y takes steps individually and through international
  assistance and cooperation to the maximum of available resources to secure the
  progressive realization of the capability to achieve an adequate standard of living
  (including adequate nutrition, clothing, and housing) for all x unable to secure
  this capability their own efforts'
- Scope: All individuals x resident in y satisfying relevant conditions all states y that
  are party to the ICESCR

Type 6:	**x has versus y claim, power, counterfreedom**
Element:	**Claim**
Explication:	it shall be the case that/y sees to it that/$S(x,y)$
Formula:	shall do [y, $S(x,y)$]
Interpretation:	y has an obligation to see to it that $S(x,y)$
Element:	**Power**
Explication:	It shall not be the case that/x does not see to it that/$S(x,y)$
Formalization:	$\sim$ Shall $\sim$ Do [$x, S(x,y)$] May Do [x, $S(x,y)$]
Interpretation:	x does not have an obligation to refrain from seeing to it that $S(x,y)$
	x may see to it that $S(x,y)$
Element:	**Counterfreedom**
Explication:	It shall not be the case that/x sees to it that/$S(x,y)$
Formalization:	$\sim$ Shall Do [x, $S(x,y)$]
Interpretation:	x does not have an obligation to see to it that $S(x,y)$

**Example 3   *The human right to sufficient food and water under Article 27 of the
South African Bill of Rights***

State of affairs $S(x,y)$: 'policies and programmes are adopted that are capable of
facilitating the progressive realization of the capability to achieve sufficient food and
water for all x unable to achieve this capability by their own efforts'
Scope: All individuals x resident in South Africa satisfying relevant conditions, the
South African government y

Type 6:	**x has versus y claim, power, counterfreedom**
Element:	**Claim**
Explication:	it shall be the case that/y sees to it that/$S(x,y)$
Formula:	shall do [y, $S(x,y)$]
Interpretation:	y has an obligation to see to it that $S(x,y)$
Element:	**Power**
Explication:	It shall not be the case that/x does not see to it that/$S(x,y)$
Formalization:	$\sim$ Shall $\sim$ Do [$x, S(x,y)$] May Do [x, $S(x,y)$]
Interpretation:	x does not have an obligation to refrain from seeing to it that $S(x,y)$
	x may see to it that $S(x,y)$
Element:	**Counterfreedom**

Box 6.14 Continued

Explication:	It shall not be the case that/x sees to it that/S(x,y)]
Formalization:	~ Shall Do [x, S(x,y)]
Interpretation:	x does not have an obligation to see to it that S(x,y)

The implication of this formulation is that all *x* anywhere have a claim against all *y* anywhere and that 'steps are taken through international assistance and co-operation to ensure that *x* has the capability to achieve an adequate standard of living'. In order to capture and formalize the idea of collective obligation and the joint specification of states collectively, an alternative would be to introduce the international community as a distinct agent:

- State of affairs *S(x,*IC): 'steps are taken through international assistance and cooperation to ensure that *x* has the capability to achieve an adequate standard of living'

- Scope: all individuals *x* resident in *y* (*a*) satisfying relevant conditions and (*b*) unable to secure the capability to achieve an adequate standard of living through own efforts; all states *y* that are party to the ICESCR

- Type of right no. 6: *x* has versus IC claim, power, counterfreedom

Membership of 'international community' could be restricted to states parties to the ICESCR, or be more broadly specified. The characterization suggests that *x* has a claim against all other states collectively that steps are taken through international assistance and cooperation, but not against specific states. However, as noted in Section 6.4, the Kanger System is 'impersonal' in the sense that rights-based statements are explicated in relation to single obligation-holders. Extending the Kanger System using iterated operators provides for the specification of obligations in multiagent systems. However, in addition to specifying the multiple obligation-holders that are collectively responsible for bringing about a state affairs, there is also a need to capture and formalize the allocation of the responsibilities of different obligation-holders in a multiagent system in relation to the joint or collective goal. For example, who is responsible (and therefore 'gets the blame') when a joint obligation is unfulfilled—the group as a whole or one or more individual members(s)? Can a member or members of the collective or group bring about the required state of affairs on behalf of the collective or group, or should individual members be modelled as having responsibility for the performance of certain tasks?[18] Modelling by Royakkers (2000), Royakkers and Dignum (2000), and Grossi et al. (2004) views rights in terms of social commitment to bring about states of affairs where the actions that should be performed by each of the multiple obligation-holders in genuine situations of cooperative obligation (where the group or collective is required jointly to bring about states of affairs) can be specified. The cooperative process is explicitly modelled as involving:

- Recognition of a cooperative obligation jointly to bring about a state of affairs
- Negotiation between members of the group of a plan that allocates individual tasks with respect to the joint goal
- Execution of the plan.

Whilst individual tasks can be specified in the Grossi et al. (2004) model, joint obligations are not simply the sum of individual obligations—they involve cooperation and coordination (including plan negotiation, sequencing of individual tasks, etc.), and cannot be decomposed into individual separate obligations in any straightforward way. This approach seems particularly appropriate for moving forward on the modelling of the international human rights system as a multiparty system where the internationally recognized human rights cannot always be adequately protected and promoted by single obligation-holders acting alone and may require international cooperation. It suggests that 'cooperation' as an international obligation is more than the sum of the actions of individual obligation-holders, and reinforces the view that there may be a need for enhanced institutional mechanisms for allocating and coordinating the individual tasks of the various obligation-holders in relation to international to cooperation in field of development and human rights (e.g. the proposals for 'Development Compacts' set out by the UN Independent Expert on the Right to Development; see Section 5.5). Formal modelling of the idea that if a particular agent is the only member of a group able to perform that part of a collective task, that agent should be responsible for performing that element of the collective task, also seems particularly relevant.

---

[18] The author is grateful for the points raised in Van Hees (2004) relating to this issue.

Conclusion

This chapter has considered emerging models of freedoms and rights in welfare economics and social choice, and highlighted the need for these frameworks to take account of internationally recognized standards in the field of poverty and human rights. The formal representation of the idea of freedom from poverty as a basic human right was analysed using the Kanger System of deontic logic. It was argued that the categorizations of human rights developed by H. Kanger failed to capture essential elements of widely accepted legal language expressions of the idea of a human right in international human rights law and authoritative international juris-prudence. These expressions suggest that all human rights incorporate common elements of claim (reflected in positive obligations to take ac-tions to protect, promote, and fulfil human rights) and immunity (reflected in negative obligations of non-intervention, omission, and re-straint).

Various proposals for developing the formal representation of the idea of freedom from poverty as a basic human right using the Kanger System were then explored. These proposals improved on past approaches by building on Sen's concepts of 'capability-rights' and 'meta-rights', and by capturing and formalizing a common element of 'claim' (as well as a common element of 'immunity'). The proposals provide a useful starting point for developing the formal representation of the idea of freedom from poverty as a basic human right, and highlight the ways in which formal representation crystallizes the nature of broader debates about poverty and human rights in ethics and international human rights law (absolute versus non-absolute human rights, negative versus positive correlative obligations, the possible dichotomy between the conditions of human rights-violation, and the conditions of rights-fulfilments) and takes such debates to a more rigorous level. The proposals set out in this paper did not, however, address certain limitations of the 'Kanger System' raised in the literature or the extensions and refinements suggested in the literature for dealing with these limitations. Furthermore, the discussion brought into focus additional complexities of the formal representation of human rights in the context of 'imperfect obligations'. Where the complete fulfilment of a human right cannot be achieved by one agent alone because of cost and feasibility constraints, or in other multiparty situations where cooperation is required to achievement the complete fulfilment of a human right, there may be a dichotomy between the conditions under which a right is completely fulfilled and the conditions under which a right is violated. Further research is required to address the need for appropriate extensions of and refinements to the 'Kanger System' to take forward the formal representation of human rights of this type.

7

Conclusion
Towards a 'Working Model' of International Accountability and Responsibility in the Field of Global Poverty and Human Rights

Could the 'capability approach' be meaningfully extended and applied as a 'Working Model' of international accountability and responsibility by linking the objective of 'capability expansion' to legally binding international standards in the field of human rights? The analysis concludes with a discussion of how the correspondences and analogues between the 'capability approach' and the international human rights framework provide a basis for the development of cross-disciplinary 'Working Models' of international accountability and responsibility in the field of global poverty and human rights bridging ethics, economics, and international law. Proposals for extending and applying the 'capability approach' on the basis of a supplementary theory of international human rights law are considered in the light of broader debates about the extension and application of the 'capability approach'. The idea of linking the protection and promotion of basic capabilities to internationally recognized standards in the field of human rights—and to institutional procedures and mechanisms for monitoring, accountability, and enforcement—is considered and the notion of an 'internationally recognized capability set' is discussed.

7.1 Extending and Applying the 'Capability Approach' as a 'Working Model' of International Responsibility and Accountability: The Underlying Theoretical Issues

The idea of linking the 'capability framework' to a supplementary theory of international legal obligation has been reflected in a number of proposals for the development of 'Working Models' of international accountability and responsibility to the UN Commission on Human Rights. Whilst these practical proposals have moved the capabilities and human rights agenda forward, they nevertheless raise important issues about the specification and assignment of duties in the 'capability framework' that have not been resolved by Sen, or indeed in the broader debates about the extension and application of the 'capability approach'. The nature of the underlying links between the 'capability approach' and the actual system of international human rights law require further examination and clarification.

The Relevance of Broader Debates about the Extension and Application of the 'Capability Approach'

The question of whether the 'capability framework' can be meaningfully and coherently combined with a supplementary theory of international legal obligation in the field of global poverty and human rights cross-cuts important debates about the extension and application of the 'capability approach'. The more general need for 'supplementary' and 'background' criteria has been discussed in the context of the charge that Sen's 'capability framework' is 'substantially incomplete' and fails to provide an adequate theoretical basis for making judgements about the relative values of different capabilities. This results in inadequate consideration of the underlying reasons in terms of which the elements of a sub-set of basic and central (or 'highly valuable') capabilities might be identified and justified. Sen has in fact defended this interpretation of the 'capability approach', highlighting the limits that diversity, disagreement, and value pluralism may impose on the development of evaluative systems, and challenging 'completeness' as a condition of evaluation in both ethics and economics. His practical proposals have emphasized that 'capability space' is consistent and combinable with several different substantive theories of value and that there is no theoretical necessity for the question of relative value to be resolved before an agreement on the choice of an evaluative space. In the absence of a complete agreement about relative weights, a focus on the 'intrinsic relevance and centrality of functionings and capabilities' can have 'substantial discriminatory power'; whilst a pragmatic consensus concerning the relative importance of a small number of central and highly valuable capabilities provides a basis for 'capability set' ranking using dominance reasoning and the 'partial order approach' (Sen 1985*a*, *b*; 1987*a*: 34; 1992*a*: 46–9, 133–4; 1993*a*: 31–4, 48–9; 1997 [1973]: 203–9). Nevertheless, whilst defending the interpretation of the 'capability approach' as 'substantially incomplete', Sen (1987*a*: 107–8) has fully acknowledged that in developing and applying the capability approach, ' . . . it is valuation with which we are ultimately concerned'. The possible grounds for distinguishing valuable capabilities from the trivial, need to be fully considered and important foundational issues regarding the identification and justification of the elements of a basic capability set need to be fully resolved (Sen 1992*a*: 42–9) and in moving forward, an ethical or social theory of value may be required to complement the capability approach (Sen 1987*a*: 100–2).

The need for a background theory of ethical or social value

Various types of background and supplementary considerations that could provide the grounds for valuing certain capabilities and functionings above others have been considered in the broader literature on the 'capability approach'. The question of the underlying relationships between the concepts of capabilities, human rights, and obligations is central to this debate. In the first wave of discussion on the issue, Williams noted that valuation exercises have traditionally been based either on some notion of what is valued as important by convention in a given social and cultural context on the one hand, or from some notion of real human nature, needs, interests, or rights on the other, or else from a combination of these grounds. He emphasizes the potential role of a background or supplementary theory of basic or human rights in identifying and justifying important and valuable capabilities:

[It has been suggested that the problem of relative value] cannot be solved by reference to capabilities in themselves, but that you have to introduce the notion of a right. The apparently innocent and descriptive-looking notions of the standard of living or well-being may then turn out to contain consideration about those goods to which we believe people have a basic right. (Williams 1987: 100)

Williams's analysis also raises the question of the relationship between human rights, obligations, and capabilities in Sen's conceptual framework.

In calling for conceptual clarity on this issue, Williams has challenged the primacy of the concept of rights (rather than the concept of capability):

> The notion of a basic human right seems to me obscure.... I would rather come at it from the perspective of basic human capabilities. I would prefer capabilities to do the work, and if we are going to have a language or rhetoric of rights, to have it delivered from them, rather than the other way round. But I think that there remains an unsolved problem: how we should see the relations between these concepts... (Williams 1987: 100)

The failure to resolve the problem of the specification and apportionment of precise obligations also received attention in the earlier literature. As Crocker's (1995: 191) discussion of the 'capability approach' and the question of relative value asked, how should obligations to protect and promote basic and central capabilities be apportioned among private individuals and organizations, national governments, groups of richer countries, and international organizations? Moreover, how much is required (duty) and how much is praiseworthy (supererogatory) but not required?[1]

7.2 Questions Left Unresolved by Sen's More Recent Treatment of the 'Capability Framework'

To what extent does Sen's more recent emphasis on the idea of fundamental freedoms and human rights resolve these debates? If the interpretation set out in Chapter 3 is correct, then the concept of 'human freedom' seems to be primary in Sen's conceptual framework. Valuable human freedoms are associated with *derivative* sets of human rights and obligations (with 'capability freedoms' and the associated human rights and obligations forming an important sub-class). On this interpretation, the idea of human rights does not seem to function as a 'background theory of ethical or social value' in Sen's conceptual framework. However, there is some ambiguity regarding the primacy of capability in Sen's conceptual framework, and at times a more fundamental role for the idea of human rights is suggested (e.g. Sen 1984: 310), whilst the concept of obligation could also be viewed as foundational. Furthermore, Sen's more recent statements do not seem to resolve the debates in the literature about 'capability set' valuation. For example, Sen (2001) emphasizes the sub-class of 'capability freedoms' *that people have reasons to value*. He suggests that the

---

[1] Glover (1995: 124–5); O'Neill (1995: 144); Alkire (2002); Robeyns (2003).

specification and justification of this sub-class should take account of both individual agency goals and contextual influences (e.g. interpersonal variations associated with 'adaptive preferences' and 'positional dependences'), and accommodate (*a*) reflective evaluation of capability achievement (taking account of individual counterfactual choices and meta-preferences); (*b*) external critical scrutiny of the 'reasons' underlying values, preference, and choice. However, the relative weight to be given to (*a*) and (*b*) is left open and the clarified approach raises far-reaching questions about the nature of the 'reasons' to be considered. In addition, Sen (2004a: 355–6) takes the analysis forward by emphasizing the Rawlsian concept of 'public reasoning' and its role in 'ethical objectivity'. However, a clear specification of 'objective reasons' is not provided.

The specification and assignment of duties in the 'capability framework'

Sen's reliance on the Kantian concept of 'imperfect obligation' raises certain additional complexities. As discussed in Chapter 2, the Kantian association between 'imperfect duties' and 'duties of virtue' is often taken to imply that the concept of 'imperfect obligation' cannot be meaningfully and coherently invoked as a basis for the conceptualization of human rights-based claims. This would seem to suggest that the concept of 'imperfect obligation' might prove a rather weak basis for the development of 'Working Models' of responsibility and accountability in the field of poverty and human rights. The discussion in Chapter 3 showed how Sen's recent emphasis on the concept of 'reasonableness' takes the debate forward here by establishing general universal positive obligations of assistance and aid 'of those in a position to help'. However, the issue of who *in particular* is responsible for fulfilling a human right, and *how far* they are obliged to go in fulfilling the human right, is left open (Sen 2000a: 494–5).

7.3 Extending and Applying the 'Capability Framework' on the Basis of Nussbaum's List

Nussbaum (2003: 33) has argued that Sen's 'capability perspective' is too vague and fails to provide a basis for distinguishing important and highly valuable freedoms from the trivial and the bad. She has defended the extension and application of the 'capability approach' on the basis of a definite list of basic and central capabilities in this context. The proposed list focuses on the following elements: 1. life; 2. bodily health; 3. bodily integrity;

4. senses, imagination, and thought; 5. emotion; 6. practical reason; 7. affiliation; 8. relationship with other species; 9. play; 10. control over one's environment. Nussbaum's earlier contributions (e.g. Nussbaum 1993, 1995) explore the possibility of a unique list of basic and central capabilities of this type in the context of an Aristotelian theory of non-relative values. Rejecting *both* the realist proposition that universal values can be identified through abstract processes of reasoning, and the relativist proposition that universal values are not possible because there is no 'objective' methodology for evaluating rival ethical claims, she contends that a universal conception of a human being is 'both available to ethics and a valuable starting point' (Nussbaum 1995: 70). Shared understandings of the constituent elements of *humanness* and a *good human life* may be available across societies and cultures, and empirical methods and anthropological research can help to identify a set of 'central and basic' capabilities that 'is not the mere projection of local preferences, but is fully international'—providing a basis for 'cross-cultural attunement' (Nussbaum 1995: 74–81). In responding to this proposal, Sen has affirmed the relevance of Aristotle's emphasis on the exercise of human capability, but has nevertheless emphasized the 'deliberate incompleteness' of the 'capability approach'.

[An objectivist normative account of human functioning] would indeed be a systematic way of eliminating the incompleteness of the capability approach.... [But] this view of human nature (with a unique list of functionings for a good human life) may be tremendously over-specified.... [T]he use of the capability approach...does not require taking that route, and the deliberate incompleteness of the capability approach permits other routes to be taken. (Sen: 1993*a*: 47)

Nussbaum on capabilities and human rights

Nussbaum's more recent contributions focus on the possibility of a list of basic and central capabilities that is explicitly introduced for political purposes (without any grounding in metaphysical ideas of the type 'that divide people along lines of culture and religion' and that is combinable with different comprehensive theories of the good) that could form the core of an 'overlapping consensus' (Nussbaum 2002, 2003: 42). Correspondences between the 'capability approach' and the idea of human rights are emphasized in Nussbaum (1995, 1997, 1999*a*, 1999*b*, 1999*c*, 2000, 2003, 2004). Basic capabilities are conceptualized as needs for functioning that give rise to claims of assistance by others—giving rise to correlative political obligations on the part of governments, and encapsulating a key element in many contemporary notions of human rights

(Nussbaum 1995: 88). The practical correspondences between the 'basic list' and internationally recognized human rights are also emphasized, with protection for liberty of conscience and religious observance built into element 6; non-discrimination and protection for freedom of assembly and speech into element 7; and political participation and protections of free speech and association into element 10 (Nussbaum 2003: 41–2). In linking the objective of 'capability expansion' to the notion of obligation, Nussbaum characterizes central and basic capabilities as 'fundamental entitlements' to be included among the fundamental purposes of social cooperation as objects of collective obligation at both the national and the international levels (Nussbaum 2003, 2004: 13). As in Sen's framework, however, the specification of obligations is general rather than specific.

'We think what people are entitled to receive and, even before we can say in detail who may have the duties, we conclude that there are such duties and that we have a collective obligation to make sure people get what they are due'. Thus the first answer to the question 'Who has the duties?' is that we all do. Humanity is under a collective obligation to find ways of living and cooperating together so that all human beings have decent lives. Now, after being clear on that, we begin to think about how to bring that about'. (Nussbaum 2004: 13)

Like Sen, then, Nussbaum fails to provide for the specification and apportionment of the precise duties to be performed by particular duty-holders in relation to 'capability expansion'. This poses a practical problem for the development of the 'capability framework' as a 'Working Model' of international accountability and responsibility. In order to move beyond the establishment of the general obligations of those in a position to help, towards the more precise specification and apportionment of obligations in the 'capability framework', supplementary criteria will be required for both Sen's and Nussbaum's versions of the 'capability approach'. Should international human rights law have a direct role in this process?

7.4 Extending and Applying the 'Capability Framework' on the Basis of International Human Rights Law

The idea of linking the 'capability framework' to a supplementary theory of international legal obligation has been reflected in a number of proposals for the development of 'Working Models' of this type to the UN Commission on Human Rights. For example, in a series of reports to the UN High Commission on Human Rights and elsewhere (Sengupta 1999,

2001, 2002*a*, 2002*b*, 2002*c*, 2004*a*, 2004*b*), the UN Independent Expert on the Right to Development (1998–2004), has set out a 'human rights-based development' framework ('HRBD Framework') that characterizes the ultimate objectives of development in terms of 'capability expansion' (rather than other informational focuses such as utility or growth), but that goes beyond the 'human development paradigm' by (*a*) viewing central and basic capabilities as the object of human rights-based claims on governments and other actors; (*b*) emphasizing the direct role that the actual system of international human rights law can play in allocating obligations to different obligation-holders (including national governments, other governments, and international organizations) in this field. The HRBD Framework links the objective of 'capability expansion' to the implementation of the broad class of internationally recognized human rights set out in the Universal Declaration and in legally binding international treaties including the ICCPR, ICESCR, CEDAW, and CRC.[2] The linkages between the 'capability approach' and the international human rights framework are also emphasized in OHCHR (2004), with internationally recognized standards being adopted as a basis for the conceptualization and implementation of PRSPs.[3]

How should the underlying links between the 'capability approach' and the actual system of international human rights law be conceived?

Whilst moving the agenda on capabilities and human rights forward, the proposals discussed above nevertheless raise important questions about the underlying links between the 'capability approach' on the one hand, and the system of international human rights law on the other. For example, Sengupta (2004*b*: 16) suggests that in extending and applying the 'capability approach' as a 'Working Model' of international accountability and responsibility, there is a need to go beyond the establishment of the general obligations of those in a position to help, and to specify and assign the specific actions that each obligation-holder is required to perform. He

---

[2] The Sengutpa framework arises in the particular context of the adoption of the Declaration on the Right to Development adopted by the UNGA in 1986 ('Declaration on the Right to Development', adopted as UNGA Resolution 41/128 of 4 December 1986). The focus on international treaties avoids some of the broader controversies associated with the notion of 'collective' and/or 'third-generation' rights relating to the possible 'collective element' of the Right to Development (and associated debates about whether states can be rights-holders and whether duties can be owed to peoples as a whole or to states). For further discussions see, for example, Higgins (1994), Alston (2001), and Sengupta (2002*a*: 861–4).

[3] Also see Osmani (2000).

envisages a relationship between the 'capability approach' and 'a process of international political consensus building' whereby 'morally binding' (general/imperfect) obligations are 'converted' or 'transformed' into 'legally binding' (specific/perfect) obligations and are made justiciable. There are two important limitations to this view of the underlying links between the 'capability approach' (as a normative framework) and the actual system of international human rights law. The first relates to the assumption that 'imperfect obligations' are located exclusively in the ethical domain. However, as discussed in Chapter 3, this assumption reflects the traditional treatment of the concept of 'imperfect obligation' in the Kantian framework. However, the analogy between the Kantian notion of 'imperfect obligation' and the concept of an 'international obligation of result' points to the possibility of important applications of a contemporary notion of 'imperfect obligation' in the legal as well as the ethical domain.[4] The second limitation relates to the implied 'conversion' between the general moral obligations associated with the 'capability approach' and the actual standards codified in international human rights law. Whilst analogies and correspondences provide a basis for practical applications of the 'capability approach', the idea of a direct transformative or intrinsic relationship could be misleading and raises important questions about the nature of the 'consensus' involved. Third, Sen has in fact often downplayed the necessity of international human rights law in codifying and reinforcing human rights (2000: 498).[5] This poses a pressing problem for the potential application and extension of the 'capability approach' as a 'Working Model' of accountability and responsibility in the field of global poverty and human rights. Although Sen's position does not preclude the possibility of pragmatic 'Working Models' that move forward by linking the 'capability approach' to the standards, codified or otherwise, established in international human rights law, the 'capability approach' does not require or entail linkages of this type.

[4] 'International legal obligations of result' focus on the evaluation of the reasonableness of action and courses of action in the light of the results achieved (rather than on the assessment of the performance and non-performance of specified types of action). Where the complete achievement of human rights is not immediately feasible (including multiparty situations where the complete achievement of a human right requires cooperation) the result required may relate to the promotion of a human right (e.g. by the adoption of an appropriate policy). In both cases the formulation of the legal obligation is general rather than specific and the obligations do not readily fall within the reach of the concept of 'perfect obligation'. See the discussion of 'international obligations of result' in Section 5.3.

[5] 'Human rights can have their own domain of influence and importance *without* being parasitic on—or even being wisely reinforced by—subsequent legislation' (Sen 2000a: 498).

7.5 Towards a Pragmatic View of the Underlying Links Between the 'Capability Approach' and International Human Rights Law

Given the unresolved nature of these broader debates, in developing theoritical underpinnings for 'Working Models' of international account- ability and responsibility in the field of global poverty and human rights, there are good reasons for adopting a *pragmatic* view of the underlying relationship between the 'capability approach' and inter- national law, that retains an emphasis on the 'capability approach' as 'substantially incomplete'. As Sen has emphasized, viewed in this way (as 'substantially incomplete'), 'capability space' is consistent and com- binable with several different substantive theories of value. A supplemen- tary theory of international obligation based on the legal commitments of governments in the field of human rights could then be viewed as provid- ing one possible 'supplementary' or 'background' theory of this type, with internationally recognized standards being viewed as a possible basis for specifying the elements of a basic capability set and for allocating the associated duties on governments and other actors.

Combining 'capability space' with a supplementary theory of international human rights law

The proposal at hand combines 'capability space' with a background or supplementary theory of international human rights law and treats inter- nationally recognized human rights and the corresponding obligations on states and other actors as being associated with an implicit or underlying capability set. Authoritative international standards in the field of human rights are explicitly adopted as a basis for the selection of central and basic capabilities and for the identification of duty-holders and the apportion- ment of general and specific duties relating to the protection and promo- tion of a basic capability set. For example, the international recognition of the human right to freedom from hunger is taken to reflect the critical importance of an underlying 'capability freedom' (the capability to be adequately nourished) and to provide a link with internationally recog- nized and established obligations on governments and other actors in relation to the protection and promotion of this underlying 'capability freedom'. The proposed approach provides a basis for the specification of an 'internationally agreed' or 'authoritively recognized' or 'legally signifi- cant' 'basic capability set'. This approach could also be used as a basis for selecting and applying a human rights-based 'international poverty line' specified in 'capability' rather than 'income' space and linked to legally binding international obligations on states and other actors, both individually and collectively. The 'Minimum Core Obligations' approach provides a legal basis for an international poverty line specified in 'capability space' rather than income space and relating to severe and extreme forms of poverty. Lists of these types would be useful for human rights advocacy purposes and should be viewed as *minimal* lists generated by just one of the various possible background or supplementary theories and methods to which Sen alludes— with other lists generated by other background and supplementary theories or participatory methods possible (and for many purposes preferable).

Building on the correspondences and synergies between the 'capability approach' and international human rights law

Nussbaum (2003: 38; 2004: 13; 2005: 174) suggests that her version of the 'capabilities list' can be characterized as one approach to the idea of human rights. Given the contested nature of the idea of human rights, she focuses attention on the merits of viewing rights as capabilities— challenging the association of the idea of human rights with negative liberty, and highlighting the importance of evaluating whether or not relevant functionings are present:

[A] focus on capabilities, although closely allied with the human rights approach, adds an important clarification to the idea of human rights: for it informs us that our goal is not merely 'negative liberty' or absence of interfering state action—one very common understanding of the notion of rights—but, instead, the full ability of people to be and to choose these very important things.

Whilst Nussbaum's list can be (and is often) conceptualized in terms of a list of minimal entitlements or human rights, given the various concerns expressed in the literature about Nussbaum's list (including concerns around democratic legitimacy and participation as well as the broad nature of the list),[6] the analysis in this monograph suggests that the repeated commitment of governments to authoritatively recognized international standards in the field of human rights can provide a pragmatic terrain for specifying the elements of a basic capability set and for allocating the associated obligations on governments at the individual level and collectively (through international cooperation). An important aim of the monograph has been to highlight the complementary and reinforcing

[6]On which, see Robeyns (2003, 2005) and Alkire (2002).

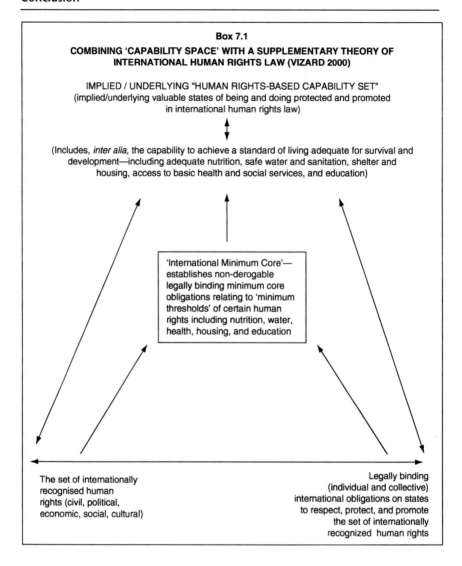

elements of the 'capability approach' and the international human rights framework, and to demonstrate that these complementary and reinforcing elements provide the basis of an integrated cross-disciplinary framework for analysing global poverty as a human rights issue that bridges ethics, economics, and international law. The discussion in Chapter 5 established eight key complementary and reinforcing elements of the international human rights framework (also see Box 1.2). The proposal does not attempt to resolve the underlying normative debates nor to fulfil the criteria required by a democratic international system or an account of objective public reasoning under free and fair conditions (the necessity of which is suggested in Sen 2004a: 355–6; 2004b). Important limitations relate to the broader criticisms of the system of international human rights law associated with the legal, power-based, and feminist critiques (relating, for example, to normative content, weak enforcement mechanisms, the focus on civil and political rights, limited procedures for democratic accountability and participation, culture-based limitations, and the ways in which the international legal system functions to promote power-based interests).[7] The advantages of the approach relate instead to the conceptualization of the links between the idea of a basic 'capability set', international human rights law, and international machinery for monitoring and enforcement. The elements of the list will vary with the degree of universality required. However, all countries have signed or ratified at least one major international human rights treaty and large numbers of countries have signed and ratified more than one treaty of this type. In the absence of complete agreement vis-à-vis the first order ethical debates (including the question of relationship of a normative theory of human rights to the actual system of international human rights law), this emerging body of international standards provides a basis for extending and applying the 'capability approach' as a 'Working Model' of international responsibility and accountability in the field of global poverty and human rights.

---

[7] See, for example, Nussbaum (2003: 37), Chomsky and Herman (1979), Gearty (2004), and, on the culture-based critique and for further references, Vizard (2000b).

References

Alkire, S.(2002). *Valuing Freedoms: Sen's Capability Approach and Poverty Reduction.* Oxford: Oxford University Press

Alston, P. (2001). *People's Rights.* New York: Oxford University Press.

Alston, P., and Quinn, G. (1987). 'The Nature and Scope of States Parties Obligations Under the International Covenant on Economic, Social and Cultural Rights', *Human Rights Quarterly,* 9/2: 156–229.

Alston, P. and Steiner, H. (eds.) (1996). *International Human Rights in Context.* Oxford: Clarendon.

American Law Institute (1987). '*Restatement (Third) The Foreign Relations Law of the United State*' in Alston and Steiner (1996), 145–7.

Anderson, E. (2003). 'Sen, Ethics and Democracy', *Feminist Economics,* 9/2–3: 239–61.

Agarwal, B., Humphries, J., and Robeyns, I. (2003). 'A Special Issue on Amartya Sen's Work and Ideas: A Gender Perspective', *Feminist Economics,* 9/2–3.

Alston, P. and Simma, B. (1996 [1992]). 'The Sources of Human Rights Law: Custom, Jus Cogens, and General Principles', in P. Alston (ed.), *Human Rights Law.* Aldershot: Dartmouth.

Aristotle (1995 [350 BC]). *Politics (Tranlsated by Ernest Barker. Revised with an Introduction and Notes by R.F. Stalley).* Oxford: Oxford University Press.

Arrow, K. J. (1963 [1951]). *Social Choice and Individual Values.* New York: Cowles Foundation for Research in Economics at Yale University, John Wiley and Sons.

—— (1995). 'A Note on Freedom and Flexibility', in K. Basu, P. K. Pattanaik, and K. Suzumura (eds.), *Choice, Welfare, and Development: a Festschrift in Honour of Amartya K. Sen.* Oxford: Clarendon Press, 7–16.

Barry, B. (1995). *Justice as Impartiality.* Oxford: Oxford University Press.

Barry, C. (2005). 'Applying the Contribution Principle', *Metaphilosophy,* 36/1–2: 210–27

Beizt, C. (1999). *Political Theory and International Relations,* 2nd edn. (first published 1979). Princeton, NJ: Princeton University Press.

Berlin, I. (1969). *Four Essays on Liberty.* Oxford: Oxford University Press.

Besley, T. and Burgess, R. (2002). 'The Political Economy of Government Responsiveness: Theory and Evidence from India', *Quarterly Journal of Economics,* 117/4: 1415–51.

Brownlie, I. (1995). *Basic Documents in International Law.* Oxford: Oxford University Press.

Brunel, A. and Salles, M. (1998). 'Interpretative, Semantic and Formal Difficulties of the Social Choice Rule Approach to Rights', in J. F. Laslier, M. Fleurbaey, N. Gravel, and A. Trannoy (eds.), *Freedom in Economics.* London: Routledge.

Centre on Housing Rights and Evictions (COHRE) (2003). *50 Leading Cases on Economic, Social and Cultural Rights: Summaries.* Working Paper No.1: ESC Rights Litigation Programme. Available at: http://www.cohre.org/downloads/50leadingcases.pdf.

——(2004). *Litigating Economic, Social and Cultural Rights: Achievements, Challenges and Strategies.* Available at: http://www.cohre.org/library/Litigating%20ESCR%20Report.pdf.

Chen, S. and Ravallion, M. (2004), *How Have the World's Poorest Fared Since the Early 1980s?* Available at: http://www.worldbank.org/research/povmonitor/MartinPapers/How_have_the_poorest_fared_since_the_early_1980s.pdf.

Chinkin, C. (2003). *Lecture at the One Day Conference on Children's Rights and Child Poverty,* LSE, 16 October.

Chomsky, N. and Herman, E. (1979). *The Washington Connection and Third World Fascism: The Political Economy of Human Rights,* Vol. 1. Boston: South End Press.

Cohen, S. (2001). *States of Denial: Knowing About Atrocities and Suffering.* Cambridge: Polity Press

Coles, J. and Hammond, P. (1995). 'Walrasian Equilibrium Without Survival: Existence, Efficiency and Remedial Policy', in K. Basu, P. K. Pattanaik, and K. Suzumura (eds.), *Choice, Welfare, and Development: a Festschrift in Honour of Amartya K. Sen.* Oxford: Clarendon Press, 32–64.

Corell, E. (2001). 'Amartya Sen's 100 Million Women', *Oxford Development Studies,* 29: 226–43.

Cranston, M. (1967). 'Human Rights Real and Supposed,' in D. D. Raphael (ed.), *Political Theory and the Rights of Man.* London: Macmillan.

Craven, M. C. R. (1995). *The International Covenant on Economic, Social and Cultural Rights.* Oxford: Clarendon Press.

Crocker, D. A. (1992). 'Functioning and Capability: The Foundations of Sen's and Nussbaum's Development Ethic', *Political Theory,* 2014: 584–611.

——(1995). 'Functioning and Capability: The Foundations of Sen's and Nussbaum's Development Ethic, Part 2', in M. Nussbaum and J. Glover (eds.), *Women, Culture and Development: A Study Of Human Capabilities.* Oxford: Oxford University Press.

Cruft, R. (2005). 'Human Rights and Positive Duties', *Ethics and International Affairs,* 19/1: 29–37.

Desai, M. (1995 [1990]). 'Rice and Fish: Asymmetric Preferences and Entitlement Failures in Food Growing Economies with Non-Food Producers', in M. Desai, *The Selected Essays of Meghnad Desai Vol. 2: Poverty, Famines and Economic Development.* Aldershot: Edward Elgar.

——(1995 [1987]). 'Story-Telling and Formalism in Economics: The Instance of Famine', in M. Desai (ed.) *The Selected Essays of Meghnad Desai Vol. 2: Poverty, Famines and Economic Development*. Aldershot: Edward Elgar.

DFID (2000). Realizing Human Rights for Poor People. Available at: http://www.dfid.gov.uk/pubs/files/tsphuman.pdf.

Drèze, J. and Sen, A. K. (1989). *Hunger and Public Action*. Oxford: Clarendon.

——and——(2002). *India: Development and Participation*. New Delhi: Oxford University Press.

Drèze, J. (2004). 'Democracy and the Right to Food', *Economic and Political Weekly*, 24 April 2004.

Eide, A. (1998). *Updated Study on the Right Adequate Food and to be Free From Hunger.* UN.Docs.E/CN.4/Sub.2/1998/9, E/CN.4/Sub.2/1999/12.

—— (1999). *Updated Study on the Right Adequate Food and to be Free From Hunger.* UN.Docs.E/CN.4/Sub.2/1998/9, E/CN.4/Sub.2/1999/12.

FAO (2004). *Intergovernmental Working Group for The Elaboration of a Set of Voluntary Guidelines to Support The Progressive Realisation of The Right To Adequate Food in The Context Of National Food Security: Final Report Of The Chair.* Available at: www.fao.org/docrep/meeting/008/J3345e/j3345e01.htm.

Fleurbaey, M. and Gaertner, W. (1996). 'Admissibility and Feasibility in Game Forms', *Analyse & Kritik*, 18: 54–66.

—— and Van Hees, M. (2000). 'On Rights in Game Forms', *Synthese*, 123: 295–326.

Freeman, M. D. A. (1994). *Lloyd's Introduction to Jurisprudence*. London: Sweet & Maxwell.

Gearty, C. (2004). *Is The Idea of Human Rights Now Doing More Harm Than Good?* Lecture, 12 October 2004, LSE

Gaertner, W., Pattanaik, P. K., and Suzumura, K. (1992). 'Individual Rights Revisited', *Economica*, 59: 161–77.

Gewirth, A. (1978). *Reason and Morality*. Chicago: University of Chicago Press.

——(1982). *Human Rights: Essays on Justification and Applications*. Chicago: University of Chicago Press.

——(1996). *The Community of Rights*. Chicago: University of Chicago Press.

Gilabert, P. (2005). 'The Duty to Eradicate Global Poverty: Positive or Negative?', *Ethical Theory and Moral Practice*, 7: 537–50.

Gordon D., Nandy, S., Pantazis, C., Pemberton, S., and Townsend, P. (2003). *Child Poverty In The Developing World*. Bristol: Policy Press.

Glover, J. (1990). *Causing Death and Saving Lives*. London: Penguin.

——(1995). 'The Research Programme of Development Ethics', in M. Nussbaum and J. Glover (eds.), *Women, Culture and Development: A Study Of Human Capabilities*. Oxford: Oxford University Press.

Gray, J. (1989). *Liberalisms: Essays in Political Philosophy*. London: Routledge.

—— (1995). *Berlin*. London: Fonatana Press.

Grossi, D., Dignum F., Royakkers, L., and Meyer J-J. Ch. (2004). 'Collective Obligations and Agents: Who Gets the Blame?' Available at: www.cs.uu.nl/~davide/pubblicazioio/grossi04collective.pdf.

Hammond, P. J. (1996). 'Game Forms versus Social Choice Rules as Models of Rights', in K. J. Arrow, A. K. Sen, and K. Suzumura (eds.), *Social Choice Re-Examined*. New York: St. Martin's Press, 2: 82–95.

—— (1998). 'Difficulties with the Social Choice Rule Approach to Rights: Some Comments on Brunes and Salles', in J. F. Laslier, M. Fleurbaey, N. Gravel, and A. Trannoy (eds.), *Freedom in Economics*. London: Routledge.

Harris, D. J. (1998). *Cases and Materials on International Law*. London: Sweet & Maxwell.

Hayden, P. (2002). *John Rawls: Towards a Just World Order*. Cardiff: University of Wales Press.

Hayek, F. A. (1960). *The Constitution of Liberty*. London: Routledge and Kegan Paul.

—— (1982*a*, 1982*b*, 1982*c*). *Law, Legislation and Society. A New Statement of the Liberal Principles of Justice and Political Economy. Volume 1, Rules and Order (1982a). Volume 2, The Mirage of Social Justice (1982b). Volume 3, The Political Order of A Free People (1982c)*. London: Routledge and Kegan Paul.

Herrestad, H. and Krogh, C. (1993). *The Right Direction*. Available at: http://www. jus.uio.no/iri/forskning/lib/papers.

—— and—— (1995). *Obligations Directed from Bearers to Counterparties*. Oslo, NRCCL and Department of Philosophy, University of Oslo. Available at: http://www. jus.uio.no/iri/forskning/lib/papers.

Higgins, R. (1994). *Problems and Processes: International Law and How We Use It*. Oxford: Clarendon Press.

HM Treasury (2004). Proposal for an International Finance Facility. Available at: http://www.hm-treasury.gov.uk/media/1C7/AB/1C7ABBFE-BCDC-D4B3-115B84EA4BD07566.pdf.

Hohfeld., W. (1925 [1919]). *Fundamental Legal Conceptions as Applied in Judicial Reasoning and Other Legal Essays, by W. Cook* (ed.). New Haven: Yale University Press.

International Committee for Human Rights (ICHR) (2004). *Non-State Actors and Corporate Responsibility*. Available at: www.ichr-law.org/english/expertise/areas/mom-state.htm.

International Law Commission (ILC) (1978). *Yearbook of the International Law Commission 1977*. New York: United Nations Publications, 2/1: 3–43.

Jasudowicz, T. (1994). 'The Legal Character of Social Rights', in K. A. K. Drzewicki, C. Krause, and A. Rosas, (eds.), *Social Rights as Human Rights: A European Challenge*. Turku: Åbo Akademi University.

Jones, P. (1994). *Rights: Issues in Political Theory*. Basingstoke: Macmillan.

Kanger, H. (1984). *Human Rights in the UN Declaration*. Stockholm: Almqvist & Wiskell International.

Kanger, S. (1971). 'New Foundations for Ethical Theory', in R. Hilpinen (ed.), *Deontic Logic: Introductory and Systematic Readings*. Dordrecht: D. Reidel.

—— (1972). 'Law and Logic', *Theoria: A Swedish Journal of Philosophy*, 38: 105–32.

—— (1985). 'On Realization of Human Rights', in G. Holmström and A. J. I. Jones (eds.), *Action, Logic and Social Theory*. Acta Philosophica Fennica, 38. Distributed by Akateeminen Kirjakauppa, Helsinki.

—— and Kanger, H. (1966). 'Rights and Parliamentarianism', *Theoria: A Swedish Journal of Philosophy*, 32: 85–115.

Kant, I. (1991 [1785]). 'Groundwork of the Metaphysics of Morals', in H. J. Paton (ed.), *The Moral Law*. London: Routledge.

—— (1996 [1797]). *The Metaphysics of Morals, Edited by Mary Gregor with an Introduction by R. J. Sullivan*. Cambridge: Cambridge University Press.

Klasen, S. and Wink, C. (2004). ' "Missing Women": Revisiting the Debate', *Feminist Economics*, 9/2–3: 263–99.

Krogh, C. (1995). *Obligations in Multiagent Systems*. Oslo, NRCCL and Department of Philosophy, University of Oslo. Available at: http://www.jus.uio.no/iri/forskning/lib/papers.

Krogh, C. (1996) *Rights of Agents*. Oslo, NRCCL and Department of Philosophy, University of Oslo. Available at: http://www.jus.uio.no/iri/forskning/lib/papers.

Lindahl, L. (1977). *Position and Change*. Dordrecht: D. Reidel.

—— (1994). 'Stig Kanger's Theory of Rights', in D. Prawitz, B. Skyrms, and D. Westerstahl, (eds.), *Logic, Methodolgy and Philosophy of Science IX: Proceedings of the Ninth International Congress of Logic, Methodology and Philosophy of Science, Uppsala, Sweden, August 7–14, 1991*. Studies in Logic and the Foundations of Mathematics 134.

MacCallum, G. (1973 [1967]). 'Negative and Positive Freedom', in R. Flatham (ed.), *Concepts in Social and Political Philosophy*. New York: Macmillan.

Makinson, D. (1986). 'On the Formal Representation of Rights Relations', *Journal of Philosophical Logic*, 15: 403–25.

Marks S. (2003) *The Human Rights Framework for Development: Seven Approaches*, available at http:// www.hsph.harvard.edu/fxbcenter/ FXBC_WP18--Marks.pdf.

Mas-Colell, A., Whinston, M., and Green, R. (1995). *Microeconomic Theory*. Oxford: Oxford University Press.

McKay, A., and Vizard, P. (2005). *Rights and Economic Growth: Inevitable Conflict or 'Common Ground'?* Concept paper available at http:// www.odi.org.uk/rights/backgroundpapers.html.

McNaughton, D. (1998*a*). 'Consequentialism', in E. Craig (ed.), *Routledge Encyclopaedia of Philosophy*. London: Routledge.

—— (1998*b*). 'Deontological Ethics', in E. Craig (ed.), *Routledge Encyclopaedia of Philosophy*. London: Routledge.

Nozick, R, (1974). *Anarchy, State and Utopia*. Oxford: Blackwell.

Nussbaum, M. C. (1993). 'Non-Relative Virtues: An Aristotelian Approach', in M. C. Nussbaum and A. Sen (eds.), *The Quality of Life*. Oxford: Oxford University Press.

—— (1995). 'Human Capabilities, Female Human Beings', in M. Nussbaum and J. Glover (eds.), *Women, Culture and Development: A Study of Human Capabilities*. Oxford: Oxford University Press.

Nussbaum, M. C. (1997). 'Capabilities and Human Rights', *Fordham Law Review*, 66: 273–300.

——(1999*a*). 'Women and Cultural Universals', in M. C. Nussbaum (ed.), *Sex and Social Justice*. Oxford: Oxford University Press.

——(1999*b*). 'Religion and Women's Human Rights', in M. C. Nussbaum (ed.), *Sex and Social Justice*. Oxford: Oxford University Press.

——(1999*c*). 'Judging Other Cultures: The Case of Genital Mutilation', in M. C. Nussbaum (ed.), *Sex and Social Justice*. Oxford: Oxford University Press.

——(2000). *Women and Human Development: The Capabilities Approach*. Cambridge: Cambridge University Press.

——(2001). 'Symposium on Amartya Sen's Philosophy: 5, Adaptive Preferences and Women's Options', *Economics and Philosophy*, 17: 67–88.

——(2003). 'Capabilities as Fundamental Entitlements: Sen and Global Justice', *Feminist Economics*, 9/2–3:33–59.

——(2004). 'Beyond the Social Contract: Capabilities and Global Justice', *Oxford Development Studies*, 32/1: 3–18.

Nussbaum, M. (2005). 'Women's Bodies: Violence, Security, Capabilities', *Journal of Human Development*, 6/2: 167–84.

OHCHR (2002). *Draft Guidelines: A Human Rights Approach to Poverty Reduction Papers*. Available at: http://www.ohchr.org/english/issues/docs/guidelinesfinal-poverty.doc.

——(2004). *Human Rights and Poverty Reduction: A Conceptual Framework*. Available at: http://www.ohchr.org/english/issues/poverty/docs/povertyE.pdf.

O'Neill, O. (1986). *Faces of Hunger: An Essay on Poverty, Justice and Development*. London: Allen and Unwin.

——(1989) *Constructions of Reason*. Cambridge: Cambridge University Press.

——(1993). 'Kantian Ethics', in P. Singer (ed.), *A Companion to Ethics*. Oxford: Blackwell.

——(1995). 'Justice, Capabilities, and Vulnerabilities', in M. Nussbaum and J. Glover (eds.), *Women, Culture and Development: A Study Of Human Capabilities*. Oxford: Oxford University Press.

——(1996). *Towards Justice and Virtue: A Constructive Account of Practical Reasoning*. Cambridge: Cambridge University Press.

——(1997). 'Political Liberalism and Public Reasons: A Critical Notice of John Rawls, Political Liberalism', *Philosophical Review*, 106: 411–28.

——(2002). 'Instituting Principles: Between Duty and Action', in M. Timmons (ed.), *Kant's Metaphysics of Morals: Interpretative Essays* Oxford: Oxford University Press.

Osmani, S. R. (2000). 'Human Rights to Food, Health, and Education', *Journal of Human Development*, 1/2: 271–96.

——(2005). 'Poverty and Human Rights: Building on the Capability Approach', *Journal of Human Development*, 6/2: 205–20.

Pattanaik, P. K. and Suzumura, K. (1994). 'Rights, Welfarism, and Social Choice', *AER Papers and Proceedings*, 84/2: 435–58

—— (1996). 'Individual Rights and Social Evaluation: A Conceptual Framework', *Oxford Economic Papers*, 48/2: 194–212.

—— and Y. Xu (1990). 'On Ranking Opportunity Sets in Terms of Freedom of Choice', *Recherces Economiques de Louvain*, 56/3–4: 383–90.

Peleg, B. (1998). 'Effectivity Functions, Game Forms, Games and Rights', in J. F. Laslier, M. Fleurbaey, N. Gravel, and A. Trannoy (eds.), *Freedom in Economics*. London: Routledge

Patten, A. (2005). 'Should We Stop Thinking about Poverty in Terms of Helping the Poor?', *Ethics and International Affairs*, 19/1: 19–27.

Petit, P. (2001). 'Symposium on Amartya Sen's Philosophy: 1. Capability and Freedom: A Defence of Sen', *Economics and Philosophy*, 17: 1–20.

Plant, R. (1991). *Modern Political Thought*. Oxford: Blackwell.

Pogge, T. (1989). *Realzing Rawls*. Ithaca, NY: Cornell University Press.

—— (2002*a*). *World Poverty and Human Rights: Cosmopolitan Responsibilities and Reforms*. Cambridge: Polity Press.

—— (2002*b*). *Can the Capability Approach be Justified?* available at http://aran.Univ-Pau.fr/ee/page3.html.

—— (2004). 'Severe Poverty as a Human Rights Violation'. (Version by personal communication dated 29 August)

—— (2005). 'Human Rights and Global Health: A Research Program', *Metaphilosophy* 36/1–2: 182–209.

—— (ed.) (forthcoming). *Freedom from Poverty as a Human Right: Who Owes What to the Very Poor?* Oxford: Oxford University Press.

Rawls, J. (1973). *A Theory of Justice*. Oxford: Oxford University Press.

—— (1993). *Political Liberalism*. New York: Columbia University Press.

—— (1999). *The Law of Peoples*. Cambridge, MA: Harvard University Press.

—— (2001). *Justice as Fairness: A Restatement, Edited by Erin Kelly*. Cambridge, MA: Belknap.

Raz, J. (1986). *The Morality of Freedom*. Oxford: Clarendon Press.

Reeder, J. P. J. (1996). *Killing and Saving: Abortion, Hunger and War*. University Park: Pennsylvania State University Press.

Risse, M. (2005). 'Do we Owe the Global Poor Assistance or Rectification?', *Ethics and International Affairs*, 19/1: 9–18.

Robeyns, I. (2003). 'Sen's Capability Approach and Gender Inequality: Selecting Relevant Capabilities', *Feminist Economics*, 9/2–3: 61–92.

—— (2005). 'Selecting Capabilities for Quality of life Measurement', in P. Anand (ed.) *Social Indicators Research: The Quality of Life and the Capability Approach*, 74(1).

Robinson, M. (1997). *Realizing Human Rights: The Romanes Lecture*. Oxford: Clarendon Press.

—— (1998). 'Foreword', in World Bank (1998), *Development and Human Rights: The Role of the World Bank*. Washington, DC: World Bank.

—— (2002). *From Rhetoric to Reality: Making Human Rights Work*. Lecture at London School of Economics, 23 October 2002. Available at:www.lse.ac.uk.

References

Robinson, M. (2004). *Health, Human Rights and Development OECD Forum*. Available at: http://www.oecd.org/dataoecd/7/27/31787614.pdf

Royakkers, L. (2000). 'Combining Deontic and Action Logics for Collective Agency', available at http://www.jurix.nl/pdf/j00-12.pdf.

Royakkers, L. and Dignum, F. (2000) 'No Organisation Without Obligations: How to Formalise Collective Obligation', available at http://citeseer.ist.psu.edu.

Sandel, M. (1984). *Liberalism and Its Critics*. New York: New York University Press.

Schachter, O. (1991). 'International Law in Theory and Practice', in P. Alston and H.Steiner (eds.) *International Human Rights in Context*. Oxford: Clarendon, 134–40.

Sane, P. (2005). *Reducing Poverty, How Human Rights Can Help*. Lecture delivered at LSE, 20 January, 2005.

Sen, A. K. (1970a). *Collective Choice and Social Welfare*. Amsterdam: Elsevier Science.

—— (1970b). 'The Impossibility of a Paretian Liberal', in *Choice, Welfare and Measurement* (1982). Oxford: Basil Blackwell.

—— (1981). *Poverty and Famines: An Essay on Entitlement and Deprivation*. Oxford: Clarendon.

—— (1981b). 'A Positive Concept of Negative Freedom', in E. Morscher and R. Stranzinger (eds.), *Ethics: Foundations, Problems and Applications, Proceedings of the 5th International Wittgenstein Symposium*. Vienna: Holder-Pichler-Tempsky.

—— (1982a). 'Rights and Agency,', *Philosophy and Public Affairs*, 11/1: 3–39.

—— (1982b). 'Equality of What?' in A.K. Sen, *Choice, Welfare and Measurement*. Oxford: Blackwell.

—— (1982c). 'Liberty as Control: An Appraisal', *Midwest Studies in Philosophy* 7: 207–21.

—— (1982d). 'The Right Not To Be Hungry' in G. Fløistad (ed.), *Contemporary Philosophy: A New Survey*, 2: 343–60. The Hague: Martinus Nijhff.

—— (1982e [1976]). 'Liberty, Unanimity and Rights' in A. K. Sen, *Choice, Welfare and Measurement*, 291–326. Oxford: Basil Blackwell.

—— (1982f [1976]). 'Poverty: An Ordinal Approach to Measurement' in A. K. Sen, *Choice, Welfare and Measurement*, 373–87. Oxford: Basil Blackwell.

—— (1983a). 'Evaluator Relativity and Consequential Evaluation', *Philosophy and Public Affairs*, 12/2: 113–32.

—— (1983b). 'Liberty and Social Choice', *Journal of Philosophy*, 80: 5–28.

—— (1984). 'Rights and Capabilities', in A. K. Sen (ed.), *Resources, Values and Development*. Oxford: Blackwell.

—— (1985a). 'Well-being, Agency and Freedom: The Dewey Lectures 1984,' *Journal of Philosophy*, 82/4: 169–221.

—— (1985b). 'Rights as Goals' (Austin Lecture), in S. Guest and A. Milne (eds.), *Equality and Discrimination: Essays in Freedom and Justice*, 11–26. Stuttgart: Franz Steiner Verlag.

—— (1985c). *Commodities and Capabilities*. Amsterdam: North-Holland.

—— (1986). 'Social Choice Theory', in K. Arrow and M. D. Intrilligator (eds.), *Handbook of Mathematical Economics*, vol. 3. New York: North-Holland, 1073–160.

—— (1987a) *The Standard of Living* (ed. Geoffrey Hawthorn, with contributions by John Muellbauer, Ravi Kanbur, Keith Hart, Bernard Williams). Cambridge: Cambridge University Press.

—— (1987b). *On Ethics and Economics*. Oxford: Blackwell.

—— (1990). 'Gender and Co-operative Conflict', in Irene Tinker (ed.), *Persistent Inequalities: Women and World Development*. New York: Oxford University Press.

—— (1991). 'Welfare, Preference and Freedom,' *Journal of Econometrics*, 50: 15–29.

—— (1992a). *Inequality Re-examined*. Oxford: Clarendon Press.

—— (1992b). 'Minimal Liberty,' *Economica*, 59/234: 139–60.

—— (1993a). 'Capability and Well-Being', in M. Nussbaum and A. K. Sen (eds.), *The Quality of Life*. Oxford: Oxford University Press.

—— (1993b). 'Markets and Freedoms: Achievements and Limitations of the Market Mechanism in Promoting Individual Freedoms,' *Oxford Economic Papers*, 45/4: 519–41.

—— (1993c). 'Internal Consistency of Choice', *Econometrica*, 61/3: 495–521.

—— (1993d). 'Positional Objectivity,' *Philosophy and Public Affairs*, 22/2: 126–45.

—— (1995). 'Rationality and Social Choice,' *American Economic Review*, 85/1: 1–19.

—— (1996a). 'Welfare Economics and Two Approaches to Rights', in J. Casas Pardo and F. Schneider (eds.), *Current Issues in Public Choice*, 21–39. Cheltenham: Edward Elgar.

—— (1996b). 'Legal Rights and Moral Rights: Old Questions and New Problems,' *Ratio Juris*, 9/2: 153–67.

—— (1996c). 'Rights: Formulations and Consequences,' *Analyse & Critique*, 18: 153–70.

—— (1997 [1973]). *On Economic Inequality* (enlarged edition with a substantial annexe, 'On Economic Inequality after a Quarter Century', by James Foster and Amartya Sen). Oxford: Oxford University Press.

—— (1997a). 'Maximization and the Act of Choice', *Econometrica*, 65/4: 745–80.

—— (1997c). 'Human Rights and Asian Values', *New Republic*, 33 (14 and 21 July).

—— (1999a). *Development as Freedom*. Oxford: Oxford University Press.

—— (1999b). 'Human Rights and Economic Achievements', in J. R. Bauer and D. A. Bell (eds.), *The East Asian Challenge for Human Rights*. Cambridge: Cambridge University Press.

—— (2000a). 'Consequential Evaluation and Practical Reason', *Journal of Philosophy*, 97/9: 477–502.

—— (2000b). 'Is Food More Important Than Political Freedom?' BBC World Service, 20 October.

—— (2001). 'Symposium on Amartya Sen's Philosophy: 4, Reply', *Economics and Philosophy*, 17: 51–66.

Sen, A. K. (2001*b*). *Global Doubts as Global Solutions: The Alfred Deakin Lectures 2001*. Available at: hhtp.//www.abc.net.au.m.deakin.

—— (2002). 'Introduction', in A. K. Sen, *Rationality and Freedom*. London: Belknap Press.

—— (2002*a*). 'Freedom and Social Choice: The Arrow Lectures—Opportunities and Freedoms' in A. K. Sen, *Rationality and Freedom*, 583–622. London: Belknap Press.

—— (2002*b*). 'Freedom and Social Choice: The Arrow Lectures—Process, Liberty and Rights' in A. K. Sen, *Rationality and Freedom*, 623–58. London: Belknap Press.

—— (2002*c*). 'Freedom and Social Choice: The Arrow Lectures—Freedom and the Evaluation of Opportunity' in A. K. Sen, *Rationality and Freedom*, 659–95. London: Belknap Press.

—— (2003). 'Preliminary Reflections on Freedom and Justice'. Paper presented at the Third Conference on the Capability Approach: From Sustainable Development to Sustainable Freedom, Pavia, September.

—— (2004*a*). 'Elements of a Theory of Human Rights', *Philosophy and Public Affairs*, 32/4: 315–56.

—— (2004*b*). 'Capabilities, Lists and Public Reason: Continuing the Conversation', *Feminist Economics*, 10/3: 77–80.

—— (2005). 'Human Rights and Capabilities', *Journal of Human Development*, 6/2: 151–66.

—— and B. Williams (eds.) (1982). *Utilitarianism and Beyond*. Cambridge: Cambridge University Press.

Sengupta A. (1999). *Study on the Current State of Progress in the Implementation of the Right to Development*. UN Docs. E/CN.4/1999/WG.18/2.

—— (2000). *The Right to Development*. UN Docs. A/55/306.

—— (2001). *Third Report of the Independent Expert on the Right to Development*. UN Docs. E/CN.4/2001/WG.18/2.

—— (2002*a*). 'Right to Development', *Human Rights Quarterly*, 24: 840–89.

—— (2002*b*). *Fourth Report of the Independent Expert on the Right to Development*. UN Docs. E/CN.4/2002/WG.18/2.

—— (2002*c*). *Fifth Report of the Independent Expert on the Right to Development: Frameworks for Development Co-operation and the Right to Development*. UN Docs. E/CN.4/2002/WG.18/6

—— (2004*a*). 'The Human Right to Development,' *Oxford Development Studies*, 32/2: 179–203.

—— (2004*b*). *Poverty Eradication and Human Rights*. Working paper series no. 2004, Harvard School of Public Health, Francois-Xavier Bagnoud Centre for Health and Human Rights.

Shue, H. (1980). *Basic Rights: Subsistence, Affluence, and US Foreign Policy*. Princeton, NJ: Princeton University Press.

—— (1984). 'The Interdependence of Duties', in P. Alston and K. Tomasevski (eds.), *The Right to Food*. Boston: Martinus Nijhoff.

Stigltz, J. (1999). *On Liberty, the Right to Know, and Public Discourse: The Role of Transparency in Public Life*. Oxford Amnesty Lecture, 27 January.

—— (2002). 'Participation and Development: Perspectives from the Comprehensive Development Paradigm', *Review of Development Economics*, 6(2): 163–82.

Sugden, R. (1986a). *The Economics of Rights, Cooperation and Welfare*. Oxford: Basil Blackwell.

Sullivan, R. (1996). 'Introduction', in Kant, I., *The Metaphysics of Morals, Edited by Mary Gregor with an Introduction by R. J. Sullivan*. Cambridge: Cambridge University Press.

Suzumura, K. (1999). 'Consequences, Opportunities and Procedures', *Social Choice and Welfare*, 16: 17–40.

—— (2000). 'Welfare Economics Beyond Welfarist Consequentialism', *Japanese Economic Review*, 51/1: 1–31.

Taylor, C. (1985). 'Atomism', in *Philosophy and the Human Sciences: Philosophical Papers*. Cambridge: Cambridge University Press. 2: 187–210.

Townsend, P. (2004). *Fighting Child Poverty Through Direct Policies*. Available at: http://www.undp.org/povertycentre/newsletters/infocus2mar04eng.pdf.

UN (1995). *The United Nations and Human Rights, 1945–1995: UN Blue Book Series*, vol. VII. New York: United Nations Department of Education.

UNDP (2000). *Human Development Report 2000: Human Rights and Human Development*. New York: Oxford University Press.

UNDP (2002). *Human Development Report 2002: Deepening Democracy in a Fragmented World*. New York: Oxford University Press.

UNESCO (2004). *Poverty: The Human Rights Approach*. Available at: http://portal.unesco.org/shs/en/ev.php-URL_ID=3905&URL_DO=DO_TOPIC&URL_SECTION=201.html.

UNICEF (2000). 'The Process: From Signature to Ratification'. Available at: http://www.unicef.org/crc/process.htm.

—— (2004a). *Convention on the Rights of the Child: UNICEF's Commitment to Child Rights Standards*. Available at: http://www.unicef.org/crc/crc.htm.

—— (2004b). *State of the World's Children 2005*. Available at: http://www.unicef.org.

United Nations General Assembly [UNGA] (2000). The Millenium Declaration, adopted as UNGA Resolution A/RES/55/2 18 September.

Van Hees, M. (1995). *Rights and Decisions*. Dordrecht: Kluwer Academic.

—— (1996). 'Individual Rights and Legal Validity,' *Analyse & Kritik*, (18) 81–95.

Van Hoof, G. (1984). 'The Legal Nature of Economic, Social and Cultural Rights: A Rebuttal of Some Traditional Views', in P. Alston and K. Tomasevski, *The Right To Food*. Boston: Nijhoff.

References

Vierdag, E. W. (1978). 'The Legal Nature of the Rights Granted by the International Covenant on Economic, Social and Cultural Rights', *Netherlands Yearbook of International Law*, 9: 69–105.

Vincent, R. J. (1986). *Human Rights and International Relations*. Cambridge: Cambridge University Press.

Vizard, P. A. (2000*a*). Conceptualising Poverty in a Human Rights Framework: Foundational Issues in Ethics, Economics and International Law. Ph.D. thesis, LSE.

—— (2000*b*). Antecedents of the Idea of Human Rights: A Survey of Perspectives. Background Paper for UNDP *Human Development Report (2000): Human Development and Human Rights*.

—— (2004*a*). 'Conceptualising Development Compacts in the Capability Framework: Issues Raised by Sengupta's "Working Model" '. Paper presented at the Fourth Conference on the Capability Approach: From Sustainable Development to Sustainable Freedom, September.

Waldron, J. (1993). *Liberal Rights: Collected Papers 1981–1991*. New York: Cambridge University Press.

Williams, B. (1987). 'The Standard of Living: Interests and Capabilities', in Amartya Sen, *The Standard of Living* (ed. by Geoffrey Hawthorn, with contributions by John Muellbauer, Ravi Kanbur, Keith Hart, Bernard Williams). Cambridge: Cambridge University Press.

WHO (2002). *World Health Report 2002*. Available at: http://www.who.int/whr/2002/en/.

—— (2004*a*). *World Health Report 2004*. Available at: http://www.who.int/whr/2004/en/.

—— (2004*b*). *Estimated Annual Deaths from Diseases Preventable by Vaccination*. Available at: http://www.who.int/vaccines-surveillance/graphics/htmls/estimateddeaths.html.

—— and UNICEF (2004*b*). *Meeting The MDG Drinking Water And Sanitation Targets: A Midterm Assessment Of Progress*. Available at: http://www.who.int/entity/water_sanitation_health/monitoring/en/jmp04.pdf.

Wood, A. (2002). 'The Final Form of Kant's Practical Philosophy', in M. Timmons (ed.), *Kant's Metaphysics of Morals: Interpretative Essays*. Oxford: Oxford University Press.

World Bank (1998). *Development and Human Rights: The Role of the World Bank*. Washington: World Bank. Available at: http://www.worldbank.org.

—— (2004). *World Development Indicators 2004: World View*. Available at: http://www.worldbank.org/data/wdi2004/worldview.htm.

World Bank Inspection Panel (1999). *Inspection Panel: Report and Recommendation on Request for Inspection, Re. Request for inspection – Argentina: Special Structural Adjustment Loan (Loan 4405-AR)*. Available at: http://wbln0018.worldbank.org/IPN/ipnweb.nsf/(attachmentweb)/SSAL_Report/$FILE/SSAL_Report.pdf.

Index